In appreciation of
your helping us share
Jesus by over-seas
radio.

Evelyn

# Two
# by Evelyn

*Evelyn Christenson*

*Assisted editorially by Viola Blake*

Evelyn Christenson's two paperback best-sellers, *What Happens When Women Pray* and *"Lord, Change Me!"* are combined in this book. A Leader's Guide for use in group studies is available for each book.

**VICTOR BOOKS**

a division of SP Publications, Inc., Wheaton, Illinois
Offices also in Fullerton, California • Whitby, Ontario, Canada • London, England

First paperback editions: *What Happens When Women Pray* 1975; *"Lord, Change Me!"* 1977.
*Library of Congress Catalog Card Number: 79-65289*
*ISBN: 0-88207-791-0*

*VICTOR BOOKS*
*A division of SP Publications, Inc.*
*P.O. Box 1825 • Wheaton, Illinois 60187*

# Contents

A Close-up of the Author by Jennifer Greene  7
*What Happens When Women Pray*  23
  Preface  25
  1  Prayer IS the Answer  27
  2  It Doesn't Take So Long  37
  3  Praying in One Accord  44
  4  The Method—Six S's  51
  5  How to Pray in God's Will  62
  6  God Never Makes a Mistake  72
  7  The Space Dimension of Prayer—Where We Pray  85
  8  The Time Dimension of Prayer—When We Pray  90
  9  The Vertical Dimension of Prayer—to Whom We Pray  102
  10  The Horizontal Dimension of Prayer—Results  107
  11  Forgiven as We Forgive  116
  12  Telephone Prayer Chains  122

*"Lord, Change Me!"*  133
  Preface  135
  Section I—Me  137
    1  Why Me?  139
  Section II—Change  149
    2  Lord, How Do I Change?  151
    3  Lord, Change Me for Others Too  165
    4  Changed—When I Study God's Word  180
    5  Changed—When the Holy Spirit Reminds  193
    6  Exchange—When I Ask God  204
    7  When I Ask Others to Pray for Me—I Change  217
    8  When I Pray for Others—I Change  226

Section III—Make Sure It Is God
Doing the Changing *237*
  9 Source No. 1, Sensual *239*
 10 Source No. 2, Earthly *248*
 11 Source No. 3, Demoniacal *258*
 12 Source No. 4, the Lord *272*

# To my 83-year-old mother.

*Watching her absolute, unwavering, childlike trust in her heavenly Father and His Word from my childhood until today has been the inspiration for my relationship with God.*

*Her unfaltering walk through deep valleys and hot fires, never doubting Romans 8:28, has been my daily model.*

*Her zest for life and tireless giving of herself to others for an entire lifetime is my priceless heritage.*

*I love you, Mother.*

*Evelyn*

# A Close-up of the Author

**by Jennifer Greene**

No two days are alike for Evelyn Christenson. But whether on the road or at home, she begins every day with the Lord about 4:30 in the morning, when she invests two to three hours in prayer and God's Word. "I find this heart preparation is a must," she says, "to keep my spiritual battery charged. Time alone with the Lord keeps my head on straight and prevents me from going off on tangents."

An exacting schedule includes many 18-hour days. Her long days have increased since her first book, *What Happens When Women Pray*, was published in 1975. Until then she was busy, conducting prayer seminars and speaking at retreats across the U.S. and Canada. But for the past few years, in an increasing manner, Evelyn has been the prayer lady on-the-go, lugging her seminar paraphernalia across the U.S. from Alaska to Florida, and from Canada to the Bahamas, speaking in seminars in churches, hotels, and even in prison. In Washington, D.C. she addressed an adult Sunday School class in the First Baptist Church, while President Carter taught in a room above. He later said to her, "I'd love to have been downstairs listening to you teach, but I had to teach my own class today." In Fort Worth, Texas she held a seminar on prayer in the federal penitentiary. A woman inmate had become so "turned on" through reading *What Happens When Women Pray* that she was searched for drugs. Later, while participating in Charles Colson's Prison Fellowship Releasee Training Program in

Washington, D.C., she helped get Evelyn invited to teach in her prison. Currently, Evelyn is booked for engagements for over a year ahead and, although it breaks her heart, must turn down countless invitations.

Despite suddenly finding herself something of a celebrity, Evelyn Christenson has remained an enthusiastic witness to the Lord's power to answer prayer and change lives. An attractive brown-eyed brunette, Evelyn conveys lively good spirits by a charming smile and warm greeting. At a recent Christian Booksellers Association Convention she was dubbed "Evelyn the hugger." People from all walks of life are attracted by her pleasant manner and the ease with which she communicates with them. She sometimes gets writer's cramp autographing books, but she never complains, giving each autograph seeker a listening ear or an encouraging remark. Autograph lines have been getting longer since her second book, *"Lord, Change Me!"* hit the religious bestseller lists in 1977. While getting her book autographed, one young woman leaned over and, as tears welled up in her eyes, whispered, "I found Christ two weeks ago while reading *"Lord, Change Me!"* Literally thousands of people have told Evelyn how her books have changed their lives. Because of this, Evelyn prays even harder that God will use her books to help people grow in their Christian faith. Joining Evelyn in fervent prayer is her prayer chain of women in the Twin Cities area. Every day since 1975

First big catch—1941

Mother, sister Maxine (right),
brother "Bud" (center), and Evelyn

one person has been committed to intercessory prayer for those who read Evelyn's two books.

As a result, cold print comes alive as biblical truths grip readers' hearts and penetrate their lives. A pastor, after reading "Lord, Change Me!" with its emphasis on changing oneself rather than everyone else, wrote this note to Evelyn, "Thanks, Evelyn, I needed that!"

A mother superior of an abbey near Toronto wrote, "Last summer, before I had any inkling that I would be asked to assume this responsibility, I was reading 'Lord, Change Me!' As I read, the Lord asked me if I would be willing to be mother superior. My first reaction was no, as I did not feel I had the necessary gifts. But when I came to chapter 6 in the book, where you [Evelyn] prayed, 'O Lord, change me. Make me only a servant. Please give me the mind of Christ,' I said 'Yes, Lord. I am willing to be the mother superior if I can be just the servant.' Thus, when the superior general of our order approached me about taking office, I was putty in her hands."

Evelyn was born and grew up in Muskegon, Michigan. The second of three children, she was an outgoing child who rarely rode a bicycle with two hands because one hand was usually in use, waving to people she passed by. Until her father, Edward Luhman, became a state highway contractor when she was 11, Evelyn's favorite play spot was among the flowers in her parents' greenhouse. Her paternal grandfather came to the

Moody Bible Institute—1941

Wedding, Valentine's Day, 1942—Muskegon, Michigan

United States from Germany and her mother, Edna, is of English and Scottish extraction. Evelyn was sent to Sunday School as a child. Her father did not become a Christian till five years before his death, and it was just before Evelyn's ninth birthday that her mother received the Lord. Soon afterward, Evelyn, largely through her mother's testimony and love, invited Christ into her life and was baptized when she was 10 years old. Her mother commemorated the occasion by giving Evelyn her first "big" Bible in which she inscribed this prayer:

> In life's great journey
> As you travel through
> May God be glorified
> In all you do.

Her mother had grown rapidly as a Christian and, soon after her conversion, the Sunday School superintendent of the church they attended asked her to start teaching a class of teenage girls. "We now don't usually give new Christians such an important job," Evelyn says, but her mother rose to the challenge and Evelyn remembers her pouring out her heart in prayer and studying the Bible. A warm, caring, and energetic person, she took the girls on overnight hikes and for many activities outside the church. Evelyn says, "I watched her living Christ in front of the girls and it made a definite impression on me. My mother had a childlike faith in Christ that never

With Air Force cadet husband—1943    Twenty-five years later

wavered. She was the only one who knew Christ of all her brothers and sisters—and my father—and she has had the privilege of leading every single one of them to the Lord.''

Evelyn and her mother have shared the principle of Romans 8:28 for many years: ''And we know that all things work together for good to them that love God, to them who are the called according to His purpose.'' She says, ''No matter what falls apart or what happens in our lives, we always look at each other and smile through our tears, or squeeze a hand, and whisper, Romans 8:28.''

As a young person, Evelyn was active in the life of her church. By the time she was 14 years of age, she was teaching in her Sunday School's Beginner Department, and through her teenage years she was always a leader in her young people's group. Church, in fact, was the center of her social life. Her vivacious personality also made an impact in high school, and she was voted the ''best all-around'' girl of her graduating class. She was described in her high school yearbook as a ''smiling, friendly, and agreeable girl . . . whose vitality comes from toboganning, which is her chief winter interest. Roller skating and swimming also have a definite part in her 'good times scheme.' Although she is a very busy girl, she always finds time to devote to her church's young people's society of which she is group leader.''

Prayer was important to Evelyn throughout her school years.

President, Bethel College Ladocian Society—1949

Secretary to Bethel College's President, Dr. Henry Wingblade 1946 to 1950

She specifically remembers praying about tests—especially math tests—starting in the seventh grade. And when she met the person who would, some years later, become her husband, she committed her relationship with him to the Lord. Evelyn's eyes sparkle when she tells how, at 14 years of age, she was introduced to a tall, thin, dark-haired boy whose parents ran a mission church in town. They discovered that they shared many interests, such as touch football, and their relationship gradually deepened.

In the fall of 1941, Harold Christenson—or Chris, as he is affectionately called—and Evelyn waved good-bye to their parents and boarded a train bound for Chicago, where they were to attend Moody Bible Institute. Chris had in his pocket a ring. They don't know on what day or in which state they became engaged, for just about midnight, when the train was crossing the Michigan-Indiana border, Chris asked Evelyn to marry him.

During the year they attended Moody, when they had spare time, they would sit beside Lake Michigan and search the Scriptures. Evelyn says, "From the outset, we wanted to be clear about God's will for us."

They were married on Valentine's Day, 1942 in the Lakeside Baptist Church, Muskegon, while a vicious sleet storm howled outside. It was a formal traditional wedding attended by 500 guests. Evelyn had several attendants, one of whom was a

Bethel College junior
yearbook picture—1950

Preacher becomes Daddy
on Father's Day, 1950

small ring-bearer who dropped the ring when he was halfway down the aisle. He had the presence of mind, however, to stop and watch where it rolled, then pick it up and proceed to the altar. Other memorable incidents during the ceremony were Evelyn's veil momentarily being caught in a vine-entwined-pillar, a smoking palm frond hanging too close to a candle, and a bug crawling out from the pastor's boutonniere and peering down inside his collar. Anxious to share their faith in Christ, the new Mr. and Mrs. Christenson knelt beneath a cross his father had made that was covered with soft lights and white lilies, while a soloist sang "Beneath the cross of Jesus I fain would take my stand."

During their first year of marriage Evelyn suffered a miscarriage. Not long afterward Chris enlisted and left for the military service, while Evelyn stayed with her parents. Some months later she gave birth to their stillborn child, just five weeks after Chris' father died unexpectedly. Chris then became a bomber pilot, stationed in England. The first purchase of their married life had been a small car. Finding it a financial burden, she decided to sell it. "With Chris and the car both gone I cried and cried," she says, "and finally my daddy's soft heart could stand it no longer. One day he came home and said, 'Honey, go look in the garage.' He had gone to the used car dealer, found the car, and bought it back."

When Chris returned from the war, he entered Bethel

Motherhood—June, 1950

Seminary dormitory days—1950

College in St. Paul, Minnesota, and after graduation continued his studies at Bethel Theological Seminary. Evelyn earned the associate of arts degree at Bethel College, took additional courses, and worked as secretary to the president for four years (1946–1950) "to help put hubby through."

Chris was dining hall manager for seven years and Evelyn got to know every student on campus as cashier three meals every day. They initiated Bethel's annual traditional Christmas smorgasbord, and Evelyn was one of the co-founders and first president of the literary society, which existed for many years. Chris and Evelyn spent their weekends traveling as part of a Gospel team till Chris took a job as a local youth pastor.

When Chris finished his training, he accepted a pastorate in a 400-member church in Stanchfield, Minnesota. It was an adjustment for Evelyn from campus life to the pastorate. "I thought," she says, "that I should do everything the way the former pastor's wife did. But I finally discovered that God had given me different gifts and talents. It was then that I learned to be myself."

They moved to Rockford, Illinois in 1955 and remained in the pastorate at the Temple Baptist Church for almost 15 years, until 1970, when he became associated with Bethel Theological Seminary in St. Paul, Minnesota. In 1968 the Rockford Church became the *What Happens When Women Pray* Church. Almost everything in *What Happens When Women Pray* and *"Lord,*

"What Happens When Women Pray" Church: Rockford, Illinois—1956 to 1970

Rockford parsonage— home to Christenson children

*Change Me!''* came out of the years in these two pastorates. "The potential of a pastor's wife is terrific," Evelyn says. "It is one of the greatest professions. There's a tendency to shy away from it, but if a pastor's wife earns the right to be followed, and builds trust and respect, she will be a leader with an automatic built-in following."

During the years at Rockford, Evelyn taught a large adult class. "I studied 25 hours a week for that class," she says, "and wrote all my own material. That's where I really learned what I know about doctrine and the life of Christ." She branched out into neighborhood Bible studies and wrote material on how to conduct small neighborhood Bible studies for her denomination's involvement in Key '73. Evelyn spoke at many functions, such as mother-daughter banquets, but found she was able to accomplish more in seminars and in-depth Bible classes.

Evelyn and her husband have three children, Jan, Nancy, and Kurt, born over a period of eight years. Daughter Judy, born in 1953, died at seven months. Growing up in a parsonage, the children learned not only to share their father with the congregation, but also the harder lesson of actually giving him to others at such times when an emergency would take him away from a planned family event. The Christenson children accept prayer as an essential part of life, for from the time Jan started kindergarten until Kurt finished high school, one of their parents prayed with each child as he or she left the

Daughter Jan's marriage to Spencer Johnson, June 8, 1971

house for school and the day's activities.

For the past 25 years, the Christenson family has spent vacation time at Pentwater, Michigan, where they rent a cottage on the bluffs of Lake Michigan. When the children were small the Christensons bought a boat. Anchored just offshore, it was the center of the family's summer activities. When Kurt was still a baby they would put a life preserver around him and he would take his nap on the boat while the rest of the family swam, water-skied, or fished. Evelyn's mother and step-father, Rollie Moss, a retired Baptist pastor, live in Pentwater as do Evelyn's sister Maxine and her husband Rudy who operate Gustafson's International Gifts. Chris' mother, sister, brother and his family from St. Paul, Minnesota vacation in the same spot. "It's not unusual to have 14 at a meal at the cottage," Evelyn says. "We are a close-knit family and enjoy boating, hiking, and watching shooting stars at midnight together."

The purchase of a king-size bed at home in Rockford provided another means for many close fun times as a family. When the children were small, all five Christensons sometimes piled into the bed, and talked and laughed or watched television together. "Our king-size bed was the best investment we ever made," says Evelyn, "because of the way it drew

Daddy marrying daughter
Nancy to Daniel Thompson,
June 15, 1974

Family vacation

our little family together."

Birthdays and holidays have always been special times for the Christensons. One family tradition allows the birthday person to choose his or her favorite dinner menu, which Evelyn then carefully prepares. She says, "We never miss the joy of spending Thanksgiving, Christmas, holidays, graduations, and other special days with our extended St. Paul family, which includes Chris' brother Carl, a surgeon, his wife and four children, Chris' mother Mae, former Bethel housemother, and Shirley, his schoolteacher sister."

For Evelyn, being a mother is "a fantastic privilege. Yes, it's a sacrificial life," she says, "yet because you love them so dearly it's the most fulfilling, joyous role in the world. It's easy to try and protect children from hard experiences. I think one of the most difficult responsibilities as parents is to give your children to God in the hard things. We would take all the hurts for them but they have to experience their own hurts so that they can grow. Every stage in rearing a child has its own fun and rewards, but the greatest of all is watching him grow up and then, after discovering his own identity, emerge as your close adult friend as well as your child."

Evelyn has balanced her responsibilities as a wife, mother, and public speaker by establishing priorities. The quality of the times her family is together is more important than how often they see each other. "I used to be a spit-and-polish mother," Evelyn says, "but I learned that at times when I can't do both it's more important to keep my relationships with my children open. Our house for a long time has been a home, not a house, with the philosophy, 'live and let live.' "

Both of the Christenson daughters are married and engaged in further academic pursuits. Jan, a doctor, is doing her residency in internal medicine and her husband, Spencer, is a family specialty physician. Nancy is completing a nursing major at the College of St. Catherine's in St. Paul. Her husband Dan is a district financial manager in the Burroughs Corporation and is also completing the master of business administration degree. Kurt rarely comes up for air from the Physics Department at Bethel College, where he, a junior, is a teaching assistant. An avid photographer, he worked and purchased all of his own darkroom equipment during high school, and develops his own film. He helps defray his college expenses by taking wedding pictures professionally.

Chris is Director of Church Relations and Professor of Evangelism and Church Growth at Bethel Theological Seminary. He also commutes to their Bethel West Seminary in California during the spring and fall quarters and conducts pastors' conferences and retreats.

Because they travel so much, Evelyn and Chris have learned the secret of having short "honeymoons" in between trips. "Our love grows deeper every day," Evelyn says. "It's a rare day when we're separated that we don't call and say 'goodnight' long distance. After 37 years of marriage (to the same man) the excitement of being alone in a motel room with Chris has not diminished. We find great joy traveling, playing, working, and praying together. In fact we just took up cross-country skiing."

Chris is Evelyn's number one fan and acts as her business manager, making all financial decisions. "I thank God," Evelyn says, "for a husband who wants God's will for his wife as well as for his own life. At times when I'm afraid of an assignment or something, he asks, 'Will God's will ever send you where His grace cannot keep you?' There are many times when we're apart that we are lonely, but we have both learned that God will and does fill those lonely hours with Himself."

The cedar split-level home in which Evelyn and Chris now live in suburban St. Paul is the first house they have owned.

Battling the tides
in the Florida Keys

Down under in the Atlantic
at Bermuda—1978

Previously, they lived in dormitories or parsonages. The living room and dining area are tastefully furnished in purple (Evelyn's favorite color) and off-white with gold. The kitchen is cheerfully accented with yellow and leads on to an oak-shaded deck, which Chris, their son, and sons-in-law built. It is the hub of all the summer fun times and meals. Evelyn's personal "Who—ME Change?," banner hangs at the sun deck doorway as a reminder to her and all her guests.

When the Christensons lived in Rockford there were frequent occasions to entertain. The large colonial parsonage could accommodate 100 sit-down guests at a time. Evelyn remembers one New Year's Eve when about 300 young people crowded into their house. "There was standing room only," she says, "and we moved about holding trays of doughnuts over our heads." In her present ministry, she confines most entertaining to their large extended family and special speakers at such functions as Bethel's Founder's Week. Evelyn has learned to define hospitality in other ways too. She says, "I give much more of myself emotionally and physically to the thousands of people I now teach, listen to, and counsel than I ever did when entertaining at home. It's a different way of giving of myself but is a much needed kind of hospitality."

An entire wall of Evelyn's study is lined with books. Her favorite is Augustus Strong's *Systematic Theology* (Revell). A close runner-up is Andrew Murray's classic *With Christ in the*

Five-hundred-thousandth copy of *What Happens When Women Pray* presented to Evelyn by David E. Hall, president of Scripture Press

Evelyn's personal, "Who—ME Change?" banner hangs in the kitchen

*School of Prayer* (Revell). Other books which have had a strong impact on her are *Joni* (Joni Eareckson, Zondervan), *Come Away My Beloved* (Frances Roberts, Revell), and writings by G. Campbell Morgan and C. S. Lewis.

Many people have wondered if Evelyn always wanted to write a book. But Evelyn says, "I hadn't the faintest idea I would ever write a book. In fact, I was a very surprised person when the people at Victor Books asked me to write my first book." For several years prior to her first book, *What Happens When Women Pray*, people at prayer seminars and retreats would tell her that the material should be in book form. She would say, "If you think this should be, pray that God will open a door if it is His will."

Then one day out of the clear blue sky, husband Chris was chatting on a plane with a longtime friend and Bethel school board member, Jim Lemon, Vice-President of Marketing at Scripture Press. When Jim asked, "What is Evie doing these days?" Chris told him about her seminars. Evelyn met them at the airport and as she and Chris gave him a ride to his motel, Jim asked Evelyn if she had her material on tape. Embarrassed, because she never carried any of her tapes with her, she replied she had recently stopped at her audio producer's office and that she just happened to have a suitcase full of tapes in the back seat. Jim Lemon took a set of tapes and dropped them on the desk of Jim Adair, the Editorial Director of Victor Books.

Prayer seminar

Autographing *"Lord, Change Me!"*

And soon afterward Evelyn had a contract.

Evelyn got in touch with Viola Blake, Assistant Editor of Billy Graham's *Decision* magazine, also in the Twin Cities. They worked from the transcribed recorded seminar and shaped the material into 12 chapters for the book, over the phone and at Viola's apartment.

Her prayer chain gave Evelyn enormous support while she wrote the book. Whenever Evelyn and Viola faced a specific problem, they called the prayer chain, "And they prayed while we wrote," Evelyn says.

God's direction and His timing are evidenced in the fact that *What Happens When Women Pray* has appeared consecutively on the National Religious Bestsellers list since April 1976. And Evelyn has personally taught this complete material to just under 200,000 people, in addition to the multitudes who have taught this material around the world from her cassette tapes, books, and leader's guides.

"How long have you had a burden for prayer?" Evelyn is often asked. She answers, "It started in my teen years and gradually grew from deep prayer for myself, on to my family, enlarged to fervent prayer for my church, and then I began to agonize in prayer for my denomination. Then God gave me a burden for all Christians in the U.S. and Canada to learn to pray. Now, for the past two years I have had a tremendous burden from God for the whole world. I am thrilled about the

Joni—1978

Evelyn, Mother, sister Maxine

invitations we are receiving from all parts of the world and am working out an overseas itinerary."

After *What Happens When Women Pray* had been out for a year, Evelyn felt that the Lord was laying it on her heart to pick up the story of her life from the conclusion of the 1968 prayer experimentation. This resulted in the book, *"Lord, Change Me!"* which describes her 14-month struggle to allow the Lord to change her—not her husband, not her children, or anybody else. The book, like *What Happens When Women Pray*, has jumped off secular racks as fast as off shelves and racks in Christian bookstores. *"Lord, Change Me!"* hit the top 10 list of religious bestsellers just six months after publication and to date has stayed there.

Evelyn is now writing a third book—on the subject of gaining through losing. It will be based on how God, throughout her life, has turned losses into gains when she has let Him take over.

People sometimes ask Evelyn if she had any idea that God might use her to minister so widely through seminars and books when she first said yes to God's will in her life. She laughs and says, "No, if God had told me, I would have probably said, 'Lord, You have the wrong gal. I have no talents along those lines.' " But today she stands in awe and humble gratitude at what can happen to a yielded and ordinary life in the hands of the omnipotent God.

Christenson family on their patio—1978

Today—
still going great

# What Happens When Women Pray

# Preface

In 1968 I was the national women's chairman for the Baptist General Conference's involvement in the Crusade of the Americas. My task was to lead the women of my own church, Temple Baptist, in Rockford, Illinois, to discover through six months of experimentation "What Happens When Women Pray." Such exciting and life-changing results were experienced from the actual praying and the methods of prayer we worked out that I began sharing them at retreats, workshops, church meetings, and conferences from coast to coast and in Canada.

In January 1972, after moving to St. Paul, Minnesota where my husband had joined the staff of Bethel College, I began six-week, and later five-week prayer seminars in this area. Since then we have added one-day seminars for which the material is consolidated and presented in three sessions of about two hours each. These have worked best for out-of-state seminars.

A steering committee made up of representatives from most of the churches of a given geographic area organizes and sponsors the seminar. Many times participants from over 100 different churches, both Protestant and Catholic, have attended.

Early in 1974 we opened the seminars to men and young people in addition to women. This has proved worthwhile as whole families have learned to pray together. Pastors take the material back to their churches to be used in prayer meetings, prayer weeks, and Sunday School classes. The results are exciting.

Rev. James Rehnberg describes what happened in his church in Thousand Oaks, California as follows: "Our Board of Trustees had called in representatives of two fund-raising organizations for we needed to raise $226,000 to build an addition to our church. After listening to both presentations and tentatively deciding which procedure to use, I asked for 15 minutes. I quickly briefed my board on your Six-S method of short, simple prayers. I reminded them that, according to Psalm 66:18, if we regard iniquity in our hearts, God will not hear us. Giving them specific instructions to pray confessing the sins in their lives before asking for God's guidance as to how to raise the money, I divided them into six small groups and sent them off to pray in different rooms of the house. After just 15 minutes of praying they came back together and unanimously voted what God had told each of them separately: *Don't use a fund-raising company. Borrow the money from the members of your own church.* Immediately we raised not $226,000 but $250,000—over and above what we needed—without even going to the local bank!"

After hearing the methods of prayer we developed, someone invariably asks, "Is this material in print?"

My answer has always been the same: "I have committed this completely to God. If He wants this in a book, He will open the doors." Then, enlisting their prayer support, I would ask them to pray specifically, *if it were God's will*, that He would open doors. So people across the United States and Canada have prayed about this book since 1968.

The preparation of the material has been a series of answers from God—from the taping of the seminar sessions, to the transcribing of the tapes, to the writing of the manuscript. God has placed on the heart of Viola Blake the conviction that it was His will for her to assist in the writing of the book.

Every step of the prayer seminars and every step in the preparation of this book has been prayed through by my Advisory Board and telephone prayer chains, with explicit instructions to pray *only for God's will*. We did not plan, or make contacts or phone calls—we only prayed.

Since we have no way of knowing who you are or what your needs may be as you read this book, our Advisory Board and prayer chains are continuing to pray daily that God will show you the next step in prayer that is *His will for you.*

# 1

# Prayer
# Is the Answer

*"The effectual fervent prayer of a righteous [person] availeth much."*
James 5:16

"Lord, help! How do I motivate eight gripers?" Here they were, on a cold January morning, sitting around my dining room table—the favored ones, those who had been chosen to learn to pray. I thought they would be enthusiastic about the idea. Weren't they all "spiritual life chairmen" of women's circles at church? Instead, they sat there griping.

Earlier, in the fall of 1967, the national committee of our denomination had asked me to do a project for the Crusade of the Americas. "Working with women in your own church, would you discover in a six-month period what happens when women pray?"

I had replied, "I'll take that little task."

It had sounded so simple in 1967. But on New Year's morning I awakened with a jolt: "It's 1968, and I have to find out what happens when women pray!" I didn't have a single thought in my head. I didn't know how to start. I didn't know with whom I should start. What would you have done? I panicked.

But as I was lying there I said, "Lord, please help. I feel negative. Everything is black. It's dark and it's cold and it's everything it shouldn't be. What shall I do? Show me."

27

Suddenly, just as if a horizontal door opened over my head, God was speaking to me, though there was no audible voice. He said, "Evelyn, if you're going to find out what happens when women pray, you are going to have to learn to use this door, the door of access to Me. This is the door of prayer. You, Evelyn, are going to have to learn to use it more effectively."

I simply said, "Thank You, Lord. Now I know just what to do."

That week I called together those eight spiritual life chairmen of the women's circles in the church where my husband was pastor. I thought, "This will really do it. These women will all be excited about learning to pray; they will be the steering committee."

Instead they griped. "I'm the spiritual life chairman of my circle," one said, "but all the president lets me do is close in prayer."

Another remarked, "My president lets me pray for the food, and that's it."

They went on and on. Evidently they didn't know what I was talking about. That's when I silently cried to the Lord for help. He answered, "OK, Evelyn, back way up and tell them about yourself."

"You know," I began, "I want to tell you something about your pastor's wife. I never teach a Sunday School class, never lead neighborhood Bible study, never speak anywhere without calling on my two strong prayer partners. The three of us pray earnestly that God will enable me to speak."

"Not you," they said. "Not our pastor's wife. You don't have any needs."

"Your pastor's wife needs prayer," I insisted; "she knows very well that she can fall flat on her face if there isn't prayer support."

I still wasn't getting through to these eight women. I had to back up some more. "In 1961, six months after I had major surgery, I was scheduled to speak at just one session of a retreat. I thought that after six months I'd be flying high, but I wasn't. A series of infections had slowed my recovery. From that standpoint, to accept the engagement was a foolish thing for me to do, but after making me comfortable in the car, my husband drove me to the conference grounds.

"All during the dinner hour I didn't say a word. I knew that if I talked then I wouldn't have enough strength to address the ladies afterward. By 10 P.M. I still hadn't been called on to speak (you know how women's retreats go on and on). Weak and trembling I searched out the chairman and said, 'Joyce, forget the whole thing. I don't have enough strength left to speak. I can't say one word.'

"Joyce replied, 'Just a minute, Evelyn.' She went to summon a very mature 'pray-er' whom she knew. The three of us found a little room with bunks in it, and we got down on our knees. Those two women prayed until I had enough strength to go out there and speak. At the end of the meeting we had a fireside service of rededication, and only 10 of the 400 women present did not rededicate their lives to Christ."

I had at last convinced my eight women that their pastor's wife depended 100 percent on prayer when she went out to minister for Christ. Slowly, they began to pray.

"Oh, Lord, show me."

"Lord, cleanse me."

"Lord, use me." That was all they prayed that first time, but it was a beginning.

### Conversion at the Country Club

Gradually, as they learned simple methods of praying effectively, God began to encourage these former gripers with beautiful answers to prayer. The first exciting result was a dramatic conversion. I had been teaching a weekly neighborhood Bible study specifically designed to introduce women to Christ, but nothing was happening. I said to the eight women, who were now praying every Tuesday morning, "I have a problem. Let's zero in on one person in that Bible study group. I know that Marion doesn't know Christ as her personal Saviour." That morning we prayed, and we prayed.

Then I told them, "I'm taking Marion to lunch." Right away they volunteered to pray while we were at lunch, and through the afternoon. As they were leaving, one said, "I'm going to pray that you take her to a place where you can really talk."

Each woman took a similar specific request home with her, and I drove on to Marion's house. When I got there she said, "Let me drive." So with my little Bible under my arm I got into her big white Cadillac convertible and we drove to her country club. Have you ever led anyone to the Lord in a country club? I hadn't, and I wasn't at all sure what was going to happen next.

Knowing that Marion's husband owned much of the stock in that country club, the host "bowed and scraped" and asked, "Wouldn't you like this nice secluded table here in the corner?" It was just the right spot for conversation. We talked and talked while the waitress kept bringing us coffee. I finally said, "You know, Marion, I think it's time we stop talking and go out to the car and pray."

What had we been talking about all afternoon? Marion had been picking my brains about Jesus. "How do you accept Jesus into your life?" "What is it like to have Jesus in your heart?" "What's it like living with Him?" So many questions. But at 3:20 Marion jumped up from her chair and together we went out to the parking lot, sat in that big white Cadillac, and Marion bowed her head and prayed, "O God, forgive all my sins; and Jesus, please come in to be my Saviour." Marion had found Christ.

Another exciting part of this story unfolded on the following Thursday morning when the dear woman who helped me clean once a week opened my front door with the immediate question, "What happened on Tuesday?"

"Why, Mary, what do you mean, 'What happened on Tuesday?' "

She explained, "Well, the Lord said on Sunday, 'Now, Mary, you fast and pray,' so I didn't eat; I just prayed from Sunday until Tuesday afternoon. Then in the middle of the afternoon the Lord said to me, 'It's OK, Mary, you can eat now.' What happened on Tuesday afternoon?"

I said, "Mary, would you believe that at 3:20 on Tuesday afternoon, Marion accepted Christ?"

Mary was huge, and she put her big arms around me, and I put my arms almost around Mary, and we stood there and cried, for she and I had prayed together for Marion by name for many months.

### Prayers, not Plans or Programs

We learned that things could happen when we didn't plan at all but just prayed. A long distance call came to our church after one of the Sunday morning services. It was Arthur Blessit calling from California. "May I use your church building for a meeting on Tuesday night?" he asked. "You won't have to do a thing. I just want to reach some hippies for Christ."

My husband said, "Fine, you may use our church."

Arthur arrived on Tuesday morning. There had been no time to advertise the meeting in local newspapers or in other churches. The only means of communication had been the hippie "underground" method. But Tuesday morning was our prayertime. The entire kitchen area of the church was "wall to wall" with women who had only one prayer—that somehow the hippies of the area would hear there was to be a meeting for them in our church that night.

As we were praying, our church secretary, Carolyn, came flying downstairs and interrupted our prayer with, "The religion editor of the newspaper came to interview Art Blessit; now they're on their knees praying!" The religion editor received Christ. Art Blessit's meeting had front-page coverage that evening. How else would you get newspaper advertising in such a short time?

We had 1,100 hippies in our church that night. They had come from as far away as Chicago—90 miles—by thumb, by motorcycle, by car. Some were on hard drugs. These characters, and I mean characters, came en masse to the service. When Art gave the invitation that night over 100 of them accepted Christ. As the Christians came forward to find a place to pray with these young people, there wasn't a closet, or a hallway, or a side room anywhere in the church where people weren't already praying!

My husband is a very organized man. In fact, he is now teaching a course in management in a seminary. But the next Sunday he laid aside his already prepared sermon and announced, "I can speak on only one subject this morning: 'What Happens When You Don't Plan, You Just Pray!'"

### Pray First, Plan Afterward
God expects us to be orderly. He expects us to manage our time, to discipline ourselves, to prepare well-planned programs, but if we could learn to pray first and plan afterward how different would be our homes, our churches, our

Christian women's clubs, our Bible studies, whatever we are doing for Christ. Maybe, just maybe, we are planning in one direction and God's will is in another direction. God might say, "Hold everything! Turn around and go this way. This is My will for you, not that way."

Even if we are plugged into God's will and know we're going in the right direction, we may be going at a snail's pace. God says, "Look, you see only a tenth of what I have for you. There are nine-tenths that you're not seeing, that you don't know anything about."

God wants us to make ourselves available to Him, and to say before we start to plan, "Lord, tell me what You want me to do, where You want me to go, how You want me to do it." Then our omnipotent God, with all the abundance of heaven at His disposal, will pour out His power upon us. Instead of following our tiny, tiny plans, God wants to open heaven and flood us. It's exciting.

In our early days of learning to pray, the best source of requests was the Christian Education Department of our church. Gail, our children's worker, came up with a fantastic idea after she witnessed some miraculous answers to prayer. Her suggestion, "Let's pray first and plan afterwards," became the slogan for our church. During Vacation Bible School that year we set up a prayer room and collected requests along with attendance sheets. Then teachers and helpers spent their break times in prayer.

An urgent request came from one department. Not one child had received Christ though the school had been in session for a week and a half. That Wednesday morning we zeroed in on that request. The same teacher was giving the same kind of Bible story, but what a difference prayer made. I stepped into the department to see 23 hands raised to receive Christ. The spiritual ceiling of our church went straight up!

### No Dry Eyes

The original notes I made for my report at our national conference in 1968 reveal what happened in six months as we were learning to pray:

January—the gripe session, "Cleanse me." "Use me." "Forgive me." "Show me." That was all.

February—eagerness had replaced complaining. They were excited. They were actually seeing the worth of themselves in prayer.

March—great joy and much sharing of answered prayer. They were talking about changes in their own lives due to praying.

April—there were no dry eyes as we were experientially learning what effectual, fervent prayer really is.

May—we were claiming victory over Satan as our specific prayers were answered in specific ways. We were learning that Satan gets busy when we actually pray, not when we study about prayer or even memorize Bible verses about prayer. But the exciting thing is that in prayer we gain victory over Satan.

June—by popular demand we opened our prayer meetings to all of our church women. In just six months we had learned that "the effectual, fervent prayer" of a righteous person avails much—not plans or programs, but effectual, fervent *prayer*.

Recently, an occult high priest was quoted in our local newspaper. He said that the churches of America had given up the supernatural. They don't deal in the supernatural; they just deal in plans and programs and social action. He said that every human being is created with a supernatural vacuum, and since Christians aren't doing anything in the realm of the supernatural, he feels that witchcraft is a reasonable substitute for Christianity.

Can we still have the supernatural in our churches? I think we can, for effectual, fervent prayer is capable of producing supernatural results.

The women of a 4,000-member church learned this in a two-session prayer seminar. A week later the wife of one of the four pastors told me, "The most amazing thing happened when we learned to pray: the Holy Spirit just went 'whoosh' through our church! I didn't tell you before, but we were just about to split. Our Christian Ed Department was deteriorating Sunday by Sunday, and members were pulling out. When nothing else worked, we decided to try prayer. Problems were solved and walls between the factions started to crumble."

I met her a year later and asked, "How is it going in your church?"

Her answer, "It's still going great."

### Unity in the Community

The "availeth much" of prayer was apparent, but there was more to come. One of the surprises was the terrific unity we found in communities where people learned to pray together. *Caution:* this refers to the body of Christ praying together, not just church members.

Last year I met the pastor of the host church where our first prayer seminar was held. He said to me, "Ev, you know our daughter was killed in a tragic accident last month, and an amazing thing happened at her funeral. There were priests and pastors and lay people from every single church in the area." And then he added, "This never would have happened if the women had not learned to pray together."

Was it because they met for a series of six meetings? No. It was because they had learned the unifying dimension of prayer.

Marcella, wife of the mayor of a northern Minnesota town, had a fantastic vision of what God can do when women pray. One day she called and said, "Evelyn, I'm concerned about our town. There are lots of Christians here, but we all go our own directions. We compete rather than work together for the cause of Christ. Could you come for a rally?"

One of the miracles at that rally was that there were representatives from every single church present. After the meeting a woman came to me and said, "I'm chairman of the women's committee here, and I know why this rally was a success."

"OK," I said, "you tell me."

"Well, Marcella told us last May, 'If Evelyn's coming for a rally, she expects you to be praying. Now get on the ball.' So we did and we have prayed in an organized fashion every other week from May to October."

I was still shaking hands with the women when a beautiful blond girl stepped up to me and asked, "Why am I here?"

I blinked and replied, "Don't you know why you're here?"

"No, I don't know why I'm here. I've never been in this church before, but this afternoon a very peculiar thing happened to me. All at once it was as if an irresistible force was urging me to come to this meeting tonight; I thought I'd better come. Why am I here?"

I looked at her and asked, "Honey, do you know Christ as your Saviour?"

She replied, "No, I don't."

Then I asked, "Would you like to?"

She said, "Yes, I would like to."

After I finished shaking hands we went downstairs and prayed together, and there she accepted Christ as her personal Saviour.

Marcella envisioned something more for the Christian women of her town—a retreat. Several months later the women who had begun to feel their marvelous unity in Christ came to the retreat. One was the same little blond I had prayed with before. "I now know what that irresistible force was," she said. "It was God's power. My husband has been a Christian for many years, and God has been calling him into full-time service, but I wasn't even a Christian. Now I'm going to be a pastor's wife. My husband has enrolled in seminary. What a horrible pastor's wife I would have made, not even knowing Jesus as my Saviour."

As we were leaving the retreat one woman remarked to me, "I think we ought to call this the 'red nose session.' Just look around at all the tears and all the red noses!" It was true. Women who formerly had crossed the street to keep from speaking to each other were now throbbing in one accord, in unity, loving each other in Christ. Something really had happened there. An irresistible force had been at work, as a result of prayer.

One day my husband walked out of the sanctuary of our church and encountered our custodian fairly dripping with perspiration. He was a giant of a Christian, but was gradually losing his ability to think and work effectively because of hardening of the arteries. As my husband saw him struggling with the vacuum cleaner he looked down, and there lying on the floor was the plug. The dear man had vacuumed the whole auditorium and didn't have the plug in the outlet!

Isn't that what happens to many of us? We work, we pull, we struggle, and we plan until we're utterly exhausted, but we have forgotten to plug in to the source of power. And that source of power is prayer—the "effectual, fervent prayer" of a righteous person that avails much.

**For you to pray:**
"*Dear God, teach me to plug in to Your power. Amen.*"

# 2

# *It Doesn't Take So Long*

*"If I regard iniquity in my heart, the Lord will not hear me." Psalm 66:18*

"How's it going, Mrs. Chris?" My very good friend Steve, one of our church boys, always asked me that question when he came home for a weekend from Harvard School of Business.

Some days I answered, "Oh, is it ever going great. We just learned this kind of prayer and look what's happening. It's going just great!"

Then, when he would come home other times and ask how things were going, I would have a different answer. "Oh, did we fall on our faces this week! It was a mess. I don't know who suggested the method of prayer we tried this time, but it sure didn't work."

Finally Steve, with his youthful fervor, was getting a little exasperated hearing of the struggles we were having as we were learning to pray effectively. I'll never forget the day he and I met down by the piano in the front of the sanctuary. He stood there with his hands on his hips, and looking straight at me, asked, *"Mrs. Chris, why does it take so long to learn how to pray?"*

I said, "Steve, I don't know. I wish I did. I'm sure it's not God's fault. This is all experimentation; it's trial and error for us. We're just learning. I really don't know why it's taking us so long."

Steve is now one of the vice-presidents of an international Christian organization, and last spring while he was teaching a management course in Atlanta, I sent him a message via one of our officers. I asked her to please tell Steve that "it doesn't take so long anymore."

Several weeks later when Steve visited us at our cottage on the shores of Lake Michigan, he said, "You know, when Jan gave me your message, 'It doesn't take so long anymore,' I had to scratch my head and wonder, *What is Ev saying to me?* Then I remembered my question back in 1968."

As I stood cooking the breakfast eggs in the cottage kitchen that next morning, I explained to Steve how and why it doesn't take so long anymore. It went something like the following.

### Effective Fervent Prayer in Only Six Weeks
Our first prayer seminar was held in White Bear Lake, Minnesota with 20 different churches represented. It was a six-week seminar, and the women were practicing simple, sometimes hesitant, audible praying. At the fifth session, one of the women shared with us that the occult had been invited into a local high school. Witches, with all their garb and paraphernalia, were instructing the students, including her daughter, in the ways of witchcraft. Of the 250 women present, many had children in that high school.

Fervent prayer really began then for those students and their teachers. In fact, women were praying so earnestly in their groups that I had to step to the microphone and tell them to conclude their praying because the baby-sitters had to go home! God had given them an urgent reason for learning to pray quickly.

God also gave them answers to their prayers. A group of Christian parents went to school officials about the matter, and, as a result, Christian speakers were given equal time to expose the errors of the occult.

Something else was stirring in that first prayer seminar. It came from a group of women from a liturgical church who sat in the second row. I could always count on them to be in the same place each week. What an inspiration they were. At the third session one of them came to me and said, "Mrs. Christenson, we want you to know that after just two weeks of praying we are already in 'April praying.' "

I had to scratch my head and think, "April praying, April praying?" Oh yes, I recalled having told the group that in 1968 it had taken us from January to April to get to our "No dry eyes," as we were experientially learning what effectual, fervent prayer really was. I said, "Tell me about your 'April praying.' "

She went on, "After the very first session, all of us from our church went home, and we promised each other that though we couldn't meet together every single day, we would pray for our church every morning at 9 o'clock. In just two weeks we are seeing fantastic things happen; we are already in 'April praying.' "

A couple of weeks later they brought me a copy of their church bulletin. One of the women said, "Look what our minister has written!"

I read, "If all these wonderful things happen to women who learn to pray, let's start praying as families."

The minister even began to preach a series of sermons on prayer because that little group practiced what they had learned the very first week.

This is what's exciting to me about the prayer seminars. There is always a nucleus of people, both men and women from all denominations, going back and turning their churches upside down.

I said to Steve, "It took only two weeks for that group from that church to learn to pray. No, it doesn't take so long anymore."

### Six Months, Six Weeks, Six Hours
One day a district leader of the Young Life Campaigners came to me with a question, "Do you think you could teach our Campaigners to pray in six hours? We're planning to meet at a college, but there's going to be a wedding there at 4 o'clock, so we have to be out of the building by 3."

I blinked, and thought, *Six hours! Six weeks is one thing; six months is how long it took us at first; but now this group is asking for only six hours!* I said, "I don't know if I can, but I'll try."

We met together at 9 o'clock in the morning. By 11 A.M. those teenagers, many of whom were disenchanted with the established church, had pushed back their chairs and were kneeling on the floor in little circles fervently praying. I felt tears spring to my eyes at that sight—after only two hours.

Recently in Fargo, North Dakota, we had our first one-day seminar. I had to tell the ladies that I wasn't sure it would work, but we plunged in, breaking just once for midmorning coffee. Then, following lunch, we had an all-afternoon session. At the end of the day, the chairman said to me, "Evelyn, the most exciting thing to me has been to hear this fervent prayer so soon by 100 percent of the people who have just learned to pray today." How long does it take? It doesn't take so long.

### Released to Pray for Others
I want to share with you one other six-week session that took place way back in the fall of 1964 when my two prayer partners, Lorna and Signe, and I began to pray together. Everything seemed to be going great in our church. In four years our membership had almost doubled, a building program was in progress, and we had a full schedule of activities to meet the needs of our congregation. Yet, the three of us sensed that there was a missing dimension. We decided to meet once a week to pray for our church—a very noble idea, we thought.

We agreed at the start to base our praying on a verse of Scripture (a good rule to follow), and right away God gave us Psalm 66:18: "If I regard iniquity in my heart, the Lord will not hear me."

"Lord, what do You mean?" we asked. "We're going to pray for our church." But He continued to apply the pressure gently: "If *I* regard iniquity in *my* heart, the Lord will not hear *me*." Wow! I, the pastor's wife? Lorna and Signe? Uh-huh.

God didn't release us to pray for other needs until we had cleaned up our own lives by confessing *our* sins. It took us, oh, so long. We prayed and prayed, and God kept bringing sins and sins to our minds. As our first prayer meeting came to a close, we thought, *"Whew! We got that one over with; next week we can start praying for the needs of the church."* But when we met the following week, we still couldn't get beyond Psalm 66:18! This was a new concept to us. God kept bringing our wrong priorities, thoughts, reactions, and attitudes to our minds. It took the three of us six weeks—six whole weeks—to get out of Psalm 66:18 and into effectual, fervent praying. I see one of those prayer partners occasionally, and we still shake our heads at that one!

You don't have that many things to be cleaned up in your life, do you? But I did, as a pastor's wife. The other day someone asked me, "What kinds of sins do pastors' wives commit, or is that too personal?"

Not knowing how to answer her offhand, I decided to compile a list, from memory, of the many sins we confessed then. Two days later Signe stopped in the Twin Cities en route back to her home. "Sig, what specific sins do you remember from those six weeks of Psalm 66:18 back in 1964?" I asked.

"The main one I remember," she replied immediately, "was our superior attitude concerning our spiritual status as compared to others and the idea that we should pray *for* them. God showed us that attitude was sin." (I added that one to the two-page list I had jotted down in answer to the question!)

What other sins had we confessed?

*Divided motives.* All of us were very involved in serving Christ, thinking our reasons were all for His glory. But God showed us how much there was of ego, self-fulfillment, self-satisfaction, and desire to build up our own worth in the eyes of our fellow church members.

*Pretense.* One said it was the first time in her life she was really honest before God. People had her on a spiritual pedestal; and she didn't dare admit, even to her family, that she wasn't as spiritual as everybody told her she was. Then she confessed to God a bad attitude toward one member of her family that no one could have dreamed was there.

*Pride.* How surprised I was when God exposed as sin the feeling of "look what I've done" that would come over me as I passed the mimeographed copies of *my* lesson outline to the members of my adult Sunday School class. I was never satisfied in the preparation of my lesson until I had exhausted the resources in my husband's library, put the volumes of notes in outline form, typed stencils, and run off copies for all.

No, none of us had been practicing any of the "dirty dozen" sins, but God exposed one by one the "little Christian sins" that Peter could have been referring to when he wrote, "For the eyes of the Lord are over the righteous, and His ears are open unto their prayers; but the face of the Lord is against them that do evil" (1 Peter 3:12).

### A Prerequisite to Answered Prayer

The three of us learned in a very practical way that there are prerequisites to effective intercessory prayer. There is one word we didn't touch on in the first chapter when we cited: "The effectual, fervent prayer of a righteous person availeth much." Did you catch what we missed? "The effectual fervent prayer" of what kind of person? A *righteous* person. It is his prayer, and only his, that availeth much.

If we are living in sin and liking it, if we are keeping it there, finding that it feels kind of good, if we're regarding— nurturing, patting that little sin along—God does not hear us.

The Prophet Isaiah gives a powerful description of someone in this plight, "Listen now! The Lord isn't too weak to save you. And He isn't getting deaf! He can hear you when you call! But the trouble is that your sins have cut you off from God. Because of sin He has turned His face away from you and will not listen anymore" (Isa. 59:1-2, LB).

Do you wonder why your prayers aren't answered? We're going to learn many reasons why they are not in the chapters that follow, but here is the first one: sin (or sins) in your life. It is "the effectual, fervent prayer of a *righteous* person that availeth much." If your prayers aren't availing much, this may be the reason. Maybe it isn't. Maybe you're long past this. But I find that when I think I'm past this one, all at once a little pride pops up, and I have to confess it quickly, get it out, and then go on.

Your problem may not be *sins*, but *sin*. And this is a very important point. When our Lord was talking to His disciples just before His crucifixion, He told them that He was going to send the Comforter, the Holy Spirit, who would convict *the world* (those who were not Christ's followers) "of sin, because they believe not on Me" (John 16:9). This is the sin that will keep God from hearing intercessory prayer—the sin of not believing in Christ as your personal Saviour. If this is your sin, the only prayer from you that God promises to hear is one of repentance and faith as you invite Christ into your life.

After we become Christians we commit sins. What do we do with them? Do we live with them? The answer is that we get rid of them. God gives Christians the formula through John, "If *we* confess our sins, He is faithful and just to forgive us *our sins*, and to cleanse *us* from all unrighteousness" (1 John 1:9). This is written to Christians, and tells us how we may be cleansed and ready for an effectual intercessory prayer life.

Even little sins can muddy up our communication system. We try to get through to God and there's something in the way. It may be an attitude, a spoken word. God wants these things cleared up. He doesn't want anything between Him and us. If there is, it's our fault, not His, when His ears are closed to our prayers.

Back in 1968, one dear woman objected to this. She said, "I don't like this one bit, this cleaning up of my life before I can be a good, strong, powerful intercessory pray-er."

Another said, "Not me. I have preschool twin boys, and no matter how much I clean up my life before I start for this prayer meeting, by the time I reach here with them in the car, there's some attitude I have to get cleaned up before I can pray for others."

I found out later that the one who objected so strenuously was harboring a grave sin in her life. She didn't like this process, but it's very definite in God's Word. This, then, is the first prerequisite—nothing between God and ourselves when we approach intercessory prayer.

How long does it take? It really doesn't take so long.

*For you to pray:*
*"Dear Father, bring to my mind that sin or sins keeping You from hearing my intercessory prayers.*
*"I confess whatever You have brought to my mind as sin.*
*"Thank You, Lord, for cleansing me as You promised in 1 John 1:9 and qualifying me for effectual, intercessory prayer. Amen."*

# 3

# *Praying in One Accord*

*"These all continued with one accord in prayer and supplication, with the women, and Mary the mother of Jesus, and with His brethren." Acts 1:14*

"Ev, this is a completely different church from what it was when we left. Why?"

To the returned missionary who asked this question, I replied, "The answer is simple. We have learned to pray in the four years that you and your husband have been in Ethiopia." Then I went on and shared with her how it all started in 1968, the experimentation with prayer techniques, and the method we finally came up with in those days—the small group method of prayer which we call "Praying in One Accord." We found this in God's Word, in the Book of Acts:

And when He had spoken these things, while they beheld, He was taken up; and a cloud received Him out of their sight. . . . Then returned they unto Jerusalem from the mount called Olivet, which is from Jerusalem a Sabbath Day's journey. And when they were come in, they went up into an Upper Room, where abode both Peter, and James, and John, and Andrew, Philip, and

44

Thomas, Bartholomew, and Matthew, James the son of Alpheus, and Simon Zelotes, and Judas the brother of James. *These all continued with one accord in prayer and supplication*, with the women, and Mary the mother of Jesus and with His brethren (Acts 1:9, 12-14).

It was a new and exciting experience for us to discover that women were included at this significant time, in the life of the early church. Among them was Mary, the mother of Jesus. In this final reference to her in the New Testament, she is on her face before God, praying with the disciples, the brethren, and the other women. Wouldn't you like to have been with them in that Upper Room? What do you suppose they were praying about? We can't answer that question, but we do know that their hearts were throbbing together as they were praying in one accord.

Jesus, their Lord, had just left Planet Earth. He had gone from their sight, yet the 120 gathered in the Upper Room had the privilege of sensing His presence in their midst. Only a short while before, He had told His disciples, "For where two or three are gathered together in My name, there am I in the midst of them" (Matt. 18:20). Jesus was speaking of those who gather together *in His name*, not of just any group of people who meet together on earth. It is only to His followers that He gives the promise of His presence. Small group praying, the method of praying in one accord, is based on the eligibility to pray in the name of Jesus; it pertains only to the followers of Christ.

### Lord, Teach Us to Pray
We can learn something else from the Upper Room pray-ers. They were putting into practice what Jesus had taught them about prayer when He was on earth. His disciples must have felt a tremendous lack in their own lives as they saw the beautiful example of the prayer life of their Lord. In their need they cried, "Lord, teach us to pray" (Luke 11:1).

Today earnest followers of the Lord sense their need just as the disciples did. It's amazing that we can knock on doors, get on the telephone, invite people to our prayer groups, only to find that when we meet together we do not know how to pray. I was one of 11 chairmen who formed 5,000 prayer groups for a

Billy Graham Crusade held in our area. Later, I will describe how I got involved in that. In any case, we heard afterward that fantastic things had happened in some of those prayer groups where women had prayed for five consecutive weeks before and during the crusade. But hundreds of women have said to me, "We did everything you told us to do. We knocked on doors, we called our neighbors. We did all these things, but we didn't know what to do when we got together. We didn't know how to pray."

Jesus' response to His disciples and to us is simple, yet so beautiful: "When you pray, say, 'Our Father who art in heaven . . . .' " You recognize that, don't you? It's the beginning of what we sometimes call "The Lord's Prayer." What is prayer? *Prayer, real prayer, is simply conversation with God, our Father.* Jesus didn't say, "Now, when you pray, say, 'My Father.' " No, He used the plural, "Our Father." He is your Father, my Father, Jesus' Father—"Our Father, who art in heaven." It's so simple. Just conversation with God.

## Changes

When people start praying together on this basis—in one accord, to our Father in heaven, in the name of Jesus—and practice praying together, things begin to change. Our lives change, our families change, our churches change, our communities change. Changes take place not when we study about prayer, not when we talk about it, not even when we memorize beautiful Scripture verses on prayer; it is when *we actually pray* that things begin to happen. And we don't suffer from the "paralysis of analysis." We are not paralyzed by analyzing prayer. Instead, we take the problems at hand and pray about them.

A newspaper reporter recently asked me in an interview, "Would you mind telling me how much you charge for these prayer seminars?"

I replied, "We don't charge anything."

"Well, then, will you tell me why you do it? If you don't charge what is your reason for spending all this time and effort?"

I had to stop and think a minute. Then I said, "The reason I teach people to pray is that I have seen so many changed lives as a result of prayer. This is what makes it so exciting. We learn not *about* prayer, but *to* pray, to converse with our Father who is in heaven."

One day I received an invitation from the women of another church in our hometown to come over and teach them to pray. I said I would. A few days later, as we drove along the main street in her little red Volkswagen, the woman who picked me up took her eyes off the road and looking straight at me asked, "Do you care if our pastor comes this afternoon?"

I was quiet for a minute because I have a "thing" about this. I thought, "Who am I to be teaching pastors?"

Noticing my hesitancy, she went on to assure me, "He really wants to come."

I said, "OK, if he really wants to come, you tell him it's all right." So the pastor sat way back in one corner of the room while the women of his church, many of whom had never prayed out loud before, learned our six little S's of prayer. Afterward we broke into smaller groups, and I know that 100 percent of those women prayed that day.

A week later at a Sunday School dinner meeting, I was sitting one place away from the speaker, who was the assistant pastor of that same church. During the meal he leaned over and loudly announced to me, "Say, do you know you turned our church upside down?"

I asked, "What happened?"

He replied, "Well, ever since our pastor heard the women praying, and learned how all this prayer works, he won't let us have a single meeting unless we pray. We can't even have a book review in our church unless we pray about it!" He didn't seem too happy about the whole thing.

"I didn't turn your church upside down," I replied. "But it's very possible that God did."

Recently a pastor greeted me at the door when I arrived to speak to the women of his church. "I'm so glad finally to see what you look like. A woman is here today who attended the prayer seminar in downtown Minneapolis. She bought a set of your tapes, and has been a little missionary circulating them among the women's circles for the last 11 months. Each circle has had its own mini-prayer seminar, with the women learning to pray. I can see such a difference in their lives."

## Not for Women Only

One night in the fall of 1969 my husband bounced in from a deacon board meeting with a message for me: "Will you please ask the women if they will take our annual Prayer Week the first week in January?"

Right away I shot back the answer. I didn't stop to pray. I didn't ask God what He thought about it at all. I just said to Chris, "You tell your deacon board, 'No.' God has called me to teach women." But I knew I wasn't really being honest with God.

My husband trotted back to the board and told them, "No, there's no way they're going to teach the whole church how to pray."

The board said, "You go back to your wife and tell her that we have been watching and we feel that the women have discovered a method of prayer that works, and we would like them to teach it to the whole church."

By this time my husband was becoming like a Ping-Pong ball being batted back and forth between two paddles—the deacon board and me. When Chris returned with the same request, I realized that I had been hasty in my reply the first time.

I said, "OK, I'll take it to the women."

Their response was also negative.

Again I agreed, but suggested that at this point we pray about it. After fervent prayer we concluded that this request was really God's way of speaking to us. We consented to take Prayer Week for 1970 on one condition—that it be held the second week in January, the first being preparation week. The board agreed. That first week we trained prayer group leaders representing every department of the church—the choir, the deacon board, the trustee board, and the Sunday School. They all came to learn the ground rules for effective praying.

In the week of prayer that followed, we discovered that we had about five times as many people participating as we ever had in the past. There were boys and girls, men and women—preschoolers to golden agers—from every area of our church life, all learning to *pray in one accord*. I don't know of one person who didn't pray, but I'll stay on the side of caution and say that of all those who attended, 95 percent actively participated in verbal prayer. Now, that's a lot of people praying, and there were some very definite answers that gave us great encouragement.

I recall, particularly, how thrilled the members of the Junior Department were after I had taught them our method of praying in one accord on the Sunday morning during Prayer Week. They came up with two urgent needs along with their other prayer requests: "We need a superintendent and a piano player in our department." That morning the Juniors with their teachers divided into small groups and prayed specifically that God would send them these workers. I cringed a little inside. What if God didn't answer their prayer?

On the following Wednesday, one of the church's business-men came to Gail, our children's worker, and said, "The Lord has laid it on my heart to be superintendent of the Junior Department, and my wife would like to play the piano for the Juniors if she can be replaced in her present department."

Meanwhile God had been working in the college-age class also. On the same Sunday of Prayer Week, along with specific prayer, they were offering themselves to God for service in the church. A student nurse wrote on her card, "I am available to play the piano where I'm needed." Gail assigned the student nurse to replace the wife in the other department, and the following Sunday the Juniors almost exploded with excitement as they were presented their new superintendent and pianist. God had really answered their prayers!

## In One Accord

We, as women of the church, had simply shared the method that God had given to us from the Bible, the method of praying in one accord in small groups. How is this achieved? *Simply by praying about only one subject at a time with one person praying aloud while the others in the group are praying silently on the same subject.* In this way everyone is praying together (in one accord) instead of planning other prayers in advance.

Have you ever been in a group when someone is praying a long prayer? And have you found that you were not really praying along with that person? Instead you were mulling over in your mind all the things you were going to pray about when your turn came? I have, and my thoughts have run like this, "Lord, now bring to my mind . . ." "Oh, I don't want to forget that one!" "Say, that's a good request" "Thank You, Lord, for reminding me of that one." Then I have gone back and reviewed the prayer subjects on my fingers. Next, I've wondered what my introductory statement should be, or how I should conclude my prayer. While someone else has been praying, I have been planning my own long prayer in advance instead of praying silently on the same subject with the person who is praying audibly. That's *not* praying in one accord.

You see, if everyone in a group is praying in one accord with the person who is praying aloud, the number of prayers ascending to heaven are multiplied by the number who are praying silently. How much more power there is in prayer when the participants are praying in one accord!

*For you to pray:*
  "*Father, teach me to pray in one accord with other people, sharing **their** burdens, joys, and petitions. Amen.*"

# 4

# *The Method—Six S's*

*"But when ye pray, use not vain repetitions, as the heathen do; for they think that they shall be heard for their much speaking. Be not ye therefore like unto them, for your Father knoweth what things ye have need of, before ye ask Him." Matthew 6:7-8*

"Well, I suppose you all know how to pray. I won't fit into this group." With that remark, Betty, my neighbor, joined the three of us meeting in a home on our block to pray for the coming Billy Graham Crusade. There she was, apparently wanting to take part, but scared to death to pray aloud, even with only three other women present.

There are thousands of people just like Betty. They are all over the country—in neighborhood prayer groups, in midweek services, and in special prayer sessions—and they are not praying audibly for only one reason: *they don't know how.*

We have found in our prayer seminars that about 50 percent of those participating have never prayed aloud before. They come from a great variety of churches, Protestant and Catholic, but talking with God in the presence of others is a very real problem to them.

My response to my neighbor, Betty, was, "Oh yes, you certainly will fit into this group. It's really not difficult. After we hear the prayer requests, we all are going to pray just one simple sentence on each one." And we did. The three of us, who had prayed for years, prayed one simple sentence following the request, and so did Betty! In fact, as we

51

concluded that session, she had prayed four times, audibly. What happens when we put ourselves on the level of the most inexperienced pray-ers? Many of them hear their own voices in prayer for the first time.

The rules we applied that morning were the ones our women devised in 1968 to implement our method of praying in one accord—praying about only one subject at a time, with one person praying aloud while the others in the group are praying silently on the same subject. There are *six S's*, six simple rules to follow, whether one is a participant or a prayer group leader, a seasoned pray-er or a shy and untrained one. These six rules serve as effective tools to help a prayer group get started, to encourage newcomers, and to motivate timid people to pray aloud. But a prayer group doesn't have to stay with these elementary rules. It's exciting to know that the participants can go on and graduate into effective, fervent, spontaneous praying.

Suppose your present prayer group is not going very well with no one wanting to join or perhaps not coming back after trying it once. Or, suppose you would like to start a prayer group in your church or in your neighborhood. You may find that these *six S's* are just what you need to encourage 100 percent participation.

### 1. Subject by Subject
The first S is *Subject by Subject*—praying in one accord about only one subject at a time. As one person prays out loud, the rest pray silently on the same subject, *not planning their own prayers in advance*. This assures complete concentration and fervent prayer on one request at a time. Also, in this way no one is deprived of the privilege of praying for the request before going on to another.

You may be accustomed to praying around the world, mentioning every person you know, every missionary in many different countries. And you may be tempted to pray this way as a prayer group leader. But your part is only to announce one subject for prayer at a time, and then to pray a short sentence prayer yourself. Sometimes it's a good idea to have a list ready and to say, "Right now we are going to pray one simple sentence about so-and-so." Then, as the leader, pray one simple sentence and wait for others to pray audibly on the same subject before going to the next request. Because the participants will have to "shift mental gears" before going on to another subject, it's a good idea to pause between subjects. Then the group will be prepared to pray again.

As the participants learn to pray in one accord, subject by subject, prayer gains momentum and becomes more spontaneous. When this happens, the leader may simply lead out in prayer on a subject rather than announcing it. When those in our groups become proficient in this method, their spiritual pulses will be throbbing together in such a way that each one will begin to sense the direction of the Holy Spirit when it is time to start a new subject. Everyone in the group will then have the freedom to initiate a new topic for prayer. It may take a while, but this is our goal. They won't have to have a leader anymore!

I remember the first time I tried this with my group in 1968. I had always come to the prayer meeting with a written list of requests at which I would peek with one eye. That day I told God I was going to hide the list and trust Him completely to bring to the minds of the pray-ers those things He wanted us to remember in prayer. Checking the list after we finished praying, I was delighted and amazed to find that He had reminded someone to pray about every single request I had written down!

When praying subject by subject, everyone is free to pray audibly in turn. But whether praying audibly or silently, all are praying in one accord on the same subject, not planning their own prayers in advance, and multiplying the power of all the prayers that are ascending simultaneously to God's throne.

### 2. Short Prayers

*Short Prayers*, the second *S*, are the secret of the success of small group prayer. Just one, or only a few sentences from each person on each subject allows time for all to pray if they wish. No one should be forced to pray aloud; let prayer be something spontaneous, something a person wants to do, even if it's only to hear her own voice in prayer.

As leaders we are responsible to see that the prayers are short. How are we going to do this? Superimpose our wills on our groups and say, "Look everybody, let's pray short prayers"? No, but at first *we* will have to back way up and start praying just one simple sentence ourselves in order to get the shy, untrained ones to pray. We make the rest of the group more comfortable by the kind of praying we do. Might it be that God is much more interested in the short statement of a new pray-er who has never prayed audibly before than He is in an elaborate prayer uttered by one who has had years of practice? It may be that we veteran pray-ers, mature pray-ers, are inhibiting the shy ones. Some of us may even have an idea that God hears us for our "much praying."

Christ had something to say about this when He was teaching His disciples to pray. He said, "But when ye pray, use not vain repetitions, as the heathen do; for they think that they shall be heard for their much speaking. Be not ye therefore like unto them, for your Father knoweth what things ye have need of, before ye ask Him" (Matt. 6:7-8).

Do we think we're going to be heard because we give an introduction, three points, and a conclusion to everything we pray about? God knows all we need, and all we have to do is to lay our requests before Him. Just think of all the requests that go unremembered when someone dominates the group with lengthy prayers on one, two, or even three subjects!

Now, there are times when long, involved prayers are very much in order. If you are asked to lead in prayer at a meeting and respond by praying one simple sentence, you will probably jar the whole group! Long prayers are appropriate at the right time and in the right place, but that time is not when the shy and untrained are learning to pray.

### 3. Simple Prayers

The third S is *Simple Prayers.* Those who have never prayed before will find it possible to utter one *simple* sentence from the heart when the leaders and other participants avoid using complicated phrases and a special prayer vocabulary. When we leave our high-sounding theological expressions at home in our prayer closets and make our short prayers simple ones, then the new pray-ers will feel comfortable about praying one simple, uncomplicated prayer themselves, and will be more apt to return the following week.

Though he didn't know it at the time, I learned a valuable lesson from one of our church leaders during our Prayer Week in 1970. He was an Irishman with a beautiful accent and a rich vocabulary. Whenever he prayed aloud our hearts soared heavenward. But we had a problem. When he finished praying nobody else dared to follow him! Why, I wouldn't be caught dead praying after he had just uttered his long, beautiful prayer, couched in lofty theological phrases. I can remember even my husband hesitating a bit to close in prayer after this man had prayed so eloquently.

As we approached that 1970 Prayer Week, I wondered what was going to happen in a group he would be leading. I soon found out, for one night he and I were leading our respective groups in areas separated only by a plastic curtain. As I presented the prayer requests to my group, I found it difficult to concentrate because I was so curious to learn what was happening on the other side of the curtain. Have you ever had your ear tuned one way and your voice aimed another?

I heard him open his prayer group with just one simple sentence. Astounded, I listened. But he didn't say another word. Soon, one by one, all the people in his group prayed their own simple sentences. Then he prayed another sentence on the next subject and stopped. Once again each one prayed. I was acquainted with everyone in his group, and I knew that many of them had never prayed aloud before; but that night every single person in his circle prayed aloud. What happens when we are willing to put ourselves temporarily on the level of those who don't know how to pray? We encourage them to pray with us.

Back in 1968 when we were practicing and experimenting with all these methods, eventually a whole room in our church was filled with women praying; but Eva, a woman who lived next door, declared that she would not join the others in prayer. She said she had never prayed out loud in a group and she never would.

I knew that Eva's family had a very fine devotional life. She was a great Christian. This wasn't her problem, but praying aloud with others was. She would shake her finger at me in other meetings and say, "Don't you ever call on me to pray; don't you ever call on me."

I assured her that we never call on anybody to pray, but still she didn't come to our prayer meetings. As we drove up to the church, we would see the curtains part as she peeked out the window, but that's as close as Eva got. Then one day, without explanation, she joined us. She came every week after that, but never prayed out loud.

As the summer rolled around, we moved our meetings to one of the parks in town. It was at one of those park sessions that I had a distinct impression from God that Eva was going to pray that day. But as I led the group in prayer, mentioning one request after another, she didn't utter a word. Though it was past time for us to start home, I kept adding requests and waiting for her. Suddenly, Eva began to pray. She forgot all the rules she ever learned. It was like Niagara Falls breaking loose! That day Eva prayed around the world.

When we had Prayer Week in January 1970, one of the groups praying was made up of all men, including the pastor and the chairman of the church board, except Eva. Again my ear was attuned in another direction. Guess who prayed *first* in that group? Eva! She has said to me since, "Ev, if I can do it, *anybody* can."

### 4. Specific Prayer Requests
S number four is *Specific Prayer Requests*. Specific requests listed and specific answers noted are a great encouragement to continuing and expanded prayer. Use a notebook or file folder for this.

If our groups start falling apart, and they may, or if people suddenly aren't interested, the best way to get things going again is to encourage them by showing specific answers to their specific requests. When there's a lag, whip out that little book in which requests and answers are recorded and point out how God has used the prayer group to change circumstances and individuals. Spend time in prayer *praising God* for His specific answers. Then watch as new life begins to flood your prayer group!

As the specific answers to their prayers pile up, you will begin to see the pray-ers change as well. By keeping records, the individuals who are praying start to *see the worth of themselves in prayer*, and this is important.

*Date* your specific requests and date the answers. God is not controlled by time as we human beings are. He is only *aware* of time. He places His answers down on Planet Earth when He knows best. Therefore, if we keep track of *time*—how long God takes to answer our prayers—we're going to learn some tremendous spiritual lessons about how God operates. As weeks and months and years come and go, we will see that His timing is always perfect.

We will also learn some *whys* when we keep track of how He answers. It may be that we are not ready for some answers. My two prayer partners and I prayed every week for two solid years before I had my first neighborhood Bible study. I wasn't ready and God knew I wasn't. If we keep a record of the specific timing of our requests and God's answers, then we can look back and see many of the reasons for His delays and His withholdings.

God may answer our prayers not only at a time when we least expect, but He may answer in a *way* we don't expect. We will be astounded at *how* God answers prayer. He may answer in a way that is completely opposite to the way we think He should. He knows what is best for us, and He never makes a mistake.

Our women experienced this great joy in praying specifically in May 1968, when we were preparing for a mother-daughter banquet. Ruth Johnson of "Back to the Bible Broadcast," a "daughter" of our church, was to be the speaker. We set up a prayer room and asked the women who came to the church to work (cook, set tables, or decorate) to spend some time, equal time if they could, in the prayer room, praying specifically for Ruth Johnson. What a great moving of God there was at the banquet that night!

On the following Sunday, with my little notebook in hand (I always recorded the results of our prayer experimentation), I said to Ruth, "Please be very careful how you answer me because we zeroed in on you in prayer, and I want a very honest answer. This will be reported to our national conference in June. Will you tell me what happened, if anything did happen, on Friday night when you spoke at our banquet."

Ruth drew a deep breath and tears came to her eyes. "Ev," she said, "the last time I was in this church it was to bury my mother. It all came back to me last Friday as I was on my way here. After I got to the church, I couldn't even bring myself to open the door. I kept thinking of my mother, and then I thought of my former Sunday School teachers who were going to be at the banquet. You know, I used to be 'naughty little Ruthie' to those teachers, and I had a feeling that they were all going to be looking at me and thinking, *There's that 'naughty little Ruthie' again.* Evelyn, I could not walk through that door. But suddenly, I felt a great sense of strength and freedom. I can't explain it, but there was complete release and I walked in. It was just fantastic. My voice has gone around the world via radio for 30 years, but never in all those years have I felt such freedom and such power as I experienced when I sang and spoke last Friday night.''

Not long afterward Ruth's missionary brother came home from India. He came to me and said, "Evie, what did you do to my sister?''

I replied, "We didn't do anything to your sister.''

He said, "Oh, yes you did. Since the women prayed, my sister has been a completely different woman.''

Now I thought Ruth was a fantastic Christian before that time, but I learned something. It was that we don't limit our praying to the down-and-outer, or to someone we think is dying or experiencing great tragedy. We also need to pray for those who are ministering, who don't appear to have any needs. What did we do? We only prayed—specifically. And God worked.

### 5. Silent Periods

The next *S* is *Silent Periods.* Silent periods between prayers are a privilege and a blessing. Don't panic when there's a lull—just listen! This is an added dimension to our definition of prayer in chapter 3. Prayer is a *two-way* conversation with God.

Today silence is almost a lost art. After a few seconds pass without audible prayer, someone usually feels compelled to clear his throat, shuffle his feet, or nervously finger a songbook. Somehow we think we have to talk *at* God all of the time, but there are marvelous things that God wants to say to us. He has answers to our questions, secrets He wants to share, yet we bombard Him with our "much praying." We forget that

God is on His throne in heaven just waiting to say something great to us, if we would only give Him a chance. How frustrated He must be (if God can become frustrated) when He has something so wonderful to tell you and me, and we aren't quiet long enough to listen to what He has to say.

One day I asked my son about a girl who lives near us, and he said, "Oh, I guess she's fine, Mom, if she'd ever keep still so we could find out."

"What do you mean?" I asked.

"Well, on the school bus that girl talks every single minute. She might be a real great girl, but she doesn't shut up long enough for us to find out."

Has God ever said that about me? Has He ever said it about you? Have we learned to keep still long enough for God to say something to us? It is in the *silence* that our communication becomes two-way.

The first time I practiced the *Six-S* method at a retreat was 1969. It was evening, and as the women finished praying in their small groups of four, I dismissed them to go out to a point near the water. "Just one rule," I said, "please don't talk while you are walking out to the point." There had been fervent prayer in their groups, and I wanted them to keep their hearts open to God's voice.

We had planned that the KTIS radio trio would come to the point by boat and, at a given signal, sing to the women on shore. But the signal somehow failed, and they waited and waited, not knowing when to start their song. The leader of the testimony meeting kept putting more wood on the fire and thinking, "I *have* to say something." But each time she thought it, God said, "Keep still, Mary." In fact, Mary told me later, "You know very well, Evelyn, that God said, 'Mary, shut up!' "

Twenty minutes went by with about 500 women sitting in absolute silence at the water's edge. Now and then we could hear soft crying. Then from the boat, totally obscured by the darkness, came the beautiful strains of "Take my life and let it be consecrated, Lord, to Thee." The common theme that ran through the testimonies that night was: "God spoke to me not so much in the songs or in the message, *but in the silence at the water's edge.*"

## 6. Small Groups

*Small Groups*, the sixth *S*, are usually best for newcomers, as well as for the shy or untrained. For some, it would take great courage to stand before a group of 100 people, or even 25 people, and raise their voices in prayer for the first time. But in smaller groups they can gain confidence in praying audibly.

In our seminars when there are several hundred participants in one room, we divide into small groups of four or five. This is quickly accomplished by standing and having every other row turn back, each two rows of people facing each other. We then just draw apart in groups of four, two from each row. How my heart thrilled at one of our prayer seminars in a large church recently when almost 200 small groups of people in the same room lifted their voices earnestly to God.

Yesterday, when one of my original prayer partners called me long distance, we chatted about the joy and the privilege of being just two or three in a little group. "Ev," she recalled, "when we started praying, just the three of us, that was the turning point in my spiritual life."

Whatever we do, we must never underestimate the value of a small group praying, for Christ promised that *where two or three of His followers are gathered together in His name, He will be in their midst* (see Matt. 18:20). What an opportunity it provides to practice the presence of Christ in our midst!

Do you remember in the account of the stoning of Stephen that he lifted up his eyes and "saw the glory of God, and Jesus standing on the right hand of God"? (Acts 7:55) The right hand of God is the place of authority and honor. Christ is still at the right hand of God today, interceding for us, but we also have His promise that He will be *with* us—where even two or three are gathered together. Now, we want to be very careful that we do not take Christ off His throne, that we do not play games with Him in prayer. He is in heaven, but *His* presence is in the midst of those who gather together in His name.

Christ helped the disciples and those who knew Him very intimately here on earth to understand this. G. Campbell Morgan, in his message "Rekindled Fire," emphasizes the importance of our Lord's vanishing and appearing after His resurrection. He explains that the disciples and His friends were learning the lesson that Christ was with them, even when they did not see Him with their physical eyes. These followers of Jesus were practicing His presence even though they could not see Him. After He had vanished from their sight for the last time at His ascension, He was in their midst in the Upper Room, and they knew it.

**For you to pray:**
*"Dear Father: Please give me the privilege of being aware of the presence of Jesus, my Saviour, in a prayer group. Teach me to help others to pray. Teach me to listen to You speaking to me in the silent periods. Amen."*

# 5

# *How to Pray in God's Will*

*"And this is the confidence that we have in Him, that, if we ask anything according to His will, He heareth us. And if we know that He hear us, whatsoever we ask, we know that we have the petitions that we desired of Him." 1 John 5:14-15*

On the morning following Lindon Karo's funeral, I posed some searching questions to those attending our prayer seminar. "What do you think went wrong? Why did this tremendous pastor, only 32 years old, die of cancer? Thousands of prayers were offered for him. Forty people in his church had covenanted to fast and pray one day a week for him. I don't think I attended a meeting anywhere during that period, but that we were all praying. Why weren't those prayers answered? What went wrong? Why did we bury Lindon Karo yesterday?"

When I reached this point in the seminar, a steering committee member (wanting to be helpful) waved her hand from the back of the church, and said, "Yes, Evelyn, and Lindon Karo's mother-in-law and sister-in-law are here with us today."

Wow! I stopped for a second and pondered, *Do I go on? Do I insult these people by teaching a lesson on how to pray in God's will? What do I do about these loved ones who buried their son-in-law and brother-in-law just yesterday? What would you have done?* I felt God was telling me to go ahead and teach the lesson I had prepared.

When the session was over, those two very beautiful Christian women came to me and said, "Please don't worry about today's lesson. Many months ago we as a family committed the whole matter of Lindon's illness to the Lord. We prayed, 'Only Your will, God, whatever it is.' We did not ask for healing only; we prayed that God's will be done in our loved one's life."

Have you come to the place where you can pray, "Only God's will"? Do you know that you are in absolute oneness with the will of God? Have you come to that place?

We read in 1 John 5:14-15 about a prerequisite to effective praying. "And this is the confidence that we have in Him, that, if we ask anything according to His will, He heareth us. And if we know that He hear us, whatsoever we ask, we know that we have the petitions that we desired of Him." Did you catch the prerequisite? How can we have confidence in anything we ask? It is by praying *according to His will*. And what is confidence in prayer? It is knowing absolutely and irrevocably that we have whatever we have asked.

### "If It Be Thy Will, Amen"

What do we mean when we use the expression "praying in God's will"? Is it simply tacking on the end of a prayer the phrase we use perhaps more frequently than any other? You know how it goes. We ask God for a whole string of things, then we piously add, ". . . if it be Thy will, Lord. Amen." Or it may be that we ask God for something we know is not good for us. Let's say, for example, that we ask for a bushel of Hershey bars! God knows very well (and so do we) that if we ate a bushel of Hershey bars we'd die of indigestion, but many times we ask Him for something just as ridiculous and tack on "if it be Thy will," just to get ourselves off the hook. This is not what it means to pray in God's will.

### The Praying Person—Not the Prayer Request

Berkeley Mickelsen, professor of New Testament Greek in a nearby seminary, said to me one day, "Evelyn, I hope that when you're teaching all those women to pray in God's will that you are teaching them that it is the person praying, and not the prayer request, that changes."

I said, "Berkeley, that's the whole gist of our lesson on God's will."

Praying in God's will is not easy, yet it's very simple. It involves a commitment of every single thing that comes into our lives to God and His perfect will. And it's exciting to live in complete oneness with the will of God. It is never dull or static because it is not a one-time, once-for-all commitment. It is something we have to work at constantly, moment by moment.

This is expressed in a beautiful definition of the word *effectual* as it is found in James 5:16. According to Vine's *Expository Dictionary of New Testament Words*, it means "the effect produced in the praying person, bringing him into line with the will of God." It is the pray-er who changes, rather than the prayer. Praying "in the will of God" means, then, *being* conformed to the will of God as we pray. Wouldn't it be great if we could always *be conformed to the will of God* (with all known sin confessed), so that we would never pray outside the will of God? The effectual pray-er, then, is a person who is completely committed to God's will for answers, and not to his own will.

After our women had been praying for a few months back in 1968, my husband exclaimed one day, "Wow, if God doesn't answer a single one of your prayers, what He's doing *in* the people who are praying will be worth it all."

What God does in the lives of people who are praying, in bringing them in line with His will, is one of His miracles here on Planet Earth. The turning point in our prayer seminars is the session where people in prayer commit their whole lives to God's perfect will. This happened to a college teacher, who sent me this note recently:

> On February 26 my sister invited me to attend your prayer seminar. I thought, *A prayer seminar? What good will it do? I have prayed and prayed, and it hasn't done any good.* But I went.
>
> You see, I have been a Christian all of my life. I was raised in a wonderful Christian home and reared in an atmosphere of loving and trusting Jesus. But suddenly I was faced with very severe testing of my faith. My husband's construction company folded, leaving a large sum of debts which we were 50 percent responsible for.

Because of this, we had to sell our home and liquidate our assets. Also, I was not well, and our little two-year-old son had just undergone surgery.

Then, the Scripture that was to change my life and my prayers, 1 John 5:14-15, "and this is the confidence. . . ." Up to that point I had not prayed for His will. I could only see what I wanted to happen.

Evelyn asked us to stand at the end of the session and form our prayer groups of four. She told us to ask God for the *one* thing we wanted most from Him. I remember saying aloud in my little circle of four Christian sisters, "Lord, I want Your perfect will for me and my family."

That was it! I was to learn later that that was what was keeping my prayers from being answered. I had never asked God for His will.

Now, I felt entirely free. I felt the whole load lift, as if the responsibility to straighten up the messy things was not mine.

Now it is nine months since that time, and I cannot begin to tell you of the peace I have in my heart. My husband's business debts are not all cleared up as yet, but God is moving. The burden is lifted. My health has improved tremendously. In fact, I got a teaching position at Bethel College this fall, a position that just seemed to come right out of heaven itself. I was not applying or seeking such a position, but was asked to join the staff. Praise God! He can "do exceeding abundantly above all that we ask or think" (Eph. 3:20).

### On Earth, as It Is in Heaven

For us to pray, "Lord, I want Your will down here on earth," is a tremendous prayer. Wouldn't it be fantastic if we could pray that prayer for Washington, D.C. today? If we could by our praying get God's will done in Moscow, or in the Middle East? While there is a sense in which we can pray that God's will be done in these places, they are not within our direct sphere of influence, are they? But there is a spot on earth, a sphere of influence that belongs only to you. It has been given to you by our heavenly Father. And it's possible for you to bring about God's complete will in your sphere of influence here on earth.

The disciples whom Jesus taught to pray: "Our Father . . . Thy will be done on earth as it is in heaven," knew they couldn't change the whole Roman Empire, but they also knew it was possible for them to change the spheres of influence which were theirs, which had been given to them by God. And they did. God changes circumstances and people when we in a very personal way pray that His will be done in the sphere of influence which is ours.

The Lord's Prayer really comes into focus right where we are when we pray, "Thy will be done on earth as it is in heaven." Is there anything contrary to God's will in heaven? No! Think of what would happen if every Christian really brought God's will to the little sphere that is his, with nothing contrary to God's perfect will! How different would be our nation, our cities, our churches, our homes.

### The Example of Christ
The supreme example of praying in the will of God is that of Christ praying in the Garden of Gethsemane on the night before He was to die on the cross for our sins. Our Lord, in His humanity, did not want to suffer. He prayed, "Father, if Thou be willing, remove this cup from Me; nevertheless not My will, but Thine, be done" (Luke 22:42). Then, after much agony of Spirit, He said, "Father, I am willing for Your will."

Have you come to the place in your life where you can say, "Lord, not my will, but Thine, be done. No matter how much it hurts, how difficult the task, how high the mountain You've given me to climb, it doesn't make any difference, dear Lord, I am willing"?

When we visited the Holy Land a few years ago, I sat alone under one of those old, gnarled olive trees in the Garden of Gethsemane, and read in Luke's Gospel the account of all my Jesus went through the night before He died, before He took upon Himself the sin of the world, including mine; when He sweat as it were great drops of blood there in the garden. With my heart absolutely breaking, I wrote in the margin of my Bible, "Lord, please, only Your will in my life, only Your will!" We don't have to sit under an ancient olive tree in His land to come to that place, but right where we are today we can say to Christ, "Lord, not my will, only Yours be done."

When we reach the place where we're really on our faces before God, does He as an "ogre" sitting up in heaven say, "Good, I have another doormat on which to wipe My feet"? Is that what He says? Do we become doormats for God to wipe His feet on when we say, "Lord, I'm willing for Your will"? Oh, no. What happened to Christ the day after He said this to His heavenly Father? He became the *Redeemer of mankind!* He became your Saviour and my Saviour.

Mary too had a tremendous privilege because she was willing for God's will in her life. Do you recall her response at the time of the Annunciation? When the angel came to her and said that God had chosen her to be the mother of the Saviour, Mary immediately responded, "Behold, the handmaid of the Lord; be it according to thy word."

Do you think it was easy for Mary to say Yes to the will of God, to being pregnant out of wedlock? When it meant vulnerability to misunderstanding, to ridicule? When it could mean possible rejection by her fiance or even being stoned to death? It was not easy for Mary, but because she was willing for God's will, she was greatly blessed by Him. She was given the great privilege of bearing the Son who became our Redeemer.

### Open Doors

What happens to Evelyn when she is on her face before God and says, "OK, Lord, I don't know what You want. That's a big mountain, that's difficult surgery, these are hard things in my life, but, Lord, no matter what it is, I want Your perfect will"? At that point does God become an ogre and take advantage of my commitment? No, at that point He starts to open doors, and fantastic things begin to happen—even prayer seminars— when I just make myself available to Him.

One day our campus pastor inquired, "Ev, how did you ever get all those prayer seminars started, anyway?"

I shrugged, "They just sort of grew, like Topsy." He looked at me, wondering at what I was saying. I went on, "You know, we really didn't plan them. They just happened. In every single step, the constant prayer of steering committees, prayer chains, and our advisory board has been, 'Lord, Your will.' Then we wait to see what His will is. We never even make contacts asking to hold a seminar, and it is so thrilling to watch God work when we let Him."

One day a young woman who had traveled almost 100 miles round trip each day to attend a Minneapolis prayer seminar asked me, "What is the procedure to get you to come to our town for a prayer seminar?"

I replied, "Pray about it, and if it is God's will, we'll come."

"Oh, three of us have been praying for several months," she replied, "and we believe God is saying we should have it."

"That's good enough for me," I said. "I'll come."

I better understood her insistence on having a seminar in her town when she handed me this note:

> Dear Evelyn: Since being in your prayer seminar at Elim Lutheran Church my life has been changed through accepting Christ. Also, my four-year-old daughter and nine-year-old son have asked Jesus into their lives. Now my husband wants me to work on him. Thank you.

God rewarded her eagerness when 30 women found Christ in "her" seminar. It was God's will!

In fact, the Bible study on prayer for all the churches in White Bear Lake, Minnesota, that automatically turned into our first prayer seminar, came into being because God took over. The chairman and I, frustrated at not being able to work my schedule into all the fall events of that area, finally in tears just prayed together, "All right, Lord, only *Your* will. Whenever *You* want this Bible study, work it out." And God timed it perfectly. He knew all along when prayer would be needed in that town. He knew that the next February, witches and occult personnel would be in one of the high schools, so He planned for those 250 women to be "praying in one accord" just at the right time.

What has turned into this whole prayer ministry in my life started in November 1967, when I was asked to work on the prayer experiment with our church women, as described in chapter 1. I hesitated at first, not knowing for certain whether to make the commitment. But one day while I was reading God's Word, a phrase in Revelation, "Behold, I have set before thee an open door," stood out as if it were in bold print. God said, "Evelyn, I have set before *you* an open door." I closed my Bible, said, "Lord, I'm willing," and went to the phone and dialed long distance to Chicago. I said excitedly to the executive secretary of our National Women's Board, "How can I say No when God has just put before me an open door in Revelation 3:8?"

Has God put before you an open door? Are you hesitating, perhaps rebelling, or holding back because of fear, when God is challenging, "Look, here's an open door, wouldn't you like to walk through it for Me? This is My will for you."

Oh, answer Him, "Lord, here I am. There is no friction between my will and Yours. Whatever You have for me, I know that You will give me enough strength, enough grace. I know You will give me all that I need, so Lord, here I am ready to do Your will."

"Try it. You'll like it!" It's amazing what happens when we step out.

### Men Too?

Sometimes I seem to need a little help from other people in going through the doors God is opening for me. "I don't think God is hung up on you teaching men to pray, but I think you are," a professional Christian counselor chided as we chatted at a Christmas party. I suddenly realized that I was so hung up that I was praying, "God, Your will," but didn't have the courage to accept it.

My prayer chains had been praying for several months about frequent requests from men to attend prayer seminars. Then I learned that, while I was planning to give a three-minute speech the next Sunday encouraging attendance at our upcoming seminar, the host church was planning for me to present the morning message. I was panicking, just *knowing* it never could be God's will for me to do *that!*

Suddenly, as we were together praying, a prayer chain member prayed, "Lord, we're sick and tired of praying this request. We're going to put out a fleece. The way the men accept Evelyn next Sunday morning will be our answer as to whether she opens the prayer seminars to men or not." I nearly fainted as she prayed. *I* never would have dared talk to God like that.

The next Saturday I received a call from a woman in one of St. Paul's suburbs. "I've met with some of our deacons (we're between pastors), and we want an evening prayer seminar in our church that is open to men, women, and young people. We definitely feel it is God's will."

"I'll give you my answer on Monday," I stalled, not daring to tell her I had to see how the "fleece" came out the next day!

With fear and trembling I shared "What Happens When We Pray" with that Sunday congregation. After the service the knuckles on my right hand were white from all those men shaking hands and thanking me. Nine days later we started our first prayer seminar for women *and men*. Sometimes I need a little pushing to go through doors God is opening. Do you?

### If You Want Me, Lord
One Friday afternoon during our first prayer seminar, I asked my small telephone prayer chain of 10 members to pray that God would keep my schedule in balance speaking against the occult and on prayer. That night, in one of those deep devotional times that come periodically in many of our lives, I prayed, "Lord, I don't know what it is, but I want Your will, just Your will." And I meant it. Then, out of the blue it seemed (but I'm sure it was God-inspired), I heard myself promising God that I would be involved in two areas if He wanted me to. One was the Billy Graham Crusade which was to be held that coming summer; the other was a national women's prayer movement.

The very next morning my telephone rang. It was Myrl Glockner. She said, "Evelyn, we've never met, but I just felt I had to call and ask if you will be one of 11 committee members to get 5,000 prayer groups going for the Billy Graham Crusade. Do you want time to pray about it? "

I was stunned. "Myrl," I stammered, "I don't need time to pray. How can I say No when just last night I said so completely, 'Lord, Your will, if You want me to be involved in the Billy Graham Crusade' "?

On the following Tuesday, after I had completed a prayer seminar session, a woman came down the aisle of the church waving a paper and calling, "Evelyn, I have a message here for you from Vonette Bright of the Great Commission Prayer Crusade. She would like you to become involved in the program."

Friday, Saturday, and Tuesday. There it was—God's opening of two doors when I told Him I was willing for His will for me with those two organizations. It's a very exciting thing. Don't say, "I want it my way, Lord," but, "Lord, Your way. Whatever You have for me, I'm Yours. You just take me, open any door, lead me in any direction." You will be astounded at what God will do. You will be panting, trying to keep up with the opportunities. Phone calls will come from people you didn't even know existed. Who inspired that person to call and ask you to go here or there to minister? Nobody—but God.

**For you to pray:**
*"O God, I want only Your will in my life. Open the doors You have for me, and give me the courage and faith to go through them. Amen."*

# 6

# God Never
# Makes a Mistake

*"Wherefore let them that suffer according to the will of God commit the keeping of their souls to Him in well doing, as unto a faithful Creator." 1 Peter 4:19*

In order to pray effectively in God's will, you may have to get a new view of God—a God who never makes a mistake. Our daughter Jan was still in high school when a friend of hers was in a serious automobile accident just before Labor Day. Not knowing whether Rick was dead or alive, she went down to the courthouse to see his demolished car. It had been placed on the lawn as a gruesome reminder to weekend travelers.

I was standing at the kitchen sink doing dishes when Jan came in trembling. Describing the car, she wondered how they ever pried Rick out of that crushed front seat. Suddenly she said, "But Mom, God never makes a mistake!" She turned and ran upstairs sobbing, and threw herself across her bed.

It was a few years later while she was in college that Jan came home because our family was going through a crisis. Once again she stepped into that same kitchen, and after we had wept together, she backed off, raised her finger at me and said, "Now, Mom, don't *you* forget, God makes no mistakes."

### An Omniscient Father
Is your God an all-wise Father, who knows the end from the beginning, who knows all the causes and all the outcomes, and

who never makes a mistake? We may pray for something that seems very good to us, but God knows the "what ifs" in our lives. He knows the calamities that might occur if He answered our prayers in the way we think best. He also knows about all our difficult situations and wants to turn them into something tremendously good.

This view of God as an omniscient Father comes into focus very clearly as the years pass. One of the advantages of growing older is that we can look back and see that God has not made a single mistake in our lives. Maybe we'll have to get to heaven before we understand some things, but it's exciting to recognize as the years come and go that everything has worked together for good if we have really loved Him. When we keep a record of what is happening to us, it isn't long before we realize that the difficult things are there for a reason, and God is making no mistakes.

### Make Requests—Don't Dictate Answers
When we first started a telephone prayer chain in our church, I, as chairman, soon learned that it was a full-time job. With 66 pray-ers signing up and averaging four, five, sometimes six prayer requests per day, it became more than I, as a pastor's wife, had time to handle, so I turned over the chairmanship to another woman. When Elmy took over I said to her, "You're going to have a problem. Some people will be calling to give you *answers* instead of requests. When they ask you to pray that such-and-such will happen, tell them kindly, 'We do not pray answers, we pray requests.'"

Do you see the difference? When we pray answers we're demanding that God do something and telling Him we want it done now—"just the way we want it, Lord." When we're bringing our requests to Him, we're saying, "Lord, here's the need" (the circumstance, the person, whatever it may be); then we ask Him to answer according to His omniscient will.

Even with pure motives, it's easy to pray answers rather than requests. One woman on a prayer chain to which I belong is a returned missionary to Africa. After she and her family came back to the States, they all wished they were back on the field, so they started to pray, "Lord, send us back to Africa." They even reapplied for the position they had vacated.

One day I received a telephone call from this dear lady. She was sobbing. "Ev, we just received word from our mission board that the position we held is filled, and we can't go back. Oh, Ev, we prayed and prayed that God would send us back to Africa."

What could I say about her praying that beautiful, noble "answer" to God? "Honey," I comforted, "you prayed the wrong prayer. If God had wanted you back on your mission station, He could have kept that position open until your letter arrived. It must not have been His will."

### A Pawn in God's Hands?

I was discussing this with a faculty wife one day, and she said, "Look, Girl, I'd feel like a pawn in God's hand if I ever prayed that way."

I thought for a minute. *Wow! Maybe so.* Then I said to her, "You know, maybe the greatest privilege in the whole world would be for Evelyn to be a pawn in the hands of God, who never makes a mistake. Just think, I'd never have to 'trial and error' anything. I'd never fall on my face (which I do very frequently). If God were in control of my every action, I would never do anything wrong." What a privilege to be a pawn in God's hands!

But God hasn't quite chosen to do things that way, has He? God has given Evelyn a free will, and He has given you a free will. He has given us the privilege of saying, "All right, Lord, I'm free. I have a free will, but I want to do what You know is not a mistake in my life." Then, it isn't God pushing Evelyn, is it?

I'm not being a pawn on a chessboard if I say willingly, "Lord, I really don't know what the best approach would be, where I should go, when I should start." With my free will I can say, "Now, Lord, You know all the 'what ifs' and all the outcomes. So, Lord, in my free will, You just use me to bring about Your perfect will on Planet Earth."

### Are You Asking Amiss?

How can we be sure that we are not asking amiss? James writes, "Ye ask, and receive not, because ye ask amiss, that ye may consume it upon your lusts" (James 4:3). Let's never insult

God by saying, "O Lord, that other woman's husband looks just a little bit good to me. Is it OK if I just sit at his feet—in my imagination? There won't be anything physical about our relationship, Lord." Let's not ever ask whether that can be God's will. We know what His will is, and He says, "Be ye holy for I am holy."

Perhaps we say, "Lord, *look* at that new car, that new house," or "Wow! Look at her wardrobe, Lord, look at it! Is it OK if I'm just a little bit jealous? " Now, we don't really ask God such questions, but we often rationalize our feelings and attitudes in an attempt to justify them, don't we?

It may be that we're a little bit touchy. We whimper and complain, "Lord, she rubs me the wrong way. Look at what she did. I really don't like her very well. Could that be Your will, Lord?" No. God's Word says, "Love does not demand its own way. It is not irritable or touchy" (1 Cor. 13:5, LB). So one sure way of not asking amiss is to know God's Word, the Bible. If God calls it sin, don't insult Him by asking about it.

But the Bible isn't all negative. We find in God's Word what we *can* do and what we *ought* to do. Responding to the positive commands of God's Word is another prerequisite to answered prayer based on obedience: "If ye abide in Me, and My words abide in you, ye shall ask what ye will, and it shall be done unto you" (John 15:7). There is nothing in God's Word that is contrary to God's will, is there? If we find it in His Word, we can believe it, we can live it, and we can act upon it.

At this point you may be asking, do we dare to pray for somebody's salvation? Is it God's will? Peter tells us, "The Lord is . . . not willing that any should perish" (2 Peter 3:9). We are to pray for those outside the body of Christ, but we must not forget that the person for whom we are praying has a free will, just as you and I have. God never superimposes His will upon anyone, but the timing and the sovereignty are His. Pray, yes. It is God's will that we pray that everyone will be saved. In answer to our prayers, the Holy Spirit faithfully woos, but we are to leave the results with God.

There is one more way we can be sure we don't ask amiss. God's Word tells us we believers have two Intercessors—Christ at the right hand of God and the Holy Spirit dwelling in us. The Holy Spirit takes our prayers *"when we don't know what we should pray for as we ought"* and brings them to the Father *"according to the will of God"* (Rom. 8:26-27). At those times when we cannot even put the deep yearnings of our hearts into words, we can rest assured that the Holy Spirit is interceding for us before the Throne of God according to the Father's will.

### When God Says No

Is it ever good when God says No? I had a meaningful No-answer when we first moved to St. Paul. I was asked to be the vice-president of a large hospital auxiliary. I knew nothing about the two hospitals they served, but was assured it was a "you-won't-have-to-do-a-thing" job.

I immediately called back home to the prayer chains I had just left, asking them to pray God's will. Soon the answer came from them and from others I had asked to pray: "God is saying No." And He was telling me No also.

When I told the committee what God had said, I almost felt the eyebrows being raised in surprise. I could not understand either why God would say No to such a great job when I was lonely with nothing to do in my new town.

A couple of weeks later, I found out why. The auxiliary's president was transferred with her husband out of state. Within two weeks, I would have been president of an organization that ran coffee shops and gift shops, and supervised volunteers and student candy stripers in two large hospitals. In addition, the whole work was needing to be reorganized through the hospital administrators and lawyers— a process which is being completed only now, four years later. What a mess I would have made of that gigantic job!

"O dear God," I prayed, "thank You for knowing the 'what ifs' and for keeping me from falling on my face in this my new hometown."

### Is Suffering Ever God's Will?

One year in our neighborhood Bible study we discovered a verse of Scripture which had a great impact on all of our lives. I knew the concept was scriptural, but I had never noticed it in God's Word before. "Wherefore let them that suffer according to the will of God commit the keeping of their souls to Him in well-doing, as unto a faithful Creator" (1 Peter 4:19).

*Those who suffer according to God's will*—is that in the Bible? Yes, it is. And almost everyone in our group that year was suffering. Of course, they weren't suffering because they were in the Bible study group. (I hope!) They were suffering in their bodies and in their spirits in various ways, but they began to see tremendous things take place. Whenever a problem arose with a crisis-impact, God gave us a specific answer immediately, in His Word, and we received strength, grace, peace, maturity in Christ—whatever was needed.

The husband of one woman in that group had a peculiar fungus growing under his skull, and his only hope for survival was in the administration of a drug that had side effects on the mind and personality. He became an entirely different person. As a result he divorced his wife and turned his back on his whole family. Recently, I had lunch with this woman. She's still radiant in Christ.

Another member's husband had contracted syphilis and had to name all his partners, a whole string of them. That woman found strength in the Word of God. Two daughters of one woman, both teenagers, were pregnant out of wedlock, as was one teenage daughter of another woman. About the least that happened to anybody was major surgery or breast cancer!

Can suffering be God's will? Yes, we all saw it come into focus in 1 Peter. If you're suffering, read that epistle. It's tremendous. We, as Christians, aren't promised that we'll be free from suffering. Sometimes we suffer simply because we have frail, human bodies, but if we're committed to the God who doesn't ever make a mistake, we can have the assurance that He has permitted our suffering and *has a specific reason for it*.

I have no way of knowing whether you are suffering as you read this chapter, but if you are, while you are, can you truly pray, "Lord, I still want Your will. Amen"? It means taking every facet, every area of our lives, and turning them over to the Lord. It's easy to pray, "Lord, how I love Your will" when we're on the mountaintop. But there are other times when we can only pray, "O Lord, I'm in the valley and it hurts. But, Lord, my answer is Yes. I know that Your will is right, and I'm willing to conform to Your will no matter what it is. For I know that You are in this valley with me."

### All Things for Good

Way back in our college days, I faced a crisis when I lost my third pregnancy. I had already had a miscarriage, then a full-term stillborn, and now another miscarriage. "Lord, Lord, why all of this?" my heart cried.

It was just after World War II, and we had returned to college after Chris had promised God in a burning bomber over Berlin that he would become a preacher after the war was over. Then God allowed us to lose this third baby. Was He turning His back and letting us suffer?

No, not at all. God gave me at that time Romans 8:28, "And we know that all things work together for good to those that love God." I loved God and Chris loved Him, and God had His reasons for not allowing those three babies to live.

What all of God's reasons were, I may never know short of eternity. But one thing God seemed to tell me was, "Do you think that you and Chris could have gone through seven more years of schooling if you had had those three babies? Your dad had become an invalid and Chris's dad had died leaving two younger children. Could you have had the courage and the financial support to face seven more years of schooling with three babies to care for?"

Did God make a mistake? No. Not at all. Romans 8:28 has been our family's life verse ever since. We know that *all* things, absolutely everything, work together for our good. This was the omniscient God who never makes a mistake dealing in the lives of those who loved Him.

Despite my earlier miscarriages, Jan came along normally, and then, when we were in our first pastorate, it seemed God was giving us a second healthy child. But Judy lived to be only seven months old. And all the pain came back again. "Lord, how come? Haven't I suffered enough? Haven't I learned?"

When God took Judy, He spoke to me so clearly from the 12th chapter of Hebrews. "For they [our earthly fathers] verily for a few days chastened us after their own pleasure; but He [God] *for our profit*, that we might be partakers of His holiness" (v. 10). God said, "Look, Evelyn, this is for your profit. If you're going to be a pastor's wife, you will have to understand some of these things." I wish I could write of all the ways that God through the years has used that experience for my profit as I've stood with heartbroken parents by tiny caskets or hospital cribs.

Ultimately God did permit us to raise three happy, healthy children, Jan, Nancy, and Kurt. And He had things to teach us through each of them, as well as through those we lost.

Do we ever arrive? My mother-in-law once said to me, "Oh Evelyn, I'm over 70 and I still haven't arrived." No, we never arrive, but God is doing something. He's making us what He wants us to be. It's in the suffering, and it's in the hard things that He wants us to say, "Lord, You never make a mistake. I want only Your will."

When I was speaking about this at an After Five Club near my home, three young women came to speak to me. I learned that one of them was going blind, one had just lost her two-year-old son in an accident, and the other was facing serious hip surgery within the next few days. As they spoke to me individually, each said that Romans 8:28 had come into focus for her that night. And each added, "I am now willing for God's will, whatever it may be."

### The Other Half of God's Will

Are you willing for God's will? In the previous chapter I wrote about the open door and the excitement. That's half of it, but the other half is being willing for God's will no matter how hard it is. At one of our church circle meetings, our spiritual life chairman, whose only sister was dying of cancer, said while leading our devotions, "I have struggled for months and months. Now I can finally tell you that if God takes my sister or lets her live, I am willing for God's will."

Her words completely broke us. We forgot everything on the agenda and started to pray. There were women there with very serious problems. A young, pregnant mother who had lost her only other child to crib death syndrome the preceding March could say, "I'm willing for God's will in this pregnancy." Another lady suffering from Hodgkins disease could say the same. Each of those women prayed and meant it, "Lord, I'm willing for Your will!" Then they immediately went to intercessory prayer for me while I spoke at the church where the youth pastor later said to me, "You turned our church upside down!" If you and I want to be powerful intercessory pray-ers, we must be willing for God's will not only in the things for which we are praying—that's only half of it. The other half is *being willing for God's will in our own personal lives.*

### Hot Fires

At Lindon Karo's funeral, my 14-year-old niece was sobbing out her heartbreak; she loved her pastor dearly. As I put my arms around her, I said, "Carla, God must have something very, very great for you if He's giving you this hot a fire so early in life." What did I mean? I meant that God has a way of making us greater persons by the "hot fires" which are preparing us for what is ahead. This is a beautiful concept. David understood it. He said, "Thou hast enlarged me when I was in distress" (Ps. 4:1). The word *enlarged* means "prepared for the task ahead."

Our Jan learned this when she was in the ninth grade. Her friend, Dave, was a fantastic boy, an *A* student, president of the student council, as well as class president. He was captain of the basketball team, and had singlehandedly pitched the local pony league baseball team to the world championship. His poetry had been published nationally—everything was going for him with two exceptions: Dave was not a Christian, and he had leukemia. But he didn't know about the leukemia and neither did Jan.

In the spring of that year, our local churches sponsored a gigantic youth rally with Dave Wilkerson as the speaker. At first Jan was timid about inviting Dave, but she finally worked up courage. On the evening of the rally, Chris and I took the car and drove them down to the armory. My husband sat close enough to Dave to hear him pray as he slipped to his knees at the end of the service: "Dear God, forgive all my sins and, Jesus, come into my heart as my Lord and Saviour."

Dave had no idea at that time that he was soon to enter into battle with a deadly killer—leukemia. By the time the junior high yearbooks came out, Dave knew he was very sick, but hardly realized how near the end was. He wrote in Jan's yearbook: "Dear Jan, Thank you for introducing me to Christ. You'll never know what He means to me now, and what He will in the future."

Two weeks later, Dave's "future with Christ" was a reality.

Early on the day he died, I was sitting alone in my purple chair in the living room. Sensing that something was wrong, Jan got out of bed, came downstairs and asked, "Where's Dad?"

I said, "He's at Dave's house, Honey."

She said, "Dave's gone, isn't he?"

I replied, "Yes."

For a little while we sat and cried together in that little purple chair. I said, "Honey, God is making you finer gold." She had heard that many times in our home. We talked about Romans 8:28, and Job's assurance that "When He hath tried me, I shall come forth as gold" (Job 23:10). That morning I said to Jan what I recently repeated to Carla at Lindon Karo's funeral, "Honey, God must have something great in mind for you to give you all this 'fire' at your age." Then Jan sobbed, "Oh, Mother, what if I hadn't invited him to hear Dave Wilkerson preach?"

Dave's funeral was the largest that had ever been held in our city. Hundreds of teenagers, teachers, and school officials were present at the mortuary. As my husband stood up to speak, he said, "I can almost hear the basketball bouncing in heaven today."

Then he told all those people what Dave had said just before he died. He had raised himself from his bed and asked, "Where am I?"

His mother had replied, "Dave, you're in Billings Hospital in Chicago and you're very, very sick. But all the doctors and nurses are here."

Then Dave had said, "Oh, no. Where I am it's all green and beautiful." And then he had died.

My husband could later tell all those teenagers and the others that Dave was with his Christ in a future that was only two weeks away when he had written about it in Jan's yearbook.

Suffering can be according to God's will. Are you willing—even if suffering is to be a part of your future?

## Committed to His Will

At our seminar session on this subject we invite participants at prayertime to commit their lives to God's perfect will. On a Wednesday morning, following such a session, one woman who attended committed her whole life, everything she held dear, to God's will. That very weekend her husband was killed in a motorboat accident! On the following Wednesday, one of the seminar members came with a message from this widow. "Please tell Evelyn that God prepared me for this experience when I committed my life to Him for His will last Wednesday."

Several months later at a prayer leaders' workshop, with tears in her eyes, she told us that she could really see God's will in this tragedy because one of her daughters who had turned away from Christ and left home had come back to Him, and was now taking her daddy's place in leading the smaller children in Bible reading and prayer each day.

After prayertime in a seminar the following February, a young woman whose husband was a seminary student said to me, "I cannot pray for God's will in my life. I cannot do it."

When I asked why, she replied, "I prayed and prayed and prayed for a baby. Then I became pregnant and was so excited, because I knew it was an answer to prayer. I knew God had given us that baby! But last December I had a miscarriage—and now I don't have my baby."

I said, "God doesn't make mistakes. He gave you the child for just the few months that you carried it. God has accomplished His purpose for that baby's life."

The young woman thought for a moment, and said, "Now I can pray for God's will." We bowed our heads and she prayed, "Lord, whatever it is, I want only Your will in my life, even though it meant losing my baby."

Again, following a seminar session on God's will, a young man who had undergone surgery for a brain tumor about five years previously struggled up the aisle with the help of two canes, and asked if he could say something. We all thought he was going to ask for prayer for healing or make some other request. But, supported on either side by his "new" mother and myself, he leaned toward the microphone and said, "I just want to thank God for these seminars and for the privilege of being here. You know, my mother died while I was still in a coma after my accident." (He called his brain tumor his accident.) Then he added, "If all these things hadn't happened to me, I would not have come to live with this new mother who is a Christian. She has introduced me to Jesus, and I have received Him as my Saviour. If I hadn't had my accident, I would never have come to know Jesus." Then he said, "I'm willing for anything that God's will has for me." And he stood there, not even able to support himself, but willing for God's will.

### The Place of Praise

We may reach the place suddenly, or it may take us years to realize that God isn't making a mistake in our lives. But then we are at the point where we can praise Him. A new Christian in my Bible study called me one day and said, "Mrs. Chris, I think I found a wrong translation in the Bible. It's there in the first chapter of James, verses two to four. Isn't it wrong when it says, 'Count it all joy when you fall into various trials'?"

I smiled over the phone and said, "No, Honey, it's not wrong. This is the place you reach when after·years and years of trials and difficulties, you see that all has been working out for your good, and that God's will is perfect. You see that He has made no mistakes. He knew all of the 'what ifs' in your life. When you finally recognize this, even *during* the trials, it's possible to have joy, deep down joy."

And Philippians 4:6 comes into focus at this point: "Be careful [anxious] for nothing; but in everything, by prayer and supplication with *thanksgiving*, let your requests be made known unto God." It is a privilege to see God being glorified in our lives. We are to give thanks always, knowing that we have a God who never makes a mistake. And if we are going to be effectual intercessory pray-ers, praying in the will of God, it's not something we tack on to the end of our prayers. It's a commitment to God's will, a way of life. It's being willing for His will in the things for which we are praying and in our personal lives. And it's "Giving thanks always for *all* things unto God and the Father in the name of our Lord Jesus Christ" (Eph. 5:20). As I said earlier, it's easier said than done—but the rewards are fantastic!

### For you to do:

*Bow your head, close your eyes, and* **think** *of the most important thing in the world to you. (It may be health, a loved one, a job, finances, schooling, etc.)*

*Now* **pray:** *"Father I want only Your will in this thing that is most important in the whole world to me. Amen."*

*Now in prayer **thank** God for however He chooses to answer, knowing it is according to His perfect will.*

*Please don't pray the following prayer unless you really mean it. "Father, I want Your will in **every area** of my life including my job, my home, my health, my children, my loved ones, and my service for You. Amen."*

# 7

# *The Space Dimension of Prayer— Where We Pray*

*"But thou, when thou prayest, enter into thy **closet**, and when thou hast shut thy door, pray to thy Father which is in secret; and thy Father which seeth in secret shall reward thee openly." Matthew 6:6*

My old green chair has long since been reupholstered, but years ago, when it was brand new, it became the quiet place to which I would steal very early in the morning to spend time alone with God. It was on my knees at that old chair that I would pour out the inmost groanings of my heart—for only God to hear. Groanings much too personal to be heard by any other. My tears stained its cushion as I knelt interceding for a loved one. It was there I was filled with awe and adoration for Him and all He is. I thought of Solomon's prayer of so long ago: "O Lord, the God of Israel, there is no God like Thee. . . . the highest heaven cannot contain Thee" (1 Kings 8:23, 27, NASB).

It was there on my knees with my open Bible that God taught me to wait on Him for every point in a series of messages. It was there with my head buried in my hands that I begged God for wisdom for a certain message that I was to give. Not getting any answers, I reached for the morning newspaper, laid it on the seat of the chair, and read in the headlines that Russia had sent Sputnik I into outer space. Then God said, "It isn't who can *conquer* outer space that counts, but He who *created* it and by whom it consists" (see Col. 1:16-17). I had my message!

### Private Prayer—Public Praying

Do you have a secret place for private prayer, a certain corner, a particular chair, or a room set apart where you can spend time alone with God? A "closet" where you daily *shut the door* to pray to your Father in secret? The group concept of prayer is important, and we do need to pray *with* one another, "not forsaking the assembling of ourselves together" (see Heb. 10:25). But the drawing apart to pray in secret is perhaps the most vital type of prayer in which we engage. It is also an indicator of the kind of prayer group participant we really are, for *it is our private praying that determines the quality and validity of our public praying*.

Though we are never to be critical of the prayers of others, we can often recognize in our prayer groups those who have spent time in private closet prayer and the others who have come perhaps to do the only praying that they have done all week. Some struggle and strain to sound pious, but it's obvious that they haven't experienced the deeper dimension of closet prayer.

Have you ever seen a bright blue iceberg? In Alaska recently I stared in awe at a mountain lake filled with beautiful blue icebergs that had broken off Portage Glacier. Immediately my mind went back to an article I had read in a *Family Tie* magazine that compared our secret praying to an iceberg. The "absolutely no boating" sign reminded me that eight-ninths of the bulk of an iceberg is below the waterline—out of sight. Only one-ninth is visible above the surface. The next day at our prayer seminar in Anchorage, I explained how prayer should be like those icebergs, with about one-ninth showing in our public group praying and eight-ninths out of sight in our secret closets.

### Other Closets

I can almost hear you saying, "I can't spend great periods of my time in a closet." No, neither can I, but I have found another kind of closet praying. It's just drawing apart to God wherever I am—at the kitchen sink, at a desk, or even in a room filled with people.

"You must have tremendous power of concentration," someone said.

No, I've just learned to draw apart from people to God. Practicing this at a California retreat with 525 people packed in a room that barely held 500, we found, though touching elbows physically, that we could each draw apart mentally to God. This too is closet praying, though it is no substitute for drawing apart to that one spot, at that one time of the day, when we really spend time with God and His Word.

One of my very favorite "closets" is my car. As I draw apart, you may be sure I don't take my hands off the wheel, fold them, and kneel. To shut my eyes would be even worse!

One morning last week, as I was getting ready to leave for an all-day prayer seminar 50 miles away, everything went wrong. My husband called from California asking me to find out when certain professors should be met at the San Francisco airport, and to give the information to his secretary so he could call her after I had gone. I couldn't find the professors; I couldn't find the secretary after frantically dialing all the possible numbers.

Then my son called from school: "Mom, I forgot all my books; could you bring them over?" I did, and was completely out of time when I left his school only to run into such a long detour that I could hardly find my way back to the freeway.

As I finally emerged on the right road, I cried to God, "O Lord, take over! Remove from me all this tension and frustration. Flow through me with Your peace and power. Make me what You want me to be by the time I arrive at the prayer seminar." And He did! My car had become my prayer closet.

Even a plane seat can be a prayer closet. For two years I had been praying with a friend about her sister who did not know Christ. Every time my friend wrote to her sis, she'd call asking me to pray for God to work in her heart as she received the letter. One day my plane had a 10-minute layover in a midwestern city with no time to disembark. I looked out over that city and thought, *That's where my friend's sister lives!* Suddenly there descended from God a heavy, overwhelming burden to pray for her. I sat in that plane in the very depths of intercessory prayer. Two days later my elated friend called to say, "I just received a letter from my sis, and she accepted Christ! " When? The exact day God had said in that plane, "Evelyn, pray."

### Which Posture?

Just as our "momentary" closet praying requires no particular place, neither does it require a certain prayer posture. In one of our seminars a man announced to me after the first session that he would not be back. "You're not praying scripturally," he said. When I asked him to please explain, he said, "You're not 'holding up holy hands.' " He could see only this one position to be used at all times even though I pointed out to him that there are many postures of prayer mentioned in the Word of God.

Jesus, when He was praying in the Garden of Gethsemane, set for us the example of *kneeling* in prayer: "And He was withdrawn from them about a stone's cast, and kneeled down, and prayed" (Luke 22:41). At the tomb of Lazarus, while standing, "Jesus *lifted up His eyes*, and said, 'Father, I thank Thee that Thou hast heard Me' " (John 11:41). Paul wrote, "I will therefore that men pray everywhere, *lifting up holy hands*, without wrath and doubting" (1 Tim. 2:8).

My husband can recall circumstances in which men experienced such grief and anguish that they have lain prostrate on the floor of his study. One was a dad who had just learned that his teenage daughter was pregnant out of wedlock. He cast himself to the floor, weeping, and my husband had to take him in his arms and gently lift him up.

King Solomon, in the Old Testament, *prostrated himself before the Lord* when he prayed in the temple. His father David communed with God upon his bed (Ps. 4:4). Whatever our posture, wherever the place, the ears of our God are open to our cry (see Ps. 34:15).

### Holy Places

God does not dwell in temples made with hands. Even so, some spots have been used as closets for prayer by so many that they seem to be holy places. Have you ever stepped into a room and felt God there? My husband and I were looking over the grounds at a midwestern retreat center last fall. We stepped into an old chapel—and I felt God's presence immediately. "Hon, please go on without me for a few minutes," I said. I knelt at that altar—not talking or praying, but just *feeling* God so powerfully there.

Another time I arrived at Bethel Seminary in St. Paul to speak at a women's retreat just as the planning committee stepped out of the Eric Frykenberg Prayer Tower, where they had been praying for our meetings. Their eyes were wide with wonder and amazement. "We felt Jesus in there!"

"Yes," I replied, "that is one of those places where I always feel a particular sense of the presence of Christ." That little circular room has no windows, no furniture—but it is filled with the thousands of prayers uttered by students and faculty of that seminary—and His presence!

Christ recognized the need for spending time alone with God. What a tremendous example Christ's prayer life was to His followers and to us. Though the disciples were Jesus' very closest friends, He knew there were times He had to pray in secret to His heavenly Father. So Christ, though He taught His disciples the concept of group prayer, as we have learned in previous chapters, also knew the importance of this private closet praying. Even though He Himself was God incarnate, He thought it necessary to withdraw to a mountain to pray all night alone before the important task of choosing the Twelve Apostles. If He—why not us?

*For you to pray:*
*"Lord, give me the joy of secret closet praying. Keep me faithful to shut the door every day and spend time with You and Your Word in secret. Teach me to draw apart alone with You, no matter where I am or with whom. Amen."*

# 8

# The Time Dimension
# of Prayer—
# When We Pray

*"Pray without ceasing."* 1 Thessalonians 5:17

Did you ever sit in a room before a glowing fire with someone you love? Did you talk every minute? Or did you feel compelled every now and then to clear your throat and say, "Now dear, I think I'll say something to you." Then with a bright introduction, did you proceed with a formal speech? Of course not. When you're with a person you love, there need not be a bit of conversation in order for you to experience real communication. If you feel like saying something, you do; if not, you don't. But the line of communication between you is always open.

Praying without ceasing is like that. How? It's simply turning the dial of our communication system with God to *on*, making possible a two-way conversation with Him at any time. When that communication line is open, we can say whatever we want to Him, and He in turn can say anything He wishes to us. Yes, it's possible to "pray without ceasing" 24 hours a day.

When we leave our daily closet praying, do we walk out and slam the door, saying, "That's it for today. Same time tomorrow, Lord, same station"? That isn't what the Holy Spirit meant when He inspired Paul to write, "Pray without ceasing" (1 Thes. 5:17). Nor is it what Christ meant when He taught His disciples, "Men ought always to pray, and not to faint" (Luke 18:1).

After Paul lists the armor with which we are to resist Satan, he goes on to say, "Praying *always* with all prayer and supplication in the Spirit" (Eph. 6:18). The source of strength in our battle with the enemy is "praying always." But when the line of communication with God closes, wham—the fiery darts of Satan strike! But that need not be the case. Let's break down the day and see how the communication system between us and God can be open all 24 hours.

### A Lark or an Owl?

How do you start your day? Are you a "lark" or an "owl"? "Larks" twitter and sing in the morning, but by the end of the day they're not doing too well; they have slowed down considerably. "Owls" take a little longer to get going in the morning. You know—"Right now I don't love anybody, but when I start loving again, you'll be first on the list." But owls gain momentum as the night progresses.

We're divided at our house. I'm a "lark" and my husband is definitely an "owl." When we pray together at night and Chris prays on and on, I sometimes have to say, "Hurry up, Chris; you're losing me." But in the morning it's a different story. Chris groans and pulls the covers up tighter when I shake him to tell him some great gem that I've just gotten from the Lord.

Because our individual, inbuilt clocks function differently, I've learned that there are no spiritual "brownie points" for being a "lark." Is it possible our heavenly Father created some of us to be "larks" and some to be "owls" so He would have somebody on the alert all 24 hours of the day?

I used to say, and I'm sure it was with pride, "I'm creative in the morning. That is my creative time." Then I realized, *Ev, you're not creative in the morning; you've just learned to listen to God in the wee hours.*

When I'm asked, "How do you get all those messages ready? How can you possibly write so many?" I have to reply, "I don't write messages, but I keep a little notebook on my bedstand at all times. Then lying there communing with my heavenly Father early in the morning, I just jot down whatever He says to me."

When I awaken, I say, "Lord, here I am. What do You want to say to me?" I usually think they should be ideas for immediate needs, but frequently He gives thoughts for retreats and messages months away. I write them down and keep them in file folders. Then when I put those papers in outline form, it's astounding to learn that God has given me every single thought I'll ever need—in time!

It's a very exciting procedure to wait upon God early in the morning while the mind is fresh, before anyone else comes upon the scene, or before the "tyranny of the urgent" rushes in. Have you learned to say in the morning, "Lord, here I am. You tell me what You want me to know today, what You want me to do"? Have you asked Him, "Is there someone You want me to call? What do You have in mind for me today? " You'll be amazed at His answers!

One morning as I was lying in bed talking to the Lord, I said, as I frequently do, "OK, Lord, whom would You have me call today?" The answer came as if it were in lights, "Mona."

"But Lord, I don't know Mona. I met her at a band concert, and at a PTA meeting—and that's it."

I waited until the kids left for school; then I went to the phone and said, "Lord, You're going to have to tell me what to say to Mona—I don't know."

I really felt a little silly about calling her, but I dialed and said, "Good morning, Mona. This is Evelyn Christenson from down the street." That's all I said. And Mona started to cry. She told me that the day before, she and her husband had been told by the doctors that their son, Dave (our Jan's friend), had leukemia and would never recover. My obedience gave me the opportunity to at least build a bridge to Mona and to comfort her in her distress.

One morning, after my daughter had asked me to pray for a girl who was feuding with her parents, I said, "Lord, if You want me to talk to her, have her call or come over." At 2 o'clock in the afternoon I answered my doorbell, and there she stood with a suitcase in her hand. "Hi, I've come to move in with you for a while."

It had been one of those unbelievably hectic days, and I glanced heavenward and sighed, "Lord, I didn't mean that *literally*."

I used to think that if one were an "owl," talking with God in the morning wasn't necessary. But one day, as I was reading Psalm 5, I saw something for the first time. I said to Chris, "Hey, it's really scriptural to talk to God first thing in the morning." In all the times I had read that psalm, it had never really hit me before. "Give ear to my words, O Lord, consider my meditation. Hearken unto the voice of my cry, my King, and my God: for unto Thee will I pray. My voice shalt Thou hear in the morning, O Lord; in the morning will I direct my prayer unto Thee, and will look up" (Ps. 5:1-3).

It doesn't say hours of prayertime are necessary, but at least we must say Good Morning to the Lord and give Him our day. So whether you are a "lark" or an "owl," God's Word says early in the morning, before the "tyranny of the urgent," before breakfast, before the school busses, before anyone says a word to you, "Early in the morning, Lord, I will look up, and pray unto You."

### Prayer Before School

After breakfast, it's time for the children to start off to school. Since our first child was in kindergarten, we have made a practice in our home of praying individually with each of our children just as they left for school. This to me has been a very precious experience. It's been more than a time to pray! We have been able to put our arms around our children, assuring them of the security of their home, and then to send them out into the big, often overwhelming world with God watching over them, in whatever they will face that day.

Every once in a while I'm told by my son, "Hurry up, Mom, make it short. The school bus is coming," and out the door he goes! Sometimes it's only one or two sentences. But meeting God with our family before we separate is a very vital part of our day.

### The Day Progresses

I have a great time with the Lord in the morning. As God and I communicate with one another, He tells me what He wants me to do, and I say, "OK, Lord." There are no problems. There aren't any people around to bother me. There are no bad reactions for me to contend with. You know, I could really be a tremendous Christian if I could stay in my "closet" with God. But I can't stay there all day. I can't even remain sheltered with members of my own family, those who love me. I have to get out and meet people—and occasionally my early morning relationship with God suddenly falls apart!

I'm a "people person," and I really like almost everybody I meet. But once in a while somebody makes me bristle, and I retaliate. There are other occasions when I just look at someone and think, "Oh, brother!"

How do I solve the problem? I've learned what I call my *SOS prayer*. I say, "Help, Lord." (But not out loud!) "Lord, give me the attitude *You* want me to have toward that person."

Perhaps you can imagine what it's like for a wife and mother to prepare to go out of town for a speaking engagement. You get all the laundry done, matching the socks with the shirts. Then you stock the refrigerator with enough food for all the days you'll be gone, outline each of your messages, try to get yourself and your clothes ready, and do the last-minute shopping. It's really hectic! In addition, you have to get "prayed up." You just can't go without spiritual preparation, so you spend extra time with the Lord. Finally you settle into the plane seat, review your notes once more, and pray.

Things had gone that way before I arrived in an eastern city for a retreat a few years ago. As I was being introduced to the ladies, a pastor's wife who was sitting next to me leaned over and gibed, almost sneering, "Do you really like these little women's meetings?"

Wow! After all I'd gone through to get there! Besides, I didn't think that meeting was so little—about 200 women were there from several states. And I was all primed and ready to share what the Lord had given me for them. Do you know what I did? I bristled!

Now, I didn't have time to say a long prayer. I had only seconds left before speaking. As I walked to the platform, I silently pleaded with the Lord. *"Help, SOS*, give me the attitude You want me to have toward that pastor's wife." And do you know, all the bristle disappeared. Because God knew I didn't have a lot of time to get this cleaned up, He answered my *SOS prayer* just like *that*! What would have happened if I had started out bristling at that audience? It would have "pulled the rug" right out from under the whole retreat.

One of the prayer requests presented at a faculty wives' prayer meeting I attended several months ago involved a serious financial problem. On the day before, the promise of a large gift of money for the new campus had been withdrawn, and we were going to pray about it.

As we were drinking coffee and chatting before the start of the prayer meeting, a woman came in whom I had never met. I didn't know who she was, but I looked down my spiritual nose and thought, *My word, she's the "squarest" woman I've ever seen in my life*. And the more she talked the more "square" I thought she was.

Then the Lord began to reprove me: "Evelyn, that's sin." Do you remember our first prerequisite to answered prayer? "If I regard iniquity in my heart, the Lord will not hear me"? I suddenly realized that I was about to spend my morning in prayer for these financial needs with sin in *my* heart! Another *SOS prayer* flew to heaven, "Lord, please, give me the attitude You want me to have toward that woman, no matter how square she is."

You know, when we pray that prayer, we never ask amiss. God knows what attitude He wants to give us. When we look at Christ's life, we can see that sometimes His perfect attitude was love, sometimes it was righteous indignation, sometimes patience, sometimes discipline, sometimes compassion. That day God gave me a surprise.

Guess who prayed first at that prayer meeting? She did. And as she started to pray, I suddenly realized that this woman had a dimension to her prayer life that I knew nothing about. She said, "Thank You, Lord, that that money didn't come through yesterday." And I blinked. She went on, "Now, Lord, You have given us the *privilege* of being on our faces before You this morning with a desperate need. Lord, what a privilege this is. Thank You, Lord. And thank You that today the school's president has the privilege of being on his face before You with this need. Thank You that the whole staff has this tremendous need, and thank You that they have the privilege of being on their faces before You."

I felt two inches high.

When I learned who this woman was, I discovered some

other things. She had an intercessory prayer life that was never less than two hours a day. She used a prayer list that was pages and pages long, containing the names of the people for whom she prays daily. And *I* had looked at *her* and thought, *Wow, is she square?*

I had a trying experience when I was teaching wives during a pastors' conference. We had gone over the material on praying in God's will, and were going to have a spiritual exercise by taking partners with whom we would share and pray. My partner was a young pastor's wife. We took our chairs to a corner as we were supposed to, and got all ready for the spiritual exercise, when suddenly she looked me right in the eye and said, "I hate you."

Do you think I smiled and said, "Oh, I just love you"? Not on your life. I said, "I guess we had better not do our exercise; we'd better just talk. Tell me why you hate me."

But as I was talking outwardly, inwardly I was praying, "SOS, Lord. Help me to have the attitude You want me to have toward this person." And God gave me the ability to sit there calmly without becoming angry and retaliating. "Would you like to tell me why you hate me?" I asked.

She said, "OK, I'll tell you. My husband has been interviewed by the pulpit committee seeking a pastor for your former church." She went on, "I didn't know who you were when I came to this meeting. I had never seen you before, had never heard one of your tapes, but I knew you were the wife of the former pastor of that church." Then she exploded, "You're everything I don't want to be and can't be in a pastor's wife, so I hate you. Look at that dress you're wearing," she said. "I'm a sweatshirt-and-jeans girl myself."

I was at a loss as to where to start, but God seemed to be saying to share deeply with her out of my heart. I told her of the hard things I had talked about in my message that morning, things that had happened *during* my time at that church. I even told her of a very personal trial I never mention in public, and how those wonderful people prayed for me—just as they would pray for her if she were their pastor's wife. It wasn't long before the two of us were in tears, clasping hands, and praying together.

As we parted, she said, "As my husband and I drive home

this afternoon, I want to tell him about how I feel now. Will you pray for me?"

I said I would, but she didn't wait until afternoon. At lunch her husband came flying across the dining room and asked, "What did you do to my wife?"

I told him I didn't do anything to his wife, but I wanted to know what happened.

He said, "You know, God is calling me to leave the church I'm now serving, and my wife has been saying, 'Absolutely not. I don't care where you're called. I won't go.' But she just came to me and said, 'Honey, wherever God leads you, I'll go along.' What did you do?"

What had I done? I had prayed, "SOS, Lord. Give me the right attitude toward this woman." And immediately He had given me an understanding attitude toward a young pastor's wife who didn't want to leave her rural community and her sweatshirt and jeans.

Not long ago a woman stopped me in a church and said, "We just called a new pastor." Guess who it was? That same young man! Then she went on, "Do you know why we called him? He's a great guy, but we were very impressed with his wife. She was so eager to have her husband where God wanted him to be, and she was undergirding his ministry like we've never seen any pastor's wife do before." I smiled and breathed a thank-You to God for that little sweatshirt-and-jeans girl who only a year before had said, "I hate you."

When we say to God, "Give me the attitude You want me to have toward that person," immediately these amazing attitudes come, the ones He wants us to have. We don't have to reach for the pill bottle. I had one toddler who I said was not just an *"Anacin* headache kid," she was a *"Vanquish* headache kid." She could paint the back fence and her hair and everything else faster than I could get out there to grab the paint can! What do we do? We pray, "Lord, right now, give me the attitude You want me to have toward that person in my family, toward that person I meet on the street, even toward the one who looks at me and says, 'I hate you.' " All day long if people rub us the wrong way, we can have the communication system open between us and God. We just pray, "SOS Lord. Give me the attitude *You* want me to have." It works all day long, the whole 24 hours.

### Bear Ye One Another's Burdens—All the Time

How about your family? Is it as easy for your children to say, "Mom, I'm having a math test at 10:30, please pray," as it is for them to ask you for $2.50 for lunch money? Do your children know that your communication system with God is always open?

One morning while she was still in high school, one of our daughters was so frightened about an upcoming important interview that I found her sick to her stomach in the bathroom. I helped her out the front door and promised to pray. Soon the phone rang. "Mother, it went great," she exclaimed, then softly, "I could *feel* you praying, Mom."

Our married daughter's father-in-law had just had open-heart surgery. Suddenly the "Red Alert" was flashed over the hospital intercom. Jan ran to a phone, dialed our number, and, with the sounds of running hospital personnel in the background, said, "Mother, Skip's dad's heart has stopped."

*My* heart stood still. I felt so helpless and so far away. "What can I do?"

There was a long pause, and then she said, "Just pray, Mother, just pray," and hung up.

I did pray, and her father-in-law revived and God gave him four more years to live. But the point is that Jan knew she could depend on me to pray about her concerns, any time, any place.

This family prayer support works two ways. After finishing a retreat at Mt. Hermon in California, I phoned home long distance. My then 10-year-old son answered with, "How did it go, Mom?"

"Oh, Kurt, it went just great."

"Well," he said with a genuine sound of pride in his voice, "how could you miss with my whole pastor's Saturday class praying for you?"

Do you have someone who will pray for you and for whom you will pray? If you don't know where to start with all these prayer suggestions, find one person with whom you can share the secret problems and needs of your life. Someone who cares and who will never, never divulge your secrets. Then fulfill the law of Christ by "bearing one another's burdens" (see Gal. 6:2).

## The Nightwatch

Are you one of these people whom God can awaken in the middle of the night to pray for one of His children's needs down here on Planet Earth? "But I need my sleep," you say. So did I, or at least I thought I did. For many years I was strictly hung up on sleeping pills. I thought I had to have eight solid hours of sleep or I'd never make it the next day. Then one summer day, I very undramatically tossed those pills into the toilet, flushed it, and said, "Lord, I'm not going to worry if I'm awake at night, because if You awaken me, there's a reason for it. I'll just ask You, 'For whom should I be praying?' "

God knows when I'm finished praying and ready to go back to sleep. And somehow there's no frustration and I never miss the sleep when God needs me to pray. It's a very beautiful, exciting thing.

One night the Lord awoke me and said, "Pray for Jacque" (a long-time prayer partner). At that time she was in San Francisco, and I learned later that she was going through a very deep spiritual battle, seemingly surrounded by forces of Satan. A letter Jacque wrote to me the next morning confirmed the reason God had awakened me. As I prayed in St. Paul, great peace had flooded her in San Francisco. *"If at night you can't sleep, don't count sheep—talk to the Shepherd!"*

Another time I was driving on the freeway in the state of Wisconsin very late on a Saturday night. It hadn't occurred to me that my gas tank might be a little bit hungry since I wasn't. All at once, *putt, putt, putt*. I was out of gas! I pulled off to the side of the road and opened the trunk (I knew that if I opened the hood, other motorists approaching from behind would see that there was a woman alone in a car).

As each set of headlights appeared behind me, I prayed, "Lord, if there's anybody in that car with whom I won't be safe, keep them going, Lord, keep them going." I sat there for 15 minutes, and every set of headlights shot right by. Nobody stopped.

Then I saw a blinking red light and heard the sound of a siren behind me. For the first time in my life I was happy and excited to hear that sound! The state trooper got out of his car and said, "You know, Lady, that you're in danger out here alone on the freeway this late at night, don't you?"

I said, "Yes, sir, I know it."

He told me that it would take about five minutes to transfer some gas from his patrol car to mine, and invited me to sit in the squad car. I noticed that he was trembling, and needed desperately to talk to someone.

He said, "I just came from an accident. A pregnant mother fell asleep, and her car veered off to the right and struck a cement culvert. I looked at the car with the right one-third sheared off and thought, *Oh, oh, this is going to be one of those messy ones.* But the first thing I saw was a little two-year-old girl walking around with just one pulled tendon in her leg. What really unnerved me, though, was that a Mrs. Beasley doll that was placed between the mother and daughter was decapitated by a piece of metal that came through the windshield, but the two of them were unharmed." He turned to me and asked, "Do you believe in God?"

I said, "Yes."

Then with deep emotion he said, "Do you think God was riding in the back seat of that car?"

I replied, "I think He may very well have been." Then I added, "Do you know that you're an answer to prayer too?"

He said, "Me? I'm an answer to prayer?"

Then I told him how I had prayed about every single pair of lights approaching my car that night.

This is only a part of the story, and we must go back to Jacque for the end of it. "Evelyn, why did I feel an overwhelming urgency to pray for you last night? We were having a birthday party and I couldn't pray right then. But again God said, 'Jacque, pray for Evelyn.' So I gathered up the birthday wrappings, excused myself to take them out, and stood by the garbage cans, and prayed." Then she told me the exact time. Can you guess what time it was? Yes, it was exactly the time I had run out of gas on that freeway!

Is your communication system so open to God that you are available to pray any time of the day or night? When God sees a need down here on Planet Earth, can He say to you, "Wake up, wake up, I want you to pray for somebody"? Or are you like I was at one time, thinking you need eight hours of sleep or you'll collapse the next day? Are you one of those with whom God can trust His burdens?

"Pray without ceasing"—all day long, all night long. It's just a matter of having the communication system open between yourself and God so you can say at any time of day or night, "SOS, Lord." And He can say to you, "Knock, knock. There's a need down there. Will you please pray?"

***For you to pray:***

*"Dear Father, I want to be available to You, 24 hours a day. Teach me to open my communication with You and never shut it. Also help me to be available to others whenever they need me to pray. Amen."*

# 9

# *The Vertical Dimension of Prayer— to Whom We Pray*

*"Draw nigh to God, and He will draw nigh to you." James 4:8*

An often overlooked but very important part of prayer is the drawing nigh to God. Before we are ready to start our intercessory prayers, we need to *wait* before God until we know we have established communication with Him. This is a time of silence when we are shutting out every other thought and distraction around us. There is no talking *to* God, just a complete mental drawing to Him; and then, as He promised, *He will draw nigh to us.*

### Drawing Nigh Takes Time
Drawing apart to God is important in groups as well as in private praying. It may be easier to do in our closets; but because of the hectic rush to arrive at a prayer meeting on time or because of the chatting after we've arrived, it is a must to pause for the seconds or minutes it takes to withdraw from all this and draw nigh to God. Often there seems to be embarrassment in a group if someone doesn't start praying audibly right away as we go to prayer—ready or not.

I remember way back in the green-chair days struggling and struggling to draw nigh to God. I can recall how I would strain and wonder where He was. And it seemed as if my prayers were only reaching the ceiling. But through the years God has taught me many things—and I'm not in the struggling stage anymore.

One thing I learned when I found it impossible to establish meaningful communication with God was that it wasn't His fault, it was mine. He is the same yesterday, today, and forever, but I am not. I let sins creep in that break my fellowship with Him, and frequently I must search my heart and confess those sins that are blocking communication between us.

I also learned the simple process of envisioning my God when approaching Him in prayer. The joy that floods my whole being as I find myself visualizing all God is—all His love, all His power, all His concern for me—defies description. What greater privilege could there be for a human being than to actually *draw nigh* to the omnipotent, omniscient God, high and lifted up on His throne in glory? This to me is the most precious part of my prayertime.

### Be Sure It's God

Why do you suppose Christ taught His disciples, and us in turn, to pray, "Our Father who art in heaven"? Have you ever thought of that? Our God, capital G, is the only God in heaven, but there are other gods. "Thou shalt have no other gods before Me" (Ex. 20:3). If there were no other gods, our God would not have given Moses this commandment.

"The god of this world [age]" is a title Paul gives Satan (see 2 Cor. 4:4). In the explosion of the occult that is sweeping our nation, we are finding that even Christians—real Christians—are getting answers that are not from God. Christ spent one-fourth of His recorded ministry dealing with the enemy, and this is a warning to us to be constantly alert that we open our minds, not to Satan, but to God who is in heaven.

In a question-and-answer period following a lecture on the dangers of the occult at a church youth meeting, a man counselor raised his hand and asked, "Why is it that when I pray I get more answers from Satan than I do from God?"

I didn't want to belittle that man before the students for whom he was responsible, but I had no choice. I looked at him, and I said as kindly as I could, "Sir, if you are getting more answers from Satan than you are from God, there's something drastically wrong with your prayer life."

Is it possible for even sincere Christians to unwittingly open themselves to suggestions from the enemy?

I know of five different pastors who claimed a voice said to them, "Divorce your wife," and each one promptly did. They said they thought it was the Lord speaking to them. But it was not surprising to learn that in every instance another woman was involved.

While flying over Canada, one pastor said to another, "I now know there is a life after death and I am preaching it from my pulpit."

"How do you know?" asked the surprised pastor sitting beside him.

"Because my stillborn baby is communicating with me. I wasn't sure before, but I know now there is life after death!"

When I speak on the occult, I find to my horror that even Christian youth are experimenting with all sorts of occult practices. As I ask them what they do at slumber parties, their response is frightening. Many have crossed the thin line between parlor games and the occult. They are hearing voices during their séances, experiencing supernatural power, and getting answers in uncanny ways from Ouija boards and tarot cards.

After I had talked with one group of teenagers in a fine local church, a mother came to me and said, "I want to tell you that those kids had a Ouija-board burning. My daughter is the ringleader of that junior high group in our church, and she came home from your meeting and said, 'Mother, playing with Ouija boards and all that stuff is an abomination to God. It says so in Deuteronomy 18.' " Yes, getting supernatural answers through any form of divination or mediums is not drawing nigh to God—and is forbidden by Him (see Deut. 18:9-14).

Halloween parties too seem to be changing in character these days. A friend of mine was having her hair done the week after Halloween. Her hairdresser said that every one of her customers who discussed attending any Halloween party said it turned out to be an attempt to draw nigh to spiritual beings other than God. What ever happened to bobbing for apples?

## Meditation Can Be Dangerous

Putting oneself into a state of passivity is a very dangerous spiritual exercise in which even true Christians are engaging. To open our minds and allow ourselves to be receptive to all the thoughts and suggestions which enter is a perilous business. We may think we are drawing nigh to God—but zing! There's Satan, and we are listening to *his* voice.

At a prayer seminar, a woman stepped up to me and said, "Do you know that I taught yoga and gave it up?"

I said, "Tell me, why did you give it up?"

"Well," she replied, "I suddenly realized that there I was in that room meditating with Buddhists, with Hindus, with people involved in every religion you can imagine. Sure, you sit there and you meditate and you get a feeling of peace and strength; but I've learned that I get all the peace and strength I need from the Lord Jesus Christ, and I don't need yoga meditation. And God told me it's a sin for me to be meditating with those others who do not know the true God in heaven."

Oh how foolish to put ourselves in such a vulnerable position! It does make a difference with whom we attempt to draw nigh to God. "What communion hath light with darkness?" (2 Cor. 6:14)

Transcendental Meditation is a guise that Satan frequently uses today to infiltrate minds. It is being taught in many of our schools, libraries, YMCAs, YWCAs, and even in some churches.

While the president of a local women's club and I were driving home together some 70 miles from a meeting, our conversation shifted to communicating. "You know," she said, "I communicate in the middle of the night. Do you?"

"Oh, yes, I communicate in the middle of the night," I replied.

She went on, "I know 'It' is out there, because I communicate with 'It.' "

I quickly changed the pronoun and said, "I know 'He' is out there. My God is out there."

She went on, "I don't know what it is I'm communicating with, but I know *something* is out there. Why don't you come to one of our meditation meetings? You can tell us how you communicate in the middle of the night, and we can tell you how we do." By that time I had an ill feeling in the pit of my stomach. I couldn't get out of that car fast enough!

Prayer is always directed from the pray-er up to God—who is in heaven. This is the vertical dimension of prayer. In the next chapter you will see how this dimension becomes a triangle when God reaches back down to earth with the answers to our prayers.

In Hebrews 11:6 we read that the faith that pleases God is two-faceted: (1) believing that He is and (2) that He is a rewarder of them that diligently seek Him. I wonder if Christians before the occult explosion really knew the full meaning of this. Have we concentrated so much on the fact that He is a rewarder that we have lost sight of *who* our God is—holy, high, and lifted up? We must draw nigh to *this* God—and then He will draw nigh to us.

Moses drew nigh to God in reality when he "rose up early in the morning, and went up unto Mount Sinai" (Ex. 34:4, 29-35). Do you remember what happened when he came down? The Children of Israel were afraid to come near him because the skin of his face shone! He had to put a veil over his face, it was so radiant. Wouldn't it be great if we could so draw nigh to God that we would become radiant? That others could tell by our very countenance that we had been with God? That we had learned the secret of His presence? That before bombarding Him with our requests, we had taken time to enter into His fellowship?

*For you to do:*

*Before starting to pray, in absolute silence, practice drawing nigh to God.*

*This may involve confessing some sin which God brings to your mind. If so, confess it, so that there is nothing between you and God in heaven.*

***Now draw nigh to Him.*** *Wait in silence until you feel God is there.*

***Now pray,*** *thanking God for who He is—whatever you want to say in adoration and praise for who He is—this God to whom you have just drawn nigh.*

***Now pray at least one request for some other person's need.***

# 10

# The Horizontal Dimension of Prayer— Results

*"But without faith it is impossible to please Him: for he that cometh to God must believe that He is, and that He is the rewarder of them that diligently seek Him." Hebrews 11:6*

With the study of the horizontal dimension of prayer, we now reach full circle. We have said that we cannot pray effectively when there is sin in our lives. We have described how to pray in God's will so that our prayers will be answered. We have spoken of the need to draw nigh to God, and to bask in the sunshine of His love because He never makes a mistake.

For what purpose have we taught about these prerequisites to prayer? Primarily, that we might become powerful, intercessory pray-ers. We are now back to the theme verse of chapter 1, "The effectual fervent prayer of a righteous man *availeth much*" (James 5:16).

*The horizontal dimension of prayer is the visible result of our effective praying here on Planet Earth.* But there can never be a horizontal dimension of prayer unless there is first the vertical dimension—that drawing nigh to God. The two are inseparable, standing as it were at the opposite points of the base of a triangle, with God at the top. The pray-er petitions God the Father, who receives the prayer, sifts it out according to His will, then reaches down to change people and circumstances on earth. *The results we humans see represent the horizontal dimension of prayer.*

### Unity

In chapter 1 I gave many illustrations to show what happens when women pray. Each was a visible result, on the horizontal level, of prayer that had ascended to God the Father, who in turn acted upon an individual or a set of circumstances here on earth. I also mentioned the tremendous unity that was experienced as members of the body of Christ prayed together. It is still happening.

Following the day of humiliation, fasting, and prayer for our country on April 30, 1974, I received telephone calls from several prayer seminar members. One woman said, "It was just beautiful in our group."

Another exclaimed, "Guess what? We finally got off the ground for the first time, really off the ground, and we're going to meet next month again, just as we did on April 30."

Another said, "We had the most beautiful experience. I helped our pastor organize the prayer meetings in our church. We used the six S's and prayed in groups of four. It was a fantastic experience."

What else happened to many of us that day? We sensed deeply the humiliation for which we had prayed. With the continuing exposure of the Watergate affair, we knew that God was bringing us as individuals and our nation as a whole to the place of humiliation. And we felt a tremendous unity not as we studied together, or talked, or met as committee members, but as we prayed together. One definite horizontal result of prayer, then, is *unity*—in the church, in the home, and in the community.

### Prayer Transcends Miles

Do you have loved ones who live a great distance from you? Perhaps a son or a daughter who is away at school? Between my mother and me lies the entire state of Wisconsin, and beyond that the vastness of Lake Michigan. Yet in prayer we both sense a oneness that transcends the miles that separate us. God is not limited to space, as we are. He is able to reach down and give the unifying sense of His presence not only to people sitting beside us in the room but to individuals who are separated by continents. We proved this to ourselves in 1965.

After I had been praying with my two prayer partners Lorna and Sig every Thursday afternoon for almost a year, my husband and I went overseas to visit the mission fields. Before leaving we noted when we were scheduled to land in Addis Ababa, Ethiopia (where Sig's daughter Shirlee and her son-in-law Cliff were stationed). Our arrival would be just prior to the corresponding time that Lorna and Sig would be meeting for prayer in Rockford, though there would be an eight-hour difference on the clock. We calculated that if all the planes were on schedule and if everything went according to plan, we would be in Addis Ababa to pray with Sig's daughter and her husband at exactly the same time Sig was praying with Lorna in Rockford.

Having slept only two out of four nights en route, we arrived in Addis Ababa exhausted, but on schedule. All the guests went to bed except me. After the house was quiet, Cliff, Shirl, and I went to prayer in the living room. We had prayed for a short while when suddenly each of us had an overwhelming sense that no miles separated us and the two prayer partners back in Rockford. It was just as if they were right there praying with us. God had transcended all the miles across half the continent of the United States, the entire Atlantic Ocean, and most of the continent of Africa, and given to us a sense of oneness in His Spirit through prayer.

After we returned home, I was anxious to learn what had happened in Rockford that Thursday afternoon. Had they felt that oneness that transcends the miles? Sig said to me then, and she has repeated it over and over since, "Ev, I have never in all my years as a Christian been so aware of God and His power, so aware of His reality, as I was when I sensed that tremendous unity we had in Him, even though we were separated by thousands of miles." This too is the horizontal dimension of prayer, *linking the pray-ers* through our omnipresent God.

## We Had Never Met

Closely related to the transcendence of miles is the *bond created by prayer* even among people who have never met. In 1968 one of the ladies in our prayer chain went to another state to purchase a poodle from a woman we knew only as Joy. Joy had had major surgery involving the insertion of a plastic esophagus, and was having an extremely difficult pregnancy. It was no wonder that our prayer-chain member came back and said, "Let's pray for Joy." We started, and week after week, month after month, we prayed for her.

One day, after Joy delivered her baby, she told her husband that it was only because those women down there in Rockford were praying that she had the strength and the courage to get through her pregnancy. And that was not all—this dear woman accepted Christ as her personal Saviour, and became the best missionary we ever had! Everyone who came to buy a poodle heard that she had found Christ, and was told about the women many miles away who had prayed and prayed for her physical and spiritual needs. I haven't met Joy to this day. It isn't likely that I will, for I don't think I'll ever buy a poodle. But God answered anyway!

On our prayer-chain lists are many whom we have never met, but God knows who they are and where they are. He knows their needs. All we do is pray our requests—we don't pray answers—and God with the mighty arm of His power reaches down to anyone anywhere on Planet Earth with His answer.

### God Is the Rewarder

Much happens when we pray. And answers come as we pray in faith believing. As I mentioned in the previous chapter, "But without faith it is impossible to please Him; for he that cometh to God must believe that He is, and that He is a rewarder of them that diligently seek Him" (Heb. 11:6). We come first of all believing that He is, and then believing unequivocally that "He is a *rewarder* of them who diligently seek Him."

As we pray believingly, we see another result in the horizontal dimension of prayer—*it is great in its working*. We are not dropping our prayers into a bottomless barrel. How do we know? One way is by the specific answers to specific requests.

We began to experience great answers to prayer early in our prayer ministry. At the very first seminar in White Bear Lake, a woman handed me a request for our intercessory prayertime. It was for her sister to receive Christ. She said, "We've tried everything we know. We've talked to her; we've taken her to meetings where she's spurned invitation after invitation to receive Him. Please pray." Though they did not even know her name, 250 women zeroed in on that unsaved sister.

The next week the woman who had requested prayer stopped me before the seminar. "Do you know what? I took my sister to a Christian Women's luncheon right after the seminar last week, and she accepted Christ within two hours of your praying!" Those 250 pray-ers gave great praise during prayertime that day.

One morning we missed one of our prayer seminar steering committee members. Someone said, "She's taking her mother, who has TB, to the hospital."

Another woman suggested immediately, "Let's stop right now and pray."

To that another steering committee member added, "But that isn't her mother's greatest need. Neither her mother nor her father knows Christ as Saviour."

Instead of doing much planning that morning, we spent most of the time praying for the mother and father of our committee member. A couple of weeks after the seminar was over, still another member of the steering committee stopped me on the street and asked, "Ev, did you hear the good news? Do you know that within two weeks after the steering committee prayed, both the mother and father found Christ?" In just two weeks! "The effectual fervent prayer of a righteous man availeth much" (James 5:16).

At a recent seminar session we prayed very definitely that a certain woman would find Christ. That very night she received Him as her Saviour. In the same week we had another answer. A mother was called out of one of our seminars because her little boy had injured his leg at school and couldn't step on his foot. We promised to pray during the intercessory prayertime. When he was told that all those women had prayed for him, he said, "Then I must be OK." He threw away the ice pack, and went riding off on his bicycle!

God gave us a beautiful answer to prayer last year. We had learned that a young woman of 23 with two children had a cancerous growth on her brain. It was the type that had spread like the tentacles of an octopus, and her doctors gave her only a few weeks to live. All of us in the seminar went to prayer for this young mother, not just praying that she would be healed, but that God's will would be done in her life. In this instance God chose to heal this young woman. A few weeks later, we learned that the tumor was shrinking rapidly and that there was not a sign of a cancerous cell in her whole body. The doctors had given her a normal life expectancy!

What happens when we pray? Things do happen. We do not drop our intercessory prayers into a bottomless barrel. We send them up to a heavenly Father, who in His time, in His way, according to His will, answers them down here on Planet Earth.

### Requests Change

We see something else taking place in the horizontal dimension of prayer—we begin to see *changes in our prayer requests*. In 1968, when our prayer experimentation started, several in our denomination were trained in Washington, D.C. for the Crusade of the Americas. We returned to our homes all excited over the prospects of prayer and evangelism. I said to my husband, "We're going to pray for a year and then we're going to evangelize for a year."

He grinned and announced, "It'll never work."

Jolted, I asked, "Why not?"

He replied, "You show me somebody who's praying and I'll show you somebody who's evangelizing. A praying church is an evangelizing church."

He was right! Our objective had been to pray in 1968, and to evangelize in 1969. But when the time came for my report to our national committee in June 1969, I had to say, "The transition has already taken place."

We found that people who prayed automatically evangelized; they naturally shared their Christ with somebody else. With prayer chains praying for each of them, we developed 35 evangelism Bible studies in our church, in homes, offices, and in a high school, among women, couples, and young people. A Bible study group entirely composed of hippies was studying regularly as a result of Art Blessit's meeting that year. New converts had already become hosts, hostesses, and teachers for their evangelism Bible studies. We had participated in the distribution of Gospels to every home in our city.

In my 1969 report, I said, "We are seeing our total church program becoming increasingly evangelistic, not superimposed by programs, but from within the hearts of the workers. . . . Our local church has been the greatest recipient of the blessings because we, as the pilot church, have put into practice the [prayer] ideas of the committee before they were passed on as being workable."

Are you concerned about outreach in your own life? In your church? When you have a praying life and a praying church, I guarantee you will have a life and a church with a vital outreach, because as we learn to pray, our prayer requests change.

It's interesting to go back and look at the careful notes I made in those months in 1968 when we first started to pray. I notice particularly that one had to have a broken leg or something equally serious to be included on our prayer lists! If we could see the need with our physical eyes—if it needed a bandage or a cast—we gave the request to our prayer chain. Otherwise it didn't get very much attention.

Gradually, though, things changed. As our spiritual eyes began to open, we saw spiritual needs and added these to our lists. God in heaven is concerned about physical needs. He expects us not only to pray about them but to put feet to our prayers, to bring in that casserole, or to help in any other way we can. But we aren't to stop there. We need to ask God to open our spiritual eyes that we might see the spiritual needs around us, especially in the lives of people who need to be transformed by Christ. This is the greatest need of every person on Planet Earth. But how can we share these prayer requests with others?

### Prayer Partners

After a banquet at which I had shared the horizontal blessings of a prayer ministry, a woman came to me with tears in her eyes. She said, "I'm overwhelmed; there's so much to remember. Where do I start?"

I told her that beyond her own personal praying, the place to start intercessory prayer is with *one prayer partner*. This is the best way I know. Find someone with whom you can share big things and little things. When you hurt or have a headache, when some little thing goes wrong or when the whole world collapses around you, have one person you can trust absolutely, and upon whom you can call at any time. Find someone who will not betray your confidence, someone who is always ready to say whenever you give her a call, "I'll pray right now." Then, as you pray together, start praying for what God wants you to do for your church, family, and those in need. And then be open to those God would have pray with you.

### Church Lists

As your intercessory prayer develops on the horizontal level through private praying and prayer partners and prayer groups, we can proceed to church lists. One church in which we held a seminar encourages members of the congregation to fill out a form early in the Sunday morning service. It reads, "During our prayertime this morning, I would like my brothers and sisters in Christ to pray for . . ." Following several blank spaces there is room for the signature of the person making the requests. These sheets are collected, and the pastor remembers the specific requests in his morning prayer.

The members of another congregation place their prayer requests on registration cards during the morning service. Later in the day these requests, along with items for praise, are listed on sheets which are distributed in the evening service. These are beautiful examples of members of the body of Christ praying for one another and bearing one another's burdens as members of Christ's family.

### Prayer Calendars

Prayer calendars represent another method of systematic prayer on the horizontal level. Usually two categories are covered—people and events. An individual may have a particular need on a certain day, or there may be a public meeting or an evangelistic effort which demands definite prayer. These requests may be on a local or a national level.

In 1968, in a circle of less than 30 women, we placed our names on a prayer calendar. Each woman prayed for a different woman each day so every person in that circle was prayed for daily. It was exciting. We heard women say, "I could feel you praying; my life was different when I knew that I was being supported and undergirded specifically by somebody in my circle."

There can be any number of variations in prayer calendars. Include missionaries, your pastor and church staff, youth ministries, and special projects. It is a great spiritual exercise.

Yes, when we started experimenting with all these methods of intercessory prayer in 1968, I wondered if anything would happen, if there would be any horizontal results. I'm not wondering any more. I know that the effectual, fervent prayer of a righteous person does avail much, and I know it from experience.

*For you to pray:*
1. *Ask God to give you the next step He has for you in prayer—a prayer partner (ask for a specific name), a group He wants you to join or start, or a new method of prayer for your church, group, family, or club.*
2. *Wait in silence for Him to speak.*
3. *Promise Him you will start **immediately** whatever He is telling you to do.*

# 11

# Forgiven
# as We Forgive

*"And forgive us our sins, just as we have forgiven those who have sinned against us." Matthew 6:12,* LB

A horizontal dimension of prayer that Christ taught is frequently overlooked by those seeking a deeper prayer life. And it relates to the thing that is *most apt to break up your prayer group*—your relationship with the other people who are in that group!

In the Lord's Prayer we read, "And forgive us our sins *as* we forgive those who sin against us" (Matt. 6:12). Your Bible translation may say debts or transgressions, but both have the same literal meaning: sins. Now, this is the Lord Jesus Himself teaching the disciples, and us in turn, how to pray. If you want to keep your prayer group intact, practice this principle of forgiveness.

That word *as* is a conditional word meaning "to the extent that"—to the extent that I forgive others, I'm asking God to forgive me.

Christ explained it like this in the two verses which follow the Lord's Prayer: "For if ye forgive men their trespasses, your heavenly Father will also forgive you; but if ye forgive not men their trespasses, neither will your Father forgive your trespasses" (Matt. 6:14-15).

Do you remember our first prerequisite to answered prayer

116

in chapter 1, "If I regard iniquity in my heart, the Lord will not hear me"? (Ps. 66:18) Christ says that if we don't forgive others, our heavenly Father will not forgive us. If He does not, our sins will keep Him from hearing our intercessory prayers. They will be of no avail.

So, unless we keep our relationships with other people clear, we cannot be effective intercessory pray-ers. Now, let's remember one more thing from chapter 1: God always hears the penitent sinner's prayer as he confesses his sins and seeks Christ as his Saviour. God also hears the plea for forgiveness of sins by the one who is already a Christian. But for us to refuse to forgive others is itself a sin. We can't be right with God and effective intercessors if we harbor the sin of an unforgiving spirit—even though we may have confessed all *other* known sins. This is a very difficult lesson for some to learn, but it is very important.

At another time while teaching His disciples to pray in faith, Jesus admonished them in rather strong words, "Listen to Me! You can pray for anything, and if you believe, you have it; it's yours! But—when you are praying, first forgive anyone you are holding a grudge against, so that your Father in heaven will forgive you your sins too" (Mark 11:24-25, LB).

## Dealing with Those Who Cause Grief

I want to share with you the way this truth was brought into focus for me in the summer of 1972. I was all set to speak at a prayer breakfast for vacationers and women from several churches in Michigan. It was possible that some people present would not know Christ, so I first made a telephone call to the spiritual life chairman of a local prayer chain and gave her my request. She jotted it down, dated it, and indicated that she would be happy to take care of the whole thing. Still feeling the need for special prayer, I called another local chain and then dialed long distance back to my former prayer chain in Rockford for their support.

When I got back home, I called the prayer chains to send through praise for God's blessing at the prayer breakfast. The spiritual life chairman to whom I spoke during my first call was very quiet for a minute. Then she said, "Um, we didn't pray."

I exclaimed, "You didn't pray!"

"No," she replied, "one of the members said, 'We don't pray for speakers on this prayer chain.' "

I was stunned, and I gathered that this woman was seeing prayer needs only with her physical eyes, not with her spiritual eyes, for this was a spiritual need. This person who had enough authority to prevent a prayer from going through an entire prayer chain stopped it dead—and no one received the request.

How did I react? Just like a human being. I admit it was wrong, but I was very grieved for several days. And my spiritual life? I can only explain it by saying it became just like straw. If you want your prayer group to fall apart, to become like straw, just become grieved with another person in the same way I did.

Soon after this incident, Chris and I took a vacation 9,000 feet up in the Rockies. It should have been a beautiful time of fellowship with God, but I couldn't get through to Him in prayer. My Bible reading was meaningless; my whole spiritual life still felt just like straw. I was grating away on the inside and feeling perfectly miserable.

Finally, by Thursday of that week, I had had it. At 5 A.M. I grabbed my Bible, went out under those gorgeous pine trees, knelt by an old pine log, and cried out to God, "Show me what's wrong with my life. I can't get through to You."

I leafed through the pages of my Bible, but found nothing that suited my need. Then in desperation I turned another page, and my eyes fell on the words right at the bottom of a page, "If any have caused grief." *Why, Lord, that's what's wrong with me*, I thought. *I've been grieved.* Then God spoke to me: "Why don't you read on." I read on—and, wow, what I discovered was a *formula* to remedy my ailment.

I remember the exact page in my King James Version, it was 1253, where God met me. This prescription was for me as an individual, and it's also for you as an individual, and for your prayer group as well. It will keep your prayer group and your prayer chain intact. The Scripture passage is 2 Corinthians 2:5-11:

*"But if any have caused grief . . ."* (v. 5). Yes, this woman had caused me grief all right! Though I was innocent, I was still grieved—and miserable.

*"Sufficient to such a person is this punishment, which was inflicted by the many"* (v. 6). I suddenly realized that she was being shunned not only by me, but by others who had learned of her refusal to let my prayer request be put on the prayer chain. The news had gotten around.

*"So that contrariwise ye ought rather to forgive . . ."* (v. 7). I saw that I had to forgive. You see, God wasn't hearing my prayers. I had asked Him for forgiveness, but I hadn't forgiven the person who had grieved me. So I prayed, "Father, give me the strength to forgive this person." He did, and I forgave her at that point.

*"And comfort . . ."* (v. 7). I was shocked. I knew that word comfort meant encouragement plus alleviation of grief. "But, Lord," I said, *"I'm* the one who's been grieved. I'm supposed to alleviate *her* grief? Lord, you have something turned around."

"No," He said, "you are supposed to comfort, encourage, and alleviate the grief 'lest perhaps such a one should be swallowed up with overmuch sorrow' " (v. 7), and suffer deep spiritual discouragement.

"Lord, do you mean that the person who has grieved me might have a reason for acting that way? Maybe feels threatened? Maybe is struggling?"

I could hear Him say, "Right."

If someone is grieving us, how many of us take the wrong attitude? Though we may not say it in so many words, by our manner we are saying, "I know you're drowning, but I'll just take my foot and push you under to be sure you go down and drown right." Aren't we guilty of this? But God's Word says we are to get underneath, alleviate, and lift! Then, after we do that, we are to:

*"Confirm your love toward him"* (v. 8). I began to see that I had no love. Oh, I might have had a little supply of the ordinary love that one has for the members of her church—you know the kind I mean. But it wasn't any special love—there was none of that. In fact, it might have been something just the opposite right then. I'm not sure what I felt, but I know it wasn't deep Christian love.

Then I had to pray, "Lord, give me the love You want me to have for this person." And kneeling by that old pine log, I suddenly had a tremendous sense of God's love being poured upon me. There it was—and I loved her.

But there was a new problem: how to "confirm it." I couldn't get myself to write a letter, but when I reached home I was still convinced that I had to confirm my love to her.

The woman who had grieved me attended the same church I did. (Chris is now Assistant Vice President of Bethel College and is not in the pastorate, so we were attending as members, not as pastor and wife.) On the first Sunday morning we were back in church, I spied her sitting on the opposite side of the sanctuary from me. I didn't hear one word the pastor said as I kept praying, "Lord, if You want me to confirm this love, You have to put her right where I'm going to run into her. I'm not going to make a fool of myself and run over to her."

You know how that kind of prayer goes. Maybe I didn't get quite that hard-nosed, but that's what I was saying to God: "I'm not going to make a fool of myself. You're going to have to put her in my path." And so help me, at the close of the service I opened the big double doors at the back of the sanctuary and almost knocked her down! There she was!

And what did I have to do? I put my arms around her and said only one thing, "I just want you to know I love you." And the tears started to roll.

She said, "And I just want you to know that my husband and I are praying for your Bible study."

She "knew" and I "knew." We got together and really worked it out a few days later.

*"That I might know the proof of you . . ."* (v. 9). Why did I have to go to her? "That I might know the proof of you"—you the member of the prayer group who has been grieved, the innocent member of the prayer group, who is responsible to forgive and to go and confirm his or her love so that God will know how big a person you are—not the one who did the grieving, but the innocent one who was grieved.

*"Lest Satan should get an advantage of us"* (v. 11). This is the most frightening thing of all. There is nothing the enemy would rather do than to see our prayer groups broken up by our failure to forgive and confirm love. Let's never be guilty of allowing him to "get his foot in the door," for we are not ignorant of his devices.

*This Is for Everybody*

I had taught a Sunday School class on this subject of forgiveness, and following the morning service that day, a leading layman who had been in the class said to me, "I just want you to know that two men in our church got together after Sunday School and resolved something that had been between them for many years, and should have been handled long ago."

A man who attended one of our seminars had loaned a relative $70, even though he could hardly spare the money. He shared his feelings with me after our session on forgiving others. "Evelyn," he said, "I just told God that I now forgive the one who borrowed that money a couple of years ago and has not even mentioned it to me since. I was becoming more and more bitter in my heart, and I now know that I have to go and confirm my love to that relative. So, after I get home tonight, I'm going to dig out that little promissory note for the $70 and write on it 'Paid in full,' and put it right in the mail."

*For you to do:*

Ask God to bring to your mind that person who has grieved you and whom you have not forgiven.

Pray and ask God to forgive you for the sin of not forgiving that person.

Now forgive that person, asking God to give you the strength and ability if you need to.

Now ask God for as much love as He wants you to have for that person who grieved you.

Next ask God how you should confirm your love to that person. Wait in silence for His answer.

Pray, promising God that you will do whatever He has told you. Go do it!

# 12

# *Telephone Prayer Chains*

*"Be careful for nothing; but in everything by prayer and supplication with thanksgiving let your requests be made known unto God."*
*Philippians 4:6*

What I missed most when I moved from Rockford, Illinois in the fall of 1970 were the 115 women who prayed for me on the telephone prayer chains. Every time I spoke, every time I was sick, every time there was a need in my family, these women prayed. I, of course, was not the only one for whom they interceded. There were hundreds of others whose physical and spiritual needs were brought before God by these faithful women.

For a long time after we moved to Minnesota, I kept a hot line going to Rockford with requests for the prayer chains. There were pray-ers in my new home area, but I hadn't found them yet. I no longer need to dial Rockford as often for there are many active prayer chains now in the Minneapolis-St. Paul area.

You don't have to be told that I believe strongly in prayer chains. They are very close to my heart since I depend almost entirely on the answers God gives when they go to prayer, and I act accordingly. When everyone is praying simultaneously for the same requests, there is really tremendous power in prayer. I know that great changes have taken place in my life because the prayer chains have prayed for me.

## Power Over the Enemy

When I first started to speak against the occult, for example, I began to experience some horrible inner feelings. At times after speaking I was so filled with resentment and anger that I actually wanted to kick my car! Members of my family remarked that I was a different person when I spoke on that subject. Why was this so? Because I was intruding in Satan's realm. Then I took the advice of one of the leading Christian authorities on the subject of the occult, and formed a 10-member prayer chain from among the strongest pray-ers I knew.

The very next time I went out to speak on this subject, all those negative feelings had disappeared. Since that prayer chain was activated, I have had nothing but a victorious experience each time I have spoken against the occult.

## Personal Needs

Before leaving for meetings in another state, I asked several prayer chains to be praying at the exact hour when I would be appearing on a TV talk show. After I completed one speaking engagement at a Christian Women's Club luncheon, I was whisked crosstown to the TV studio to take part in the second half-hour of the program. Arriving during the commercial between the two segments of the hour, I was not aware that a well-known false evangelist from Korea had just preceded me on the program. Had I known this, I would have been completely unnerved. Instead I chatted enthusiastically on the subject of prayer—how, when, and where God answers. Friends who watched both half-hours of that talk show told me the astounding difference there was between them. God had guarded me—because of all those simultaneous prayers.

I have a file folder bulging with recorded prayer requests and answers that were handled through our Rockford prayer chains. As I reviewed these in preparation for the writing of this book, I was overwhelmed at the number of times my name appears—on an average of four times a week! There are requests for my speaking engagements, for physical strength, and for help at times when I was ministering for Christ. Here's one example: "April 14: Pray for strength for Evelyn. She has the flu, and is scheduled to speak at Janesville tonight. The ladies want to learn about prayer chains and how to pray effectively."

"April 15: Evelyn made the meeting. She had great praise. Many ladies were touched and eager to be changed." It was always understood that they were to pray that God would make me well enough to go if it was His will that I be there.

You may feel that you could not have such a prominent place in the prayer concerns of a large group. Perhaps that is true. I have a wonderful privilege to be prayed for so much. Nevertheless, you can reap great benefits by finding just one or two prayer partners and praying regularly for and with one another. But remember, my prayer chains started with just eight members. Why don't you start one?

### A Teaching Instrument for the Family

One exceptional thing about prayer chains is what they do for your home. If you want to really teach prayer to your children, I know of no better way than prayer-chain procedures.

As the children hear Mother calling through the prayer requests, and then watch as she bows her head immediately after putting down the receiver, they know that Mother believes in prayer. When the answer comes through they can hear her say, "Oh, that's great!" They watch her as she dials the next person on the prayer chain, and they listen as she says, "Praise God. He answered our prayer." They take note of her joy as she bows her head and thanks God for answering.

As prayer-chain calls come into the home, the children and other members of the family can observe the progress of prayer, taking note of specific requests, specific answers, God's timing, and the flow of praise.

For our family this has been one of the greatest teaching instruments through all the years of bringing up our children. They believe so much in prayer chains that both our daughters, when they were out of town, have spent their own money to call long distance with requests. Now our son, Kurt, the only child still living at home, every once in awhile comes out with, "I think it's time to call the prayer chain!"

Once while Kurt and I were painting the ceiling of our sun porch, the telephone rang, but I wasn't in any particular hurry to answer—you know how it is—being up a ladder and with the paint dripping down my arms! Our daughter Nancy picked up the kitchen phone, and in a few seconds she called in, "Never mind, Mother, it's *just* another answer to prayer."

Nancy herself was a subject for prayer on her wedding day. The note from my file reads: "June 8—6:30 P.M. Chris called the prayer chain with a specific request: 'Pray for Nancy who is vomiting and has diarrhea. Pray for God's divine healing as she will be married at 7:30 tonight.'"

The entry on June 9 reads: "Praise the Lord. Nancy was a bit queasy in the tummy, but came through in fine shape for the wedding!"

In Rockford we had an amusing illustration of the way children are impressed by the prayer chains. Our children's worker, Gail, was teaching prayer to a group of fifth- and sixth-graders. While meeting one Saturday, Gail said to the youngsters, "Would you please pray for the pastor's wife? She's speaking in Chicago today."

Just then a little boy raised his hand and said, "Never mind. You know that thing, that prayer chain thing? They've already prayed. It's all done."

Prayer chains provide a wonderful method of teaching complete confidence in answered prayer, and in the God who answers prayer. Let your children hear these specific answers that are reported over your telephone. It will do something for your entire family.

Not only mothers, but whole families are involved in the ministry of prayer chains. I remember one Sunday in Rockford a well-known Gospel singer and his family were visiting his parents. He is paralyzed from the waist down, and on that particular day his urinary tract had stopped functioning. By 6 P.M. the family was quite alarmed and had called the hospital emergency room.

As they were ready to leave for the hospital, his mom said, "Let's try the prayer chain first." At 6:20, when everybody was scurrying around getting ready for the evening church service, the prayer chains were activated. The request could not have come at a better time; everybody was home. Members of whole families stopped what they were doing and prayed for him. Later his mother said, "A very amazing thing happened. While the prayer chains were praying, suddenly, it was just as though an electric shock whizzed right through our house, and through my son's body. We didn't have to take him to the hospital because his whole system started to function normally once again."

### Church Families Too

Another beautiful illustration of family involvement was the result of a request dated Sunday, March 23: "Please pray for Becky. She has started labor pains. The baby is not due for seven or eight weeks." (Becky is the one mentioned in an earlier chapter whose only child was lost through a crib death.) That morning, before Sunday School, 120 homes received this specific request through the prayer chains. Mothers, fathers, and children all stopped to pray.

Later, the burden was shared in every department of the Sunday School; the whole church family joined in prayer for Becky. The notation made on Monday, March 24, reads: "Pray for Becky, and especially for her 3 lb., 8 oz. daughter." On Tuesday, March 25, the request was urgent: "Becky's baby has developed lung complications. Pray that God's strength will sustain Becky and Eddie, that the God who never makes a mistake will do what is best." God worked in a wonderful way.

Becky and I belonged to the same circle in our church. Every month she brought that healthy, happy little "answer to prayer" to our meetings and set her on a blanket in the middle of the floor—what a precious reminder of God's ability to answer prayer!

### Felt in Hospitals

Many prayer-chain requests are for those who are confined in hospitals. I have one note in my folder which reads: "Alice went to see Inez, who remarked, 'Your friends must be really praying. God was so near to me, and I'm not afraid anymore.' Her tests show a malignancy, and the nurses and her roommates can't understand the change in her attitude. She tells them God did it, and she's not afraid anymore."

There was also praise from Florence: "I'm so thankful God took me through this last experience. I was never more conscious that He was near. Each day I felt upheld by your prayers." As we received thank-you notes and telephone calls from patients for whom we prayed, most of them said, "I could feel you praying."

### In Bible Study Groups
Some of the most exciting answers to our prayer-chain praying have come out of Bible study groups. There was Lynn, for example. She had threatened to break up our meeting the first time she attended one of my Bible studies. She stood on her head, showing us how *she* had learned to meditate in her search for answers to life. Our prayer chains were already praying for her, and Lynn found Christ when she attended the Bible study the second time. After receiving Him she said to me, "I want to be on the prayer chain that prayed for me." Immediately she requested prayer for her friend, Sandy, to find Christ. Then came the day when she called, full of excitement, "Sandy just accepted Christ!" After a long pause, she said, "Now I'll have to find somebody else to put on the prayer chain."

Do you believe that thoroughly in prayer, in answers to prayer? Lynn does.

Among my notes, I have a request dated March 19, pertaining to Friendship Bible Coffees: "Lee would like us to pray for the seven Bible studies this morning and others this afternoon. Pray especially that the Holy Spirit will convict of the need for salvation." The answer: "Four found Christ that day!" One of the requests our prayer chains honored every day was to pray specifically for the women who attended the Bible studies.

### Seminars
Recently I received a call from the chairman of one of our previous prayer seminars. It illustrates the way prayer chains grow out of these sessions. She said, "This is the week you're going to teach prayer chains in your present five-week seminar, isn't it?" I told her it was. Then she went on, "Well, I'm leaving for California, but I want you to know what we have done in our area. We have just started six prayer chains, and we have almost enough people to form a seventh. We have three morning chains, an evening chain, and an emergency chain that operates around the clock. Both men and women

take part in this one. And we average three to nine requests per day on those prayer chains."

I then asked, "What's happening?"

She answered, "We're taking requests for physical and spiritual problems, from those who are having difficulties in their homes, and we're seeing things cleared up with beautiful answers to prayer. This is the most exciting thing that has come out of our prayer seminar. We're finding a unity among people from all the different churches that are represented on our prayer chains, and we feel this is a real service to the Lord."

The woman who was chairman of our retreat at Forest Home in California wrote, "Prayer chains are springing up all around now—men's, women's, and even children's prayer chains!" Prayer chains are not just for women. It's exciting to see everyone in a church involved—the pastor, members of the various boards, the Sunday School—everybody. A host pastor at one of our prayer seminars started an all-men's prayer chain with a challenge to the men in one of his church groups. "You know," he said, "there are certain things I cannot give to women to pray about. I need some men volunteers." He got them—one hundred percent!

A national youth speaker called me long distance and said, "I just listened to your prayer tapes while I was driving from Michigan to Pennsylvania. Now I feel that I wouldn't dare go through these 14 speaking engagements where I'll be bringing messages against the occult without prayer." We prayed, and when I next heard from him, he wrote, "I could feel you praying and I never before had such freedom, such attentiveness, and discipline in the schools where I spoke."

### The Chairman

In Rockford we had 10 prayer chains with 10 or so persons on each chain. Because we wanted to have as many people as possible praying simultaneously, our chairman, after receiving the calls and recording the requests verbatim, called person number one on all 10 of the prayer chains, and in 15 minutes 115 people were praying.

Incoming prayer requests may come from any source, but it's important that only the bare essentials be communicated in the request. A discerning chairman will sense when something is too personal, and will ask, "Have you checked with the person for whom you're requesting prayer?" As I look over the recorded requests in my folder I am amazed at the spiritual insight of our chairman and the careful wording she used in the prayer requests. For years she had helped me with housework in the parsonage, and we had spent many hours there in prayer together. But there came the day when after much surgery, she could no longer do housework and felt that God was calling her to be our prayer-chain chairman.

When she accepted the position, she stood up in our women's meeting and said, "I thank God for all the pain and the surgery, for He has shown me that there's something much greater that I can do for Evelyn than ironing and baking cookies."

## No Gossiping

A testimony by one of our prayer recipients attests to the strong commitment of our prayer-chain members. It happened that the woman who was my Bible study hostess for three years had a daughter who had left home and strayed far from Christ. Through her broken marriage, a divorce, and her remarriage, our prayer chains kept praying for this dear girl, and then for her new mate.

One day, while they were traveling in the East, this couple stepped out of their car, knelt in a parking lot, and without any human intervention, both accepted Christ as their personal Saviour. When they came back to our church in Rockford, the husband gave a testimony during a Sunday morning service. He said, "My wife and I owe our eternal salvation to the prayer chains of this church."

After they had gone away to study at a Christian college, the wife, as she related her experience to a group of faculty wives, said, "The thing that really astounded me after I came back home was that not one person of the 115 on those telephone prayer chains gossiped. They all knew I had been married and divorced, and that this was my second husband, but no one else knew about it."

That is the way it should be.

It's possible that some may find it difficult to keep juicy information confidential. If such is the case, they could call the chairman and say, "I would like my name removed from the prayer chains." This hasn't happened yet in our experience, but someday it might!

We have found that it is a great source of strength for prayer-chain members to sign the list of rules governing chain procedures at one time, while they are all together. In this way it is not a commitment to a group, or to a prayer-chain chairman, but it is a commitment to God.

Our basic rules are few and simple. Members promise to pray *immediately* when receiving requests by telephone. They also promise to pass on the request immediately to the next person in the prayer chain. They are not to delete anything or add anything to the request. And they are to keep it confidential—no gossiping.

### The Strongest Link

Ordinary chains are as weak as their weakest link, but a prayer chain is as strong as its strongest link. Why is this so? Because every single link in a prayer chain, every member, is united from here on earth to God the Father in heaven. All, the weak and the strong, are praying simultaneously to God the Father, and we see the dramatic, exciting results here on Planet Earth.

In January 1968, we started with eight gripers, and in just a few months we had 66 pray-ers. From March to December, these 66 pray-ers prayed for 508 requests which multiplied to 33,528 prayers to God the Father, who sent back as many answers. Multiply your prayers on a chain and watch exciting things happen!

### A Chain Reaction

Prayer chains have a peculiar and wonderful way of linking people together. We found this out when our Jan made a long distance telephone call from college to our prayer chairman in Rockford—325 miles away. The chain reaction started with her request on Tuesday, May 12, 1970: "Pray for God to be with and help a professor [Jan's chemistry teacher] at Bethel, whose wife has a serious back problem. She was to have had immediate surgery, but they just found out that she is pregnant. She has to be in bed much of the time and cannot take many pain pills as it might hurt the baby." Periodically after that we prayed for Sharon, and also for her unborn baby.

Two years later, after moving from Rockford, I was having my first Bible study class in St. Paul, when a young mother with a toddler in tow introduced herself to me in the church parking lot: "I'm Sharon," she said.

"Are you *the* Sharon for whom our prayer chains prayed when our Jan was so concerned about her chemistry professor's wife?" I asked.

As she grinned and nodded, her girlfriend spoke up, "Oh, Sharon, *that's why* you had such an easy delivery!"

Not long after that I was almost 2,000 miles away teaching the Six S's and telephone prayer chains at a women's retreat at Forest Home in California. I read some illustrations of prayer-chain requests directly from the bulging file folder—my most powerful teaching tool! As I read the request Jan had phoned in from Bethel in 1970, a woman sitting in the back of the auditorium waved her hand to get my attention. She said, "I have an urgent request from Sharon's mother-in-law. She just found out today that Sharon's husband's brother has an extremely serious brain tumor." God gave to that roomful of women a tremendous sense of urgency as we broke into groups of four to practice and experience the reality of "praying in one accord."

Returning to St. Paul, I immediately placed this pressing request with the faculty wives' prayer chain which we had recently started. Through the long, difficult illness and death of his brother, we continued to pray for this professor's need. And now, who do you think has been the telephone prayer chairman of this faculty wives' prayer chain for the past two years? Yes, Sharon.

Sharon was also one of those chosen to be on my first personal prayer chain in the Twin Cities. The chain is still active, and this last year the other members and I prayed for Sharon through another difficult pregnancy, through the baby's late arrival (timed to be after the brother-in-law's out-of-state funeral), and the new baby's surgery. And we continued to pray about Sharon's back problem—for which we started prayer four and one-half years earlier in Rockford! In December 1974, Sharon had that surgery, and mother and baby are now doing beautifully.

Yes, telephone prayer chains (as all forms of prayer) have a unique way of joining the human links together on a horizontal plane here on earth. But the marvel of it is that each individual is directly connected to the source of power of the whole universe, who is up in heaven—God Himself!

*"Lord, teach me to pray! Amen."*

# "Lord, Change Me!"

# Preface

When I finished the *What Happens When Women Pray* project of the first six months of 1968, I thought it was time to relax. The job was done. But God had other plans. Before I left the conference at which I reported the outcome of that experimentation in prayer, God had begun a new process in me. I came home, not to look on the things which were behind, but to press on in another personal project, this time praying, "Lord, change me—not my husband, not my children—just me!"

I struggled alone with God for 14 months, allowing Him to change me. And all during this time He was clearly putting the emphasis for changing on ME, not anybody else.

God used the seven methods I have outlined in chapters 2 through 8 of this book to teach me how He wanted me to change and how He would provide the direction and the means for my changing. These methods have been used successfully for Christian education retreats, teacher training sessions, church prayer weeks, women's retreats, Sunday School classes, and Bible studies.

This process of waiting on God brought forth the theme, *Lord, Change Me,* spontaneously and unplanned at a retreat I was conducting 14 months after He began teaching it to me. Then the theme gathered momentum as I began sharing it at retreats, conferences, and studies around the United States and Canada.

But I discovered one danger in this process. I had to make sure I was being changed by the Lord and not by the other three possible sources of wisdom James lists in verse 15 of his third chapter. The last four chapters of this book (Section III) deal with the subtle or deliberate ways our thinking is influenced by other people, our own sensual selves, demons, or by God. And what we think eventually produces our lifestyles. We can tell the source of our instruction by what this wisdom produces in our lives—how we are changed. And this is an ongoing process of becoming more like Christ—until we see Him face to face.

# SECTION 1—ME

# 1

# Why Me?

"Lord, I will never speak again—never—if this is the price my husband has to pay for my being a public speaker." And I wept as I prayed, "Lord, I want You to change me into the kind of wife *You* want me to be."

I had crept out of bed at 5:30 A.M. to seek the Lord in my private "prayer closet" by my old green chair. And as the minutes ticked into hours, I stayed on my knees struggling.

Why was I telling God I would never speak again? Was I disappointed, disillusioned, tired out? Oh, no—just the opposite. Flooding over me as I agonized with God was the enormity of what I was promising. I was willing to give up a way of life to which I was sure He had called me: my weekly women's neighborhood Bible study, the large adult Sunday School class—one of the greatest joys of my life—I had been teaching for almost 12 years, and my busy banquet-speaking schedule. Then my mind turned to all the retreats in the United States and Canada, where I had seen God work in such quiet, yet powerful, ways. I thought of the Vacation Bible Schools, teacher-training classes, conferences, conventions—the list parading through my mind seemed endless. But I prayed, "Yes, Lord, *all*!"

My husband, Chris, missed me, and suddenly I was aware of his footsteps on the stairs. He paused halfway down and asked, "May I join you?" I looked up at him and sobbed, "Chris, I'm not praying for *you*, I'm praying for *me*! I'm praying that the Lord will change *me*." (The Lord may have had some changing to do in Chris's life, but that was not *my* concern that morning. That was between the Lord and Chris.)

### Why Me, Lord?

But why did I need to be changed? Hadn't I cried over my sins all one Sunday afternoon when I was only nine years old? I had heard Evangelist Harry McCormick Lintz preach in church that morning in Muskegon, Michigan, and I thought the evening service would never come—and then that it would never end—so eager was I to respond to his invitation to those who wanted to invite Jesus into their hearts. I almost ran down the aisle, then opened my heart completely to Jesus, as our Sunday School superintendent knelt beside me and carefully explained from the Scriptures how I could become a Christian.

And hadn't I really made Him *Lord* in addition to Saviour that Sunday? Yes, I had. From that day on I had grown steadily—sometimes in little baby steps and at other times in giant steps of faith—but always I had wanted and sought His will. Hadn't I even spent months praying about my first and only boyfriend until I was positive he was the one God wanted me to marry? And hadn't Chris and I, as engaged students at Moody Bible Institute, spent our free moments poring over Walter A. Maier's *For Better Not for Worse*, the Christian classic in those days for brides and grooms who wanted a Christ-centered marriage? And hadn't I, in agreement with my husband, sought only God's will as we struggled to find His spot for us in full-time Christian service, and later as we served Him as pastor and wife for 16 years? Yes, I had.

And in that last pastorate hadn't I spent six miserable weeks confessing sins to God with Lorna and Signe, my two prayer partners, before He released us to pursue our goal—prayer for our church? Hadn't God given us three years of deep intercessory prayer? And hadn't He done a Herculean job *in* and *on* and *through* us as the women of our church experimented in prayer in 1968?

### So Then, Why Me?

My personal agony that early morning by my old green chair was precipitated by what had happened at our denomination's annual conference in Davenport the week before. It was June 1968, and I was flying high. Earlier, in the fall of 1967, the national committee of our denomination had asked me to do a project for the Crusade of the Americas: "Working with women in your own church, would you discover in a six-month period *what happens when women pray*?" I had accepted the challenge with enthusiasm. Now I had a fantastic report to give to the 600 women attending the opening banquet of our conference. Women from all over the United States and Canada, as well as foreign missionaries, would hear the results of our six-month experiment. Just before the banquet started, a man carrying what looked like a movie camera arrived and said to me, "Wave your arms and make believe you're speaking." As I complied, our national director, sitting at my right, whispered laughingly out of the corner of her mouth, "Psst. I think that's a TV camera!" And I was horrified to discover that she was right!

Early the next morning the jabs started—not at me, but at my husband—from fellow pastors and friends. "Hey, I saw your wife on television last night." "How does it feel to be the husband of Mrs. Christenson?" One pastor remarked to Chris, as he glanced at the shocking pink dress I was wearing, "I saw your wife on TV. Wow! It wasn't in technicolor, though." To my horror, the local TV station had chosen the segment showing my pseudospeech to represent our entire national conference on its news telecast. All week long Chris had borne the brunt of this cruel teasing. It became so embarrassing that I was the most crushed wife you could possibly imagine when we left the conference. I arrived home in Rockford, brokenhearted and puzzled. That is what had brought me to my knees beside my old green chair.

## Why Not Victory Day?

All through breakfast that same morning, the first Tuesday in July, and while dressing for our women's weekly prayer meeting at Alpine Park, I kept dabbing away the tears. Even as I drove to the park I kept telling myself, "This is victory day, and we are going to have a victory celebration." But the tears persisted—not tears of joy, but tears of brokenness.

Eagerly the pray-ers gathered, waiting expectantly to hear

what had happened in Davenport. These were the women with whom I had experimented in prayer the previous six months. These were the women, their ranks now multiplied, who had pled daily with God during the whole week I was in Davenport, that He would undergird me and that what they had experienced would spread to other women.

I felt strongly that these women waiting at Alpine Park deserved to know that after I shared what had happened in those six months when *they* prayed, every one of the 600 women present at the banquet stood to her feet and promised God that she would go home and start proving that God does answer "when women pray." They deserved to learn the outcome of their praying as they arbitrarily picked out one of the conference speakers to zero in on in prayer. I wanted to tell them that after he had spoken I had followed him into the wing of the platform area and asked, "Rev. Hanstad, would you tell me how it was preaching out there today? You see, our ladies in Rockford picked you from among all the conference speakers as a special subject of prayer for many days. Did it make a difference?" He drew a quick breath and said, "Oh, I've never had such *freedom*. I'm usually so uptight and nervous when I speak before all my peers and those administrators, but today it was different. I felt so free; there was no tension at all."

These women who had prayed for me so faithfully while I was in Davenport also deserved to know that I had awakened on the morning of the banquet with a burning sore throat and a throbbing, stuffy head. I had been too sick to pray for myself. All I could do was mumble weakly from my bed, "Oh, God, tell somebody to pray; tell somebody to pray." And without knowing of my condition, these women who were waiting in the park had prayed all that day for me. They deserved to know that God had heard and answered their prayers, for after I had crawled out of bed to get ready for the banquet that evening, still unable to talk out loud or breathe freely, a miracle had happened. I had bent over to brush my teeth, and, when I raised my head, I was well. My voice was normal, my head was clear, the sore throat and miserable aching had disappeared.

I had planned the victory speech they deserved. Their six-month job was done. But God had further plans. He was leading us up the next rung of the spiritual ladder. He had already started the process in me, bringing me down to the depths of despair that I might rise to something higher. He had some more changing to do in me. So, instead of the victory speech, I told them the whole story of what had transpired earlier that morning by my old green chair.

Trying to hide my stubborn tears, I shared the pain of my experience with the women. They all wept with me. We were feeling an unexpected and different kind of victory. I remember Katy praying that morning, "Lord, I don't care what it is, take it from me so that I can serve You effectively. Lord, I don't care what it is." Now, Katy is a sharp gal. Her husband is a tennis champion, and they have two beautiful children. She is one of those women you watch to find out what the styles are going to be next year. But Katy wept along with the rest of us that morning as we prayed, "Lord, change me." Our hearts were all echoing her prayer, "O God, take away anything—so that You can really use me." Katy desperately wanted God to be first in her life.

But a strange thing happened. Following that meeting, and for over a year afterward, we never used the phrase, "Lord, change me." It was to go underground, to emerge 14 months later.

### A New Process
God didn't take me up on my offer to give up my speaking and teaching, but He did begin that day to answer my prayer, "Lord, change me." He already had the next step in my spiritual maturity planned and ready for me. He started that morning to teach me a great principle which began a process in my life that is still at work. I have discovered through the years that surprising things happen when I pray, "Lord, change *me*—don't change my husband, don't change my children, don't change my pastor, change *me*!" This doesn't mean that I approve or even condone everything they do, but rather that I concentrate on how *I* handle my actions and reactions. More and more the fact comes into focus that they, and not I, are responsible before God for their actions. But I am responsible for the changes that need to be made in *me*.

This concept became the process whereby Evelyn was to become more Christlike, conformed to *His* image, as stated in

Romans 8:29, "For whom He did foreknow, He also did predestinate *to be conformed to the image of His Son.*" And since being Christlike is my goal, I must expect this process to continue throughout my life and end only "when He shall appear" and I shall be "like Him" (1 John 3:2).

Although it was to be 14 months before the Lord-change-me concept was to become an actuality, the process had started. God had launched me personally on a 14-month gestation period. The "birth" would not take place until over a year later. This was the process of facing the reality of *my* need to change—again and again and again.

The struggle was like a hot iron inside me. That's the only way I can describe it. And it took 14 solid months of turning to the only adequate, worthy Source of change—God Himself—and of searching His Word and allowing Him to make changes in my life, not in anybody else's.

"O God," I kept praying, "don't change anybody else, not my husband, not my children, just change ME!"

### Me Again?

That same month, June 1968, I had some more changes to make. (What a horrible month that was!) I discovered something new about myself—because my daughter told me!

At the dinner table one evening Jan, our just-turned-18 eldest, abruptly announced, "Mother, I don't ever want to hear your philosophy again. Do you know that the tone of your voice actually changes when you start giving your philosophy? I know what's coming every single time."

"*Me* again?" I pushed my chair from the table, flew up to my bedroom and threw myself, sobbing, on my bed.

What was God teaching me *this* time? Jan always had been an independent first child, determinedly doing her own thing—following the encyclopedia's instructions for formal table settings while still in second grade; conquering the world of reading in sixth grade by winning our denomination's national reading contest. Her "I can do it myself, Mother" personality had been there from birth, but always under mother's guidance. So what was happening to her now? What had legally becoming an adult at her 18th birthday done to her?

Then, agonizing in my soul, I prayed, "Lord, don't change

Jan. I know she's a teenager who needs to find her way in the world. Just change me! Lord, make me the kind of mother You want me to be. O God, I know she's growing up. Show me, please, how You want me to change!"

Then began in earnest what was to stretch into 14 months of soul-searching for me.

### Without a Word

As I looked in the Bible for direction, God gave me a *principle* from 1 Peter 3:1-2 that guided my "changing" and carried me through those difficult 14 months. At that time the emphasis for me from God was that others were to *observe my* chaste and reverent behavior. "So that some . . . may be won *without a word"* (RSV).

Although this verse speaks specifically of the husband-wife relationship, I was to find that the "without a word" principle also worked with mothers and daughters. I determined not to impose my philosophy on Jan again. No more "preachy" mother!

Keeping my advice to myself, especially with my personality, wasn't easy. And Jan even enrolled at my alma mater as a freshman that fall! Oh, how I could have helped her by telling her just how to do everything. After all, hadn't I spent seven years with her daddy on that campus (and with her as a little baby)? And hadn't I, as secretary to the president, typed the disciplinary letters to parents and worked with the details of scholarship and college administration? But I restrained myself from offering my help. She didn't want it. Her independent attitude prevailed. She had to find out who *she* was—by herself.

I've learned since that that time wasn't easy for Jan either. She has confided to me that frequently, those first few weeks, she would sit in her dorm, bite her lip and blink hard to keep back the tears—determined not to call home every time she felt lonely—determined to become independent—determined to make her own decisions in college. And at the same time I was sitting home just as determined—blinking back my tears— determined to let her find her own philosophy of life, to find her own way in the world.

When the first child turns 18 and decides to cut the apron

strings, parents (especially mothers) almost bleed to death. Their wounds seem to be much deeper than those of the children, and heal so much more slowly. Letting go of Jan was one of the most devastating things that had ever happened to me. How I thank God for five years of preparation before our next child became of age. I didn't bleed nearly so much, for I had had five years to change my "smotherhood" to "motherhood." And Nancy could walk with much more confidence in the field which Jan had plowed as virgin soil those many years before.

### It Works

By February following that horrible June, my then eight months of silence about my philosophy was starting to bring results, although I honestly wasn't looking for them. I was only concentrating on the Lord changing me. That He might in turn be changing my daughter hadn't occurred to me. Our first visit to her college was for Founder's Week. As we sat conversing at dinner with Jan and the boy she was then dating, I sat in stunned silence as she carefully, deliberately kept saying to him, "My mother thinks this about that. And she thinks this about that." The other part of those verses in 1 Peter 3 was proving to be true, "That some . . . *may be won* . . . when they [observe] your reverent and chaste behavior" (3:1-2, RSV). But this wasn't the time to say anything.

Multiplying my prayers for her, I entrusted Jan to God and kept my "hands off" policy going those 14 months. Without mentioning to anybody what I was doing, I silently stayed in God's Word, wept and prayed, "Lord, don't change Chris, don't change Jan, don't change my other children, don't change the people in my church, don't change anybody else—but Lord, change Evelyn."

I recently checked with Jan about this, and she said, "Oh, Mom, you really never did open your mouth to me once with any of your philosophy for all those months. You never did."

Now eight years later, I have just had the shock of my life. A doctor's wife from our church greeted me one Sunday morning and said, "I was chatting with your Jan at our Christian Medical Society's retreat, and she told me that she gets her philosophy of life from her mother." And it was Jan herself who had said to me just days before that, "Mother, your next book has to be, must be, *Lord, Change Me.*"

But the most surprising and thrilling thing to come out of those 14 agonizing months of keeping my mouth closed and letting God change me was a birthday card the next year from my Jan. It was signed: "To my mother—who says so much in her silence."

I had learned the first step in becoming more Christlike—*admitting* that I was the one who needed changing, and in silence *living* my life before others.

The struggle paid off in many ways, but one of the most gratifying was when Nancy, our middle child, came home from her part-time job four years later, burst into the living room and said, "Mother, I found you in the Bible! I was just reading my *Living Bible* and found you in Titus 2:7." Tears came to my eyes as she read it to me. "And here you yourself must be an example to them of good deeds of every kind. Let everything you do reflect your love of the truth and the fact that you are in dead earnest about it."

I cried in my heart, "O God, have I really *lived* in front of Nancy an 'example . . . of good deeds . . . love of truth . . . and . . . in dead earnest'? Are there really those who are being won, not with my words but by observing me?"

# SECTION II—CHANGE

# 2

# *Lord,*
# *How Do I Change?*

"Lord, I want to change. But how do I discover *Your* 'chaste and reverent' behavior, mentioned in 1 Peter 3:1-2? Especially since I've been trying so hard for so long? Is there more, Lord? How should I go about becoming what You want me to be now?"

**Let Him Ask of God**
When I asked God these questions, He showed me that *He* gives answers. All I needed to do was ask: "If any of you lack wisdom, let him ask of God, that giveth to all men liberally, and upbraideth not; and it shall be given him" (James 1:5). One definition of wisdom is "that endowment of heart and mind which is needed for the right *conduct of life.*" Wisdom is not just philosophic speculation or intellectual knowledge, but a practical, applied lifestyle. It is not only knowing something in your head, but applying it to your life so that it becomes a part of you.

**If Any Lack Wisdom**
In 1966 God had taught me the *process* of seeking wisdom from His Word. I had been given my first denominational assignment—to bring four messages to women's and girls' work directors from our 18 districts in the United States and Canada on the theme, "God's Word for a New Age." I was to prove that the Bible was an adequate guide for this new age—an age

of exploding knowledge, with technical libraries becoming obsolete every six months, and with a whole new world being conquered in outer space.

Trying to come up with the material for my messages, I drew a blank month after month. Finally, on July 8, 1966, I panicked, realizing I had only two months left to find the solution to this mind-boggling challenge. So, at 5:30 one morning, I sought my green chair "prayer closet," fell on my knees, and begged God to give me the answer. I prayed and pleaded for over an hour—but no answer came. In desperation I reached for my Bible, opened it to where I was reading devotionally, and started to read Psalm 25.

Suddenly one little four-letter word in the fifth verse almost jumped off the page at me. It seemed to be in very black bold type. W-A-I-T. "Lead me in Thy truth, and teach me: for Thou art the God of my salvation; on Thee do I *wait* all the day."

"O Lord," I cried, "I'll take You at Your Word. I'll trust You. I won't read any books on the subject. I'll just stay in *Your* Book and let You tell me what I should teach those women."

Then every day for the next six weeks I read the Scriptures, not consecutively in one book, but at random. And each time God stopped me (as He had at the word *wait*), I would jot down the specific thought on a separate piece of paper. When I finished this process during our vacation at the cottage on Lake Michigan that summer, God had a surprise for me. I looked at the hopeless pile of random notes and announced to the family that I needed to use the dining room table to divide these into some semblance of order.

As I read through these disconnected, scattered thoughts gleaned from my Bible reading, I realized that they were logically dividing themselves into four specific subjects. And I no longer had one large pile but four smaller piles of paper. With mounting enthusiasm and curiosity, I reread each grouping and discovered that these random notes fell into a natural outline form. (They reminded me of my college freshman English class where we learned to make notations from our research on index cards.) In almost a state of shock I, who had always thought of myself as the "commentary kid," looked at the four piles of notes in outline form for the four messages which would prove that God's Word is an adequate guide for our sophisticated, proud minds. Wow! The Bible was alive—sufficient for our new age!

The process of obtaining wisdom from God was indelibly impressed on my mind. For six weeks He had been carefully guiding and directing my "random" reading, speaking specifically to the subject through scattered Scriptures.

### Who Giveth to "All" Men Liberally

God had another surprise for me in this process of seeking wisdom from His Word. After giving these four messages at the Regional Chairmen's Conference in Chicago and sharing them at a retreat in the foothills of Mount Rainier in Washington, I taught them at the annual fall "Learning for Serving" seminar at our church. Soon afterward a visiting college president was our guest speaker on a Sunday morning.

After the service my phone began to ring. "Did you recognize your outline this morning, Evelyn?"

"That was not *my* outline," I assured the caller. "I know that man never heard a word I ever taught. That was *his* outline, not mine."

God had taught both of us the same truths from His Word! I don't know the method God used to give our guest speaker his message, but it overwhelmed me that identical instructions had been given to both of us.

The following January I kept my radio tuned to Moody Bible Institute's annual Founder's Week broadcasts while doing my housework. Day after day I listened in stunned silence as two nationally known speakers used the same points and illustrations God had given me in that random reading the previous summer for my "God's Word for a New Age" project. Finally I pressed the "off" buttons of the washer and dryer, ran into the dining room and dropped my head in my arms at the table. "O God," I sobbed, "You gave *me* the same information out of Your Word that You gave those two great men of God with earned Ph.D. degrees! *Me*—a nobody!"

### Read Until

Two years later, in June 1968, God offered me a new project which originated with my oldest daughter's criticism, described in the last chapter. This time I was to let God *change me through His Word* while I kept my philosophy to myself. Most mothers go through a time of deep introspection when their children leave the nest. Now I had joined their ranks. I too reevaluated myself—soon to be out of a job just as I was becoming experienced at being a mother.

I set out in earnest using the process God had taught me, allowing Him to tell me *how* He wanted me to change. Staying in the Scripture for instruction, I would read only *until* He spoke. Then I would stop to pray about what He had said, analyze His reason for stopping me at that particular point, discover the need He knew I had, and then determine what I could do to change. I underlined hundreds of verses during those 14 months, but I'll share here only a few that were the most meaningful to me.

As I read in the Psalms, day by day, starting in June 1968, God gave me the *source* of wisdom that would effect changes in my life. First, He gave me Psalm 1:2, "But his delight is in the law of the Lord; and in His law doth he meditate day and night." In the margin of my Bible by that verse I wrote: "24 hours" and "all undergraduates, no alumni." I was to meditate in His law day and night, and not consider myself as having graduated from God's school of learning and changing. There was still more for me to learn.

*How I was to approach this process* was shown to me in Psalm 25: "The meek will He guide in judgment; and the meek will He teach His way" (v. 9), and "What man is he that feareth the Lord? Him shall He teach in the way that He shall choose" (v. 12). Coming to God humbly and meekly, admitting that *I* needed to be changed, was a new, emerging thought to me in those days.

Then underlined heavily in my Bible was *the promise of authoritative direction from God* for me in Psalm 32:8: "I will instruct thee and teach thee in the way which thou shalt go; I will guide thee with Mine eye." There was no question about it; God would instruct me and guide me in my quest for instruction as to *how* I was to change.

As God spoke to me forcefully out of the 139th Psalm, the idea of Scripture being profitable for reproof (2 Tim. 3:16) became evident. "Search me, O God, and know my heart; try me, and know my thoughts; and see if there be any wicked way in me, and lead me in the way everlasting" (vv. 23-24). God had to show me through His Word what displeased Him and what needed to be changed in me. In the margin I penciled, "Prayer: 'Lord, change me.' "

Then, as I read until God spoke from the Book of Proverbs during those 14 months, He gave me much instruction about *obtaining wisdom*: "Yea, if thou *criest* after knowledge, and *liftest up thy voice* for understanding; if thou *seekest* her as silver, and *searchest* for her as for hid treasures; then shalt thou understand the fear of the Lord, and find the knowledge of God. For the Lord giveth wisdom; out of His mouth cometh knowledge and understanding" (Prov. 2:3-6, italics mine). Once again God was impressing upon me the truth that "the fear of the Lord is the beginning of wisdom" (Prov. 9:10). And that wisdom was to be found in His Word.

### Transformed—by the Renewing of Your Mind

Some specific points on *how* I could change began emerging during those 14 months as I searched the Scriptures. I remember rising early in the morning in a Fort Lauderdale condominium, struggling with what God meant when He had given me Romans 12:2 the month before: "But be not conformed to this world: but be ye *transformed* by the renewing of your mind, that ye may prove what is that good, and acceptable, and perfect, will of God."

On December 29, 1969, I wrote in the margin of my Bible, "Transformed—same word as Christ's transfiguration." Did God want me changed as dramatically as Christ was on the Mount of Transfiguration when His face shone as the sun and His raiment was white as the light? Then I wrote, "Changed—from worm to butterfly." I almost felt like the surprised worm I had seen on a poster. Watching a butterfly soar overhead, the worm was saying, "Who, *me* change?" Then I wrote in the margin of my Bible beside Romans 12:2, "Pronouns—does God want *me*?" The pronouns were so very, very personal. I circled them. No mistaking it. God wasn't talking to my husband, my children—but to me. Then the abrupt note in my Bible said, "Spiritual maturity—period." Yes, that's what all that changing was about—to be mature in Him. Like Him. Proving what is His good and acceptable and perfect will—for me.

God also told me how I *didn't* have to change. Although I felt no inner compulsion to give up my teaching and speaking after I had told God I would that previous June, it was such a thrill to get the confirmation directly from Him. As I was reading in Ephesians 6, I blinked in surprise and then tears of relief swelled in my eyes as He stopped me at: "And for me, that utterance may be given unto me, that I may open my mouth boldly, to make known the mystery of the Gospel, for which I am an ambassador in bonds; that therein I may speak boldly, as I ought to speak" (vv. 19-20). This was one of the greatest things God taught me those 14 months. He told me to continue speaking and teaching even though I was willing to give it all up if it was going to hurt my husband. My final affirmation to this came last fall from my husband himself when he said to me, "Honey, I'm your greatest fan."

God continued to show me how to change. On February 18, 1969, I read Galatians 2:20: "I am crucified with Christ; nevertheless I live; yet not I, but Christ liveth in me; and the life which I now live in the flesh I live by the faith of the Son of God, who loved me and gave Himself for me." Then, in my Bible, I wrote, "Ego moves to the side—Christ to the center of me." The *how* to change was becoming obvious. I was to let Christ live in me, transforming me into the likeness of Himself.

There were many specific instructions, but Philippians 2:3, with the notation, "Humility—April 1969," was so meaningful to me at that time: "Let nothing be done through strife or vainglory; but in lowliness of mind let each esteem other better than themselves."

God even showed me some affirmation of the learning in silence through my 11-year-old Kurt as we were reading together that January. "Isn't it amazing how much you can learn when you don't argue? " he commented on Philippians 2:14: "Do all things without murmurings and disputings." Renewing my mind!

God seemed to reassure me through one verse of Scripture in my struggle to become changed, more Christlike. In February I had a heavy speaking schedule and was utterly exhausted at a retreat in Mount Hermon, California. I fervently prayed for God to change me before the Saturday night banquet. Two days later, after an almost miraculous rejuvenation for the banquet, I marked this in my Bible: "Being confident of this very thing, that He who hath begun a good work in you will perform it until the day of Jesus Christ" (Phil. 1:6).

A verse I would only be able to understand later prompted me to write "me" in the margin beside it on February 1, 1969. Like Paul, would I be a more effective servant of Jesus after this? Would my ministry for Christ be more effective because of the experiences of these 14 months? "But I would ye should understand, brethren, that the things which happened unto *me* have fallen out rather unto the furtherance of the Gospel" (Phil. 1:12).

### Precept upon Precept

Then God gave some more specific instructions about His method of teaching me those 14 months. On March 23, 1969, He showed me emphatically that He was the Teacher. "But the anointing which ye have received of Him abideth in you, and ye need not that any man teach you but as the same anointing teacheth you of all things, and is truth, and is no lie, and even as it hath taught you, ye shall abide in Him" (1 John 2:27). "Whom shall He teach knowledge? And whom shall He make to understand doctrine? Them that are weaned from the milk, and drawn from the breasts. *For precept must be upon precept*, precept upon precept; line upon line, line upon line; here a little, and there a little" (Isa. 28:9-10, italics mine).

That was it. Through hundreds of verses God spoke directly to me during that time. He had piled precept upon precept and line upon line, showing me what needed to be changed, and how to depend completely upon Him for wisdom to change. This maturing was for those who were weaned from milk, those who were growing up—by the renewing of the mind!

### And Upbraideth Not

Never once in those 14 months did God scold me for asking for more wisdom. Over and over again He reassured me that He wanted to give me all the wisdom I needed. The gift of wisdom is the only gift promised to *all* who ask for it. The other gifts are given by the three Persons of the Trinity as They please to distribute them.

In 1 Corinthians 12:8-11 we read that the Holy Spirit divides gifts to every man as He wills. Romans 12:3-6 shows us that "God hath dealt to every man the measure of faith . . . having then gifts differing according to the grace that is given to us." Then, in Ephesians 4:7 and 11, we read, "But unto every one of us is given grace according to the measure of the gift of Christ . . . and He gave some, apostles; some, prophets; and some, evangelists; and some, pastors and teachers." Thus Christ too gave people of differing gifts to the churches as He desired. But the gift of wisdom is different. Every believer can ask for and receive the precious gift of wisdom for making changes in his life. He is given a renewed mind to know the perfect will of God.

### Changed—Through My Spiritual Diary

But receiving wisdom for my life from His Word has not been confined to those 14 months. Recently I did a project in preparation for an assigned retreat theme of "God's Living Word." To prove to myself—and those at the retreat—that the Bible had been alive in my own life, I dug out the three Bibles from which I had read devotionally since I was 18 years old. I went through those Bibles, systematically and laboriously, and recorded in three columns (one for each Bible) the most significant underlined, and usually dated, Scriptures. As I pored over these three Bibles for a month I had a surprise. I could tell from the passage I had underlined whether I had been in victory or defeat, joy or depression, death, birth, surgery, illness, open doors, challenge, or closed doors. And as the evidence piled up, I slowly began to realize that God had *always* given *specific answers for specific needs at specific times.*

As column after column on page after page filled up on the legal pad I was using, something overwhelmingly significant came into focus. I had in three Bibles a *spiritual diary of my life* from the time I was 18! For all of those years God had been instructing me specifically out of His Word. The process that came into focus as "Lord, change me" that June 1968, actually had been an unrecognized goal of my life since I had graduated from high school in 1940.

May I share a few of the verses that are most precious to me, selected from the thousands underlined and usually dated in those three Bibles?

* * *

At our first pastorate in the fall of 1953 God spoke definitely to me the day the doctors told us our baby, Judy, could not live. I remember taking her to the hospital, coming home with aching, empty arms and a horrible rebellion in my heart—stubbornly hanging on to my right to keep her. I struggled alone in my bedroom for hours over a statement our former pastor had made, "God must love Harold and Evelyn a lot to give them all that sorrow." As I thought about the Scripture he was referring to in Hebrews 12:6, "For whom the Lord loveth He chasteneth," I became more and more angry at the man for saying such a terrible thing.

But as I fought with God in my solitude, He seemed to be saying to me, "Read on." So I opened my Bible and read verse 7: "If you endure chastening, God dealeth with you as sons; for what son is he whom the father chasteneth not?" Then verse 10 says that our earthly fathers "chastened us after their own pleasure; but He [God] for our profit." God seemed to be whispering to me that, if I was going to be a pastor's wife, I would have to understand some of these things. I would need compassion when I was called upon to stand beside a crib in a hospital or by a little casket. I could only be all He wanted me to be as a pastor's wife as I experienced this chastening. Then verse 11 explained it all: "Now no chastening for the present seemeth to be joyous, but grievous; nevertheless *afterward* it yieldeth the peaceable fruit of righteousness unto them which *are exercised* thereby" (italics mine).

I felt my stubborn will go limp within me—at the same moment my tense, rebelling body crumpled on the bed beside which I was kneeling. I had surrendered to His will, whatever that might be. And at that point God changed me. My battle was over. My rebellion ceased. From that point on there was no struggle, although there were two more months of watching Judy slowly burn out. I was filled with grief on the day she died—but there was no rebellion. He had prepared me for those difficult days—but even more so for all the years ahead. God had changed me by *exercising* me with chastening. But it was all for my profit—so that I could be a "partaker of His holiness." And that "peaceable fruit of righteousness" did come at last.

* * *

In 1973 I was quite shaken when a pastor's wife accused me publicly of leaving out a theologically important point in a message. Checking the tape of the message later, and finding that I really *had* said it, didn't ease the embarrassment. But God had the answer for me. The next morning as I read Psalm 19 one word stood out in the 14th verse—*Thy*. "Let the words of my mouth, and the meditation of my heart, be acceptable in Thy sight, O Lord, my strength, and my Redeemer."

In the margin of the Bible I wrote, "In *Thy* sight, not in people's sight." And then I prayed, asking the Lord to remove all the negative thoughts I had had the night before. I asked Him to forgive me and "make EVERY thought and ALL my words acceptable to YOU, LORD!" Immediately I sensed His affirmation, His OK on that message. The desire to defend my innocence melted. God had changed me!

* * *

It was pouring rain as I started for an out-of-state retreat in April 1973. Three miles from home a truck, a compact car, and Evelyn stopped for a red light, but the car behind me didn't. Crunch. And all four vehicles accordioned into one. I recovered from the jolt to my back but evidently not from the jolt to my nervous system, for as I drove during the following week I kept my eyes as much on the rearview mirror as I did on the road ahead of me! And the next weekend I was to drive to a northern Minnesota retreat. I couldn't. I felt nothing but apprehension and fear at the possibility of being hit from behind. And the theme for the retreat was to be J-O-Y! But just before I was to drive to the retreat, God gave the answer as I was reading in the Psalms. A smile spread over my face as I read: "But let all those who put their trust in Thee rejoice; let them ever shout for *joy*, because Thou defendest them; let them also that love Thy name be joyful in Thee" (Ps. 5:11). Immediately I saw my problem—failing to trust Him! At that moment He exchanged my fear for His—yes, literally—His joy. The apprehension disappeared, and I drove, a changed woman, to that J-O-Y retreat, really experiencing what I was to preach.

My spiritual barometer for years has been 1 John 1:4: "These things [are written] that your joy may be full." I can always measure the amount of time I'm spending in the Scriptures by how much joy (not superficial happiness, but deep down abiding joy) I have. When I find a lack of joy in my life, the first thing I check is how much time I'm spending in God's Word!

\* \* \*

I'll never forget speaking at a convention where our schedule included breakfast, morning coffee and rolls, lunch, afternoon coffee and rolls, dinner, evening snack with sweet rolls! I had a badly sprained ankle at the time and was forced to go to my room to elevate it several times during each day. My car driver and I took that time to read the Bible together, practicing the "until He speaks" process.

One afternoon Luke 4:4 took on a completely new meaning: "Man [or woman] shall not live by bread alone, but by every word of God." I actually found myself thanking God for my sprained ankle so I could exchange some of the sweet rolls for the Bread of Life. I wrote in the margin of my Bible: "Plenty of time for coffee and rolls, but not enough time for God's Word alone."

\* \* \*

I'm convinced that God has a sense of humor. In 1965 our church experienced a great moving of God, and every Sunday for four months I had the privilege of praying with at least one, and frequently with many, who came to find Christ as their Saviour. It was exciting. But suddenly I had pain in my middle and was hospitalized for tests. A "No Water" sign was hung on the end of my bed, and by early morning the real or imagined desperation for water had set in. In my discomfort I prayed, "God, please give me something to read in my Bible that's just for me, right now." And Psalm 63 popped into my head, although I didn't have the foggiest idea what it was about. I grabbed my Bible, turned to the Psalm and read: "Oh, God, Thou art my God; early will I seek Thee." So far so good. It was 5:30 in the morning.

As I read on in that first verse, I cried, "Lord, is this a joke? " "My soul thirsteth for Thee, my flesh longeth for Thee in a dry and thirsty land, where no water is."

Then I saw in verse 2 what God was really trying to say to me: "To see Thy power and Thy glory, so as I have seen Thee in the sanctuary." God showed me that my real problem was not the lack of water, but in not wanting to miss seeing Him move in the sanctuary. My real rebellion was at being put on a shelf in the midst of the action!

* * *

When the tests were over I remembered smiling bravely as my doctor told me that I would have to have surgery right away. I nodded and smiled until he disappeared out the door, and then burst into tears. Reaching for my Bible, I prayed, "Oh, God, give me something for *right now!*" Immediately Romans 12:1 flashed into my mind, and I turned to it, "I beseech you, therefore brethren, by the mercies of God, that ye present your bodies a living sacrifice, holy, acceptable unto God, which is your reasonable service."

Now I had His answer. I had given Him so completely my spirit—my mind, my emotions, my energy. All that I was, I thought. But *I had never given Him my body!*

Surgery and days of recuperation came and went, but I was still kicking at being left on a shelf when so much was going on in "the sanctuary." Not until the next Sunday when I tuned into a pastor friend's radio program did I obey God's instruction to me. I was still kicking because *my* body was in a hospital bed instead of at church that morning. But a little poem he read, "Gaining Through Losing," struck a responsive chord, and I gave God my body—once and for all. (I knew the verb tense of "gave" was a once-for-all and not continuous action.)

Gradually my attitude toward my health changed. Illness didn't disappear completely (although its diminishing frequency has been rather amazing), but my *attitude* toward it changed. I relaxed. I felt somewhat like the pastor who called his banker saying *our* car is in the ditch. Through the years I have learned to say, "God, *our* body is sick."

God changed me from an overprotective guardian of my body to one who entrusts that body to Him. What a great way to live! No friction, no hassle. Whenever I don't feel well, I just say, "Lord, if You want me to be well enough to do the job for

You that's coming up, thank You. But if not, just teach me what You have for me to learn while I'm on a shelf." This obedience to His specific instruction has done more than anything else in my life to take the pressure off and change my whole outlook on life.

\* \* \*

One of the favorite things we do during our vacation in Michigan around August 12 is to lie on the beach at midnight and watch the fantastic display of shooting stars. The summer our Kurt was seven I read an article in the *Reader's Digest* about a father who got his seven-year-old boy up in the middle of the night to see the shooting stars because, he reasoned, there were some things more important than sleep. So, when the exhibition was at its peak, we decided it was time for Kurt to join the rest of the family on the beach. The excitement and the "oh's" and "ah's" mounted with each display of God's celestial fireworks.

But the real excitement came the next morning when, as a family, we read at the breakfast table Psalm 33, and especially the fifth to ninth verses: "The earth is full of the goodness of the Lord. By the word of the Lord were the heavens made; and all the host of them by the breath of His mouth. . . . Let all the inhabitants of the world stand in awe of Him, for He spake, and it was done." I found myself not only excited over an astronomical wonder, but changed into a mother awed at God's timing and selection of our daily reading—overawed that He wanted to tell us that He only had to speak and all this was done!

\* \* \*

The beach at Lake Michigan is also my favorite place to read God's Word and let Him speak to me. Every day while we are on vacation I rise early and, weather permitting, take my Bible down to the edge of the lake and read until He speaks. One morning I read such a great psalm about our God that I found myself skipping down the beach instead of doing my usual hiking. God had changed an ordinary, run-of-the-mill vacation day into one of exhilaration and exploding joy, joy that could not be contained in ordinary steps. The thrill that sent my body soaring like the eagle's burst out in impromptu songs of praise as I adored Him for who He is and praised Him for what He is. Changed by a psalm? Yes, changed!

Thirty-six years of underlining answers for actual situations have proven to me that the Bible truly is a *living* Book. "For the Word of God is living and active," Hebrews 4:12 (NASB) tells us. Yes, it is alive. It has answers in the midst of our knowledge explosion today—or tomorrow—on this planet and in outer space. And precept upon precept as I let it renew my mind and my attitudes, I am changed. Changed into what is His perfect will for me to be.

### Treasure

I packed those three Bibles in my tote bag to show at that retreat where I was to speak on "God's Living Word." As I headed for the plane in Minneapolis, the security guard started systematically to check my carry-on luggage. When he pulled out the first Bible he gave me a "that's-a-nice-lady" smile. The second one produced a puzzled expression on his face. But, at finding the third, he was sure I had hidden something valuable in those Bibles, and proceeded to search each one diligently. He even held one up by its binding and shook it vigorously.

That guard never discovered the treasure I had hidden in those three Bibles. The omniscient Lord Jesus Christ, "in whom are hid all the treasures of wisdom and knowledge" (Col. 2:3), had given it to me. Underlined and marked on those pages was all the direction I had needed for a "chaste and reverent" lifestyle since I was 18 years old. Line upon line, precept upon precept, God had taught me how to change.

When I have needed direction for my life, has He ever left me groping in the dark, trying to find my way? Oh, no! He has given me His Word as a "lamp unto my feet, and a light unto my path" (Ps. 119:105). And, as I have obeyed His instructions, He has *changed me*, step by step, into the person He wants me to be.

# 3

# *Lord, Change Me for Others Too*

The 14 months marched silently along with God continuing His rebuking, refining, enlightening, changing. I was aware of each step, but still had not thought of it as anything more than a process for me.

But suddenly the months of searching Scripture "without a word" were over. The "Lord, change me" gestation period which started in June 1968, came to an end and the hidden theme was born. What had been a very private experience in my own life erupted, unplanned, at the 1969 Minnesota Baptist Women's Retreat at Big Trout Lake, Minnesota. Unannounced, it became a principle to be shared with others.

"Did the theme of this retreat change? " asked a committee member.

"To what do you think it changed? " I asked.

"I think it changed to 'Lord, Change Me.' "

"I think it did too. But I didn't change it. God did."

No, I hadn't changed the theme. I had diligently prepared my messages on the theme those 800 women had chosen for their retreat—but God had other ideas.

Just before I started to speak on the Wednesday night of that retreat, someone slipped a note to me: "Please come to our cabin. We have a problem." I tucked the note in my Bible, promising myself to see about the need after the service.

While I spoke that night, one illustration from a previous women's retreat was to trigger the change of theme. I told these Minnesota women that back in September 1966, right after I had found such exciting answers when I had read only the Bible, I decided to try the *wait* process on the 400 women attending a retreat in the foothills of Mount Rainier in Washington. Having no idea of what God was going to say to them, I sent those women out to read Colossians 3 by themselves. I had instructed them to read only *until* God spoke, and then to stop and pray about what He was saying to them.

In addition to speaking at that Mount Rainier retreat, I told them I had also served as a counselor. A steady stream of women came to me for advice—talking to me while I brushed my teeth, and even shouting over the shower curtain. I knew I didn't have professional answers for those women, so every time one came to me I listened to her problem and then asked the question: "And where did God stop you in your reading of Colossians 3 today?" I felt I was on safe ground asking that question.

And do you know what happened? *In every instance* the Lord stopped *each one of them* at the answer to her problem. I didn't have to offer a single solution, because the Lord did. In fact, on Saturday night the retreat committee said to me, "God is doing such a great thing, let's not structure the Sunday morning service. Let's just ask the women to share what God has been saying to them out of the Scripture."

That Sunday morning for one and one-half hours the women kept popping up like popcorn sharing what God had said. I was so overwhelmed that I finally asked them all to jot down on a piece of paper what God showed them when He stopped them in Colossians 3. I went home to Minnesota with a large manila envelope bulging with specific answers—not from me but from God.

I told the Minnesota women that as I was hurriedly throwing things into my suitcase to catch a plane for Minneapolis, a very angry and distraught woman burst into my room. I explained that I really didn't have time to talk with her, but she told me to keep packing while she talked. She trembled with anger as she ranted on about a woman she couldn't stand, a woman who was also attending the retreat. "Why," she exploded, "she actually talks and gossips about our pastor. And I won't go to prayer meeting if she's going to be there because I get so furious when she prays. Would you believe she actually prays against him right in front of him? "

As she raved on, I paused in my packing, turned to her and asked, "And where did God stop you in Colossians 3? "

"In verse 13."

"What does it say? "

"It says, 'Forebearing one another, and forgiving one another, if any man have a quarrel against any; even as Christ forgave you, so also do ye.' "

"Is that where He stopped you? " (Nod.) "How long have you been a Christian? "

"Three months."

"Did Christ forgive anything in you when you became a Christian? "

A look of shock crossed her face. Then she put her head on my shoulder and began to weep. "Oh, it's *my* fault, isn't it? I'm the one who needs to change, not her. I'm the one God needs to change." She had seen that she was to forgive others *as* He had forgiven her—forgiven her of all her past sins when she accepted Him as her Saviour three months before.

I went to the airport with a wet shoulder, but left behind a woman who had learned to forgive as Christ had forgiven her—because God had shown her what was wrong with herself, not with the other woman.

That's the story I told at the 1969 Minnesota retreat before going to the cabin whose members had sent me a note just before the meeting. Though it was a warm September night, when I entered the cabin, I was sure there were icicles hanging from the ceiling. I have never felt a colder atmosphere. All the women were sitting there in sullen silence with their chins slightly jutted and arms crossed.

I soon discovered that they were all from the same small town where their church had recently split. Half of them had stayed in the church and the other half had left. At home they weren't speaking to one another. But the unknowing camp registrar had put them all in the same cabin!

And there they sat—each one blaming the other. My first suggestion was that they read Colossians 3.

"No!" One lady was sitting cross-legged on her bed right

beside me, holding her Bible. I asked her several times to read Colossians 3:13 for us, but she stubbornly repeated, "No, I won't."

A couple of hours passed, but I was getting nowhere. They finally agreed on one point: the problem in their town was all the fault of one man—*he* did this, and *he* did that. And if *he* hadn't done that, *we* wouldn't have done that. "Yes," they all agreed, "it is all his fault because our church broke up."

"He sounds like a pretty horrible guy, and I guess it is probably all his fault—or at least most of it is. But," I said, "do you think one percent of the blame might be in this room? "

"No! Uh-uh! There's nothing wrong in *this* room."

But I kept pushing the point. "Could there *possibly* be just one percent? "

Then from the far corner a woman said hesitantly, in a barely audible voice, "I think there's one percent over here."

Then someone else said, "I think maybe there's, ah, ten percent here."

Finally the woman with the Bible, sitting cross-legged on her bed, looked at me and stammered, "I—I think I can read Colossians 3:13 now." And slowly she read: "Forgiving one another, if any man have a quarrel against any; even as Christ forgave you, so also do ye."

At a quarter to one in the morning, we finally ended the encounter with our arms around each other, weeping and praying. And those women prayed only one prayer, "Oh, Lord, don't change that guy back home. *Change me!*"

The next night at our campfire sharing time, the "Lord, Change Me" theme continued. Woman after woman kept saying, "I needed changing—not everybody else." One women's society president said, "Nine of my women had made reservations for this retreat, and I kept saying of each one, 'Isn't that wonderful; does *she* need it!' And then my phone started ringing, and one after another was saying that she couldn't make it. I would hang up the phone and think, 'Isn't it too bad; *she* needed it so badly.' Finally there were just four going from our church. But tonight I realize that it wasn't all the women who couldn't come who needed this retreat; *I* am the one who needed it."

Yes, I knew the theme of the retreat had changed. I had

watched it change. But I hadn't changed it—God had. Thus "Lord, Change Me" for groups was launched—to be used with thousands of people, always with the same results, all over the United States and Canada.

### Another Surprise

On the first Monday following that Minnesota retreat, God had another surprise for me in the unfolding of the "Lord, Change Me" theme.

Early in the morning our front doorbell rang and there stood a man my husband had counseled many, many times. He had been married, divorced, and remarried to the same woman. And his life was still a horrible mess. "Could I see the pastor?" he asked.

My mother-hen defense for Chris went up and I said, "It's terribly early and Chris is still asleep. Could you come a bit later?"

"I *have* to tell somebody. Could I tell *you?*"

Monday morning! But I said, "Wait until I turn off the washer and dryer." I returned, pulled my robe tighter around me as I sat down on the davenport and said, "OK. Tell me."

He said, "Do you know what? The most amazing thing happened to me."

And I halfheartedly countered, "Really? "

"Yup. A week ago I was driving my truck down Broadway, and I was blaming everybody for what was going on in my home—my kids, my wife, my employer. But suddenly the Lord said to me, '*You* are the one who needs to be changed, not all the rest of the people. *You* need to be changed.' As I drove I think I even closed my eyes once and prayed, 'Lord, change *me*; Lord, change *me*.' "

I sat there in amazement: *Lord, change me!*

It was all coming into focus. The "Lord, Change Me" concept had been given to him too. It was spreading. God was spreading it!

"I have had the most marvelous experience," he continued. "I went home, and there was that wife that I had married, divorced, and remarried. We were having such a rough time. And the next morning when I woke up there she was, the same wife. But I loved her with a love I didn't know was possible. I took her in my arms and said, 'Oh, honey, how I love you.' It was just great. I loved her, and I loved the kids.

"Now, I hadn't gotten along with my dad. We hadn't really spoken for many years. I got in the car and went out to see my old dad who had been an invalid for a long time. I went to his bedside, took his hand, and said, 'Dad, I just came here for one reason. I came here to tell you I love you.' And the tears started to trickle down his face as he took my hand and said, 'Sonny, I have waited since you were that high (measuring three feet from the floor with his hand) to hear you say that.'

"Then I went to church on Sunday morning, and there was my wife's lawyer who knew all the dirt about me. I thought I was ready to join the church that morning, but I knew that I had some unfinished business. Instead of going down front to say that I wanted to join the church, I turned around and swung over to my wife's lawyer. The two of us put our arms around each other, and stood there in the sanctuary and wept. The next person I saw was a businessman who had done me dirt—a Christian, a member of our church. I got to thinking, 'I haven't been so honest with him either.' And I walked up to that man, looked him right in the eye, and stuck out my hand. We shook hands.

"Mrs. Chris, I *had* to tell somebody, because all I've been praying is 'Lord, change me.' *And all of these things have happened in my whole relationship with people—just because I prayed 'Lord—change—me!'* "

This is the exciting part of the changing process! Relationships with people do change when we pray, "Lord, change *me*." And I now realized that God had not given this fabulous thought to me to be kept selfishly to myself—only to see myself change. But He had intended all along that it was to be shared with others whom He also wanted to change.

### *"We Want a 'Lord, Change Me' Retreat Too"*
The next morning I went to our weekly prayer meeting with my heart absolutely overflowing. I decided it was time to share "Lord, Change Me" with my dear women. I told them what God had been doing in my life for 14 months, and then how the process had miraculously erupted, unplanned, at the Minnesota retreat the preceding week. Then I shared the startling

story that had been told to me the morning before. When I finished, one wide-eyed member of our prayer group said, "I think we need a 'Lord, Change Me' retreat too."

So we planned what was to be my first "Lord, Change Me" retreat. For the next month our president and I struggled, trying to put together an agenda, but to no avail. The day before the scheduled retreat, we communicated five times trying to figure out what to do all day long, but the Lord kept telling both of us, "Just trust Me. Just trust Me."

The next morning I was a little apprehensive as the church parking lot started to fill with cars. The officers of our women's organizations were gathering to form a caravan to a cottage in Wisconsin for our first "Lord, Change Me" retreat. They were trusting me, as their pastor's wife, just as I was trusting God, and the responsibility was a bit overwhelming. Armed with nothing but our Bibles, we wended our way to our all-day retreat. As we traveled I kept praying silently, "Oh, Lord, just You—just You."

The great part of trusting the Lord is that He never lets you down. I spent the first 20 minutes of that retreat sharing my excitement over what God had done in my own life for 14 months: the Minnesota retreat, the Monday morning visitor, and then the prayer group's request for this retreat. That was all.

From then on that day we let God be in command. I assigned a portion of Scripture, instructing them to "take this portion of Scripture, find any spot you want in this cabin, and read until God speaks to you. Read *only until* He speaks. Don't read any more. If you read on after He speaks, you'll get confused, not knowing what you should pray about. Then, ask God *why* He stopped you at that point, *what needs changing* in your life, and then *what He wants you to do* about it. Be sure to listen as He gently brings answers to your mind. God's speaking to you in the Scripture may be only a little nudge, or you may think some words are popping out in bold print."

Then we prayed a simple prayer. "Lord, remove all our preconceived ideas about this portion of Scripture. We want You to tell us *afresh* what You want changed in us *today*." I asked for complete silence, explaining that it is impossible for God to speak to us if we are chattering, discussing, and talking to each other. So, a slightly bewildered but willing group sought their private spots with the Lord and began reading.

I sat in the living room wondering what would happen. For almost two years these women had been experimenting with what happened when they prayed, learning to pray first and plan afterward, and then to bear one another's burdens in prayer. Did God have another step for *them* too?

At 11 o'clock we came back together and formed a large circle of prayer on our knees in the living room. Then the miracle began. We had agreed not to talk to each other, but we prayed aloud to God about where He had stopped us in the Scripture portion. I can't find any word to describe what happened next but "revival." Those women wept and prayed on their faces before God, confessing what He had told them was wrong in their lives.

"Lord, I'm sorry. Forgive me. Lord, change me," they all prayed. He had put His finger on specific needs in their lives—all of them out of the same portion of Scripture. Tears were abundant, including those in my own eyes as I listened in amazement at the way God had been faithful to His "just trust Me" promise the day before.

Through the years I have never ceased to be astounded at this process as I've led thousands to read *until* God speaks. He who knows the thoughts and intents of every heart digs deeply into the hidden recesses to search out sins and shortcomings we are often not aware of. And He does it in response to our sincere prayer to be shown what *He* wants to change in us.

During lunch we continued our silence so that we could keep listening to God. As the leader, I thanked our hostess in advance for the noodle casserole, and once again felt a slight anxiety in my heart about the unaccustomed silence. But I was put at ease at our very next session when one woman reported, "It was embarrassing when I first sat down. I sat there eating my hot dish, and I didn't know what to do. And then all at once God started to talk to me about the thing in my life He had convicted me of that morning. He penetrated deeper and deeper. I wasn't aware that there was anyone else at the table because I was alone with God, and He was speaking to me." Most of the women agreed that this was their experience during that time of silence.

In the afternoon of our first "Lord, Change Me" retreat, we concentrated on what God wanted to change in our circles and women's church meetings. Assigning another portion of Scripture, we prayed asking God to show us specific things He knew needed changing in our organizations. After listening to God speak to us from Romans 12, we prayed together as officers of our individual circles about what God had shown us. Then, just before our day apart was over, we gathered and asked our secretary to take notes as we shared all the things God had said needed to be changed in our circles. Those ladies bombarded our secretary with the ideas God gave them:

Circle officers should meet before each meeting to ask God's guidance.

Pray about purpose of our circles.

Do what *God* says to do.

Make inactive members feel wanted.

We must meet the needs of *all* ages in our circles.

Have a "Lord, change me" night in our circles next month.

Show compassion and love by doing kind deeds, invite, offer to pick up.

Postcards to tell them they were missed.

Help and teach, don't push.

Everyone has a talent; use it to make all feel needed.

I was so astounded at God's advice that when I got home I reread that portion wondering how He ever found some of those things in that passage to tell those ladies.

But the climax came when our shocked president looked in amazement at the women and then at a list she had dug out of her notebook. "Ladies, I have here a whole list of things I thought needed changing in your circles, and gripes from people who have wanted to see this or that changed; but I don't have to read it to you. God has told one or the other of you every single problem I have listed here and what should be done about it. I don't have to say a word! "

Yes, God had another exciting experiment for the "what-happens-when-women-pray" ladies of our church. And He had indelibly written on my heart how He can speak to specific personal and organizational needs without the president or pastor's wife saying a word. "If any of you lack wisdom, let him ask of God, who giveth to all men liberally" (James 1:5).

### A Reality: 2 Timothy 3:16

"All Scripture is given by inspiration of God, and is profitable for doctrine, for reproof, for correction, for instruction in righteousness" (2 Tim. 3:16).

Sometimes God stops us on something He wants changed in our beliefs only—in our doctrine. But most of the time He deals with the three other facets in this verse—what He wants changed *in our actions.*

God frequently uses this method of reading until He speaks for *reproof*—the process of exposing and convicting of things He is dissatisfied with in our lives. One woman kept coming to me at a retreat asking me what to do about her husband who was not assuming his role as spiritual head of the house. I used every scriptural approach I knew, but nothing seemed to provide the answer.

When I arrived home, I received a letter from her. She wrote, "Dear Evelyn: Please forgive me. I wasn't honest with you, so you couldn't possibly have known my real problem and given me the right answer. But when I was reading our assigned chapter, God stopped me on my real problem—a little three-letter word 'own.' I am the secretary for a pastor. He's my ideal. I get all of my spiritual insights and help from him. At the retreat God showed me while reading His Word that I should 'be in subjection to my *own* husband.' "

About six months later I was visiting in her church, and after the service I heard, "Here's Larry, Evelyn. Here's Larry, Evelyn."

"Who's Larry?" I wondered.

I looked up to see this woman with her *own* husband in tow, happily beaming at me. Then I remembered—he was her *own* husband, the now obvious spiritual head of her house.

A young convert had been invited to one of my retreats to be our Sunday School speaker. It was obvious from the beginning that she had come to show us that she had arrived spiritually and we had not. But at our Saturday night testimony meeting around the campfire, she stood up and said, "I would give anything if any one of you would take that Sunday School hour tomorrow morning. I came here feeling so superior to you. But I took my Bible this afternoon as I was told and read God's Word. And," she said as her voice choked, "He stopped me on the word *humbleness,* and I know now that I came here because of pride. God had to show me that He wanted me to be humble and have humility. All I have is pride in my own self-attainment. Please will one of you take that Sunday School hour tomorrow morning?"

I was really shocked at a not-so-typical example of God stopping at specific problems at one retreat. During our sharing time there was absolute silence as four pastors' wives stood up at different times and said, "My husband left the pastorate (each said some time within the last 12 months), and God has told me out of His Word today that it was all *my* fault." How God reaches down and puts His finger of reproof right on the word or words we need.

It is interesting to watch God use *restoration to an upright state* from 2 Timothy 3:16 at our retreats. One Friday night at a weekend retreat the wife of a seminary student said her roommate was so angry that she was just about kicking the furniture because her seminary-student husband had received a call to a place to which she did not want to go. She asked me if I would see if I could calm her down and counsel with her.

"Let's wait until we read in God's Word tomorrow, and see what *He* says to her," I suggested, and she agreed.

At sharing time the next day so many in the group were stating that God stopped them in Galatians 5 concerning the leading of the Holy Spirit, that I finally said, "Everybody whom the Lord stopped on the Holy Spirit's leading and their following, please stand up." To my surprise, the angry wife of the night before stood up (with nearly half the whole audience—another surprise). As she was telling us all about it, I leaned over the pulpit and asked, "Does that mean to so-and-so city too?"

"Yes, it does," she beamed back at me.

I didn't have to say a word. God had put His finger on her problem, and she had said in her heart she was willing to be changed into a willing follower of the Holy Spirit's leading.

A thank-you letter after a retreat said it so well, and only God could have known the need in her heart.

"Dear Evelyn: I'm so thankful for the Key '73 retreat. I learned what it means to have real joy! You see, I was raised in a Christian home, and I knew everything a Christian should do

and be. I had it all in my head. But I found Him in my heart.
God changed me that day, and I am so thankful. What
impressed me was when you sent us out, alone, and without
speaking, to read until He spoke to us."

Another note recorded the place God stopped one woman:
"Galatians 6:2. 'Bear ye one another's burdens'—and the name
of a specific person came to me immediately. Praise the Lord
for His *living* Word."

*Instruction in righteousness* from God was evident in this note:

"Dear Evelyn: There wasn't time to share publicly, but my
husband and I have considered adopting a child and adding to
our family since we have the room and the money. . . . I
wasn't sure if it was God's will or just our do-gooder thoughts.
I now know that God thinks I can and should do this. James
1:27, 'The Christian who is pure and without fault, from God
the Father's point of view, is the one who takes care of orphans
and widows, and who remains true to the Lord' " (LB).

### 100 Percent of Us?

Every fall our church had a kick-off for our Christian Education
administrators and paid staff who were to decide on the
direction of their ministries for the coming year. In September
1970, I was asked to conduct a "Lord, Change Me" retreat for
them. All the C.E. board members, departmental superintendents, the general Sunday School superintendents, staff, and
pastors were there. I briefly explained the process of reading
until God spoke to them and assigned Galatians 5:1—6:10, then
sent them off alone to read.

When we came back together we knelt to share in prayer
what God had told each of us. Something astounding began to
emerge: person after person prayed about God stopping him or
her on some thought concerning the importance of the Holy
Spirit's leading in the Christian Education activities in our
church. It soon became evident that God had stopped every
single administrator and staff person on the same principle—
let the Holy Spirit lead. My pastor husband and our assistant
pastor, Gary Smalley, were kneeling side by side. When the
pattern took shape and included where God had stopped them
also, they both put their heads in their hands and wept!

Even more amazing than the fact that God speaks to all

individually is that He speaks to many collectively about the same thing. Every time I assign this portion in Galatians, never fewer than 50 percent and up to 100 percent of the participants are stopped on the passage dealing with the Holy Spirit's leading. And this always is absolutely without any instruction as to what they are to look for or expect from God. Whenever this happens, I feel a sense of holy awe sweeping over me. God's *instruction in righteousness*—showing us the direction He wants us to go!

### Write God a Letter

Frequently at our retreats, after God has spoken to us through His Word, we write Him a letter. We tell Him what we will change in our lives because of what He has pointed out to us. After having each one seal his letter to God in a self-addressed envelope, I collect the letters and keep them for about a month. Then I put them in the mail so the writer can check up on herself to see if she really *did change*—or if she forgot and went on in the same old condition.

I always "read until" with the others at retreats, and here is one letter I wrote:

"Dear God: You told me that I am hung up on not really accepting 'that person' back into the fellowship of the beloved, and that I am to restore that person who was overtaken in a fault—lest I, Evelyn, should be tempted like that—even though I don't think that is one of my weaknesses. I will restore that person in every possible way. Lord, open doors, make me comfortable around that person again."

The very next day God honored my prayer, and arranged a surprise breakfast meeting. I keep that letter as a constant reminder of how *I* had to change in my attitude toward one who had slipped—of how God had told *me* to change and I had obeyed.

The changes come, however, not when God speaks but when we *obey* what He has told us. We are changed only when we *apply* to our lives what He has said.

A pastor and his wife were chatting with me at a conference last summer. She said, "After our 'Lord, Change Me' retreat, Evelyn, I went home and practiced letting the Lord change me according to what He had told me at your retreat. And it really worked. Now there is someone else I need to pray 'Lord, change me' about."

"There surely is," agreed her smiling husband.

### All-Church Prayer Week

Conduct an all-church prayer week with God speaking instead of people? To do this took courage, but the results of our "Lord, Change Me" prayer week in January 1970, were fantastic. We observed a strict rule of no preparation, no leading. The week before, we trained all those who would be leading the groups. If they had not had an experience of God speaking personally to them from His Word, they were to find others to lead for them. We formed no new prayer meetings, but used only the existing classes, organizations, and boards of our church as groups.

Spreading this "Lord, change me" process to the whole church resulted in great things. One Sunday School superintendent said, "Every member of the C.E. board had been in a different preparation week prayer meeting, so our chairman had each share how God had already spoken and changed his life. Each one gave a specific request from his area; then we all prayed about it. Nobody was pulling for his pet project; all prayed only for what God wanted done through the C.E. board. There's a different feeling in the C.E. board now."

A woman who had been at the center of our church's prayer life for several years said, "As I walked into the church and saw the 'Silence, Please' signs, sensed the reverence and hush, and then saw the sanctuary set up for prayer with circles of chairs even on the platform, I felt as if something new was coming to our church." And it did. We used the "Lord, Change Me" Bible-reading process and our "Six S" prayer method—subject by subject, short prayers, simple prayers, specific prayer requests, silent periods, small groups. And we had almost 100 percent participation in audible prayer, and at least five times as many people attended as had ever come before.

Our children's worker said, "As a church staff, our feet really never touched ground as we led several training sessions a day during preparation week and watched hearts, attitudes, and lives change as God spoke and these leaders were being prepared by Him to lead prayer week meetings in their respective groups. By the time we got to our weekly church staff prayer meeting during prayer week, there was such a sense of God's presence that tears replaced audible praying.''

The results of my 14 agonizing months of letting God change me privately can well be summed up in the words of our deacon chairman when he reported about that first all-church "Lord, Change Me" prayer week: "The tremendous problems we faced ceased to be problems because of prayer week. We found a unification of spirit that never had been in our board before. Our meeting ended with all of us standing in a circle, holding hands, and singing 'Blest Be the Tie That Binds'—with tears flowing. God moved in that meeting. It was 'preparation week,' with God preparing hearts, that made the difference. I think every church meeting should be run like this.''

# 4

# *Changed—When I Study God's Word*

"Should I let God change me through devotional reading or Bible study? " That is not a fair question, because *both* are essential for a well-rounded, transformed life. Devotional reading is never a substitute for deep, systematic Bible study—but it is a complement to it. And the Lord does change me *when I study His Word.*

Paul gave Timothy excellent advice when he said, "Study to show thyself approved unto God" (2 Tim. 2:15). He also counseled him to: "Remember that from early childhood you have been familiar with the sacred writings which have power to make you wise and lead you to salvation through faith in Christ Jesus. Every inspired Scripture has its use for *teaching* the truth and *refuting* error, or for *reformation of manners and discipline in right living,* so that the man who belongs to God may be efficient and equipped for good work of every kind" (2 Tim. 3:15-16, NEB, italics mine).

I'm so grateful that God did not ask me to give up teaching when I prayed, in June 1968, that He would make me the kind of wife He wanted me to be, for this would have deprived me of great joy. Digging into the Bible always produces a joy and an excitement that *changes* me into a different person. My spiritual barometer, 1 John 1:4, applies here, "These things [are written] . . . that your joy [might] be full." Even if I'm willing to be changed by what God is teaching me, the end result is always joy. Deep Bible study also produces spiritual maturity.

One of the guidelines we gave to each participant of Key '73 neighborhood Bible studies was "The purpose of this study is for us to find our lifestyle out of God's Word. This will include accurately observing what the Bible really says and applying it to our daily lives."

This chapter is not intended to be an in-depth guide on how to study the Bible. Its purpose is to show how life-changing a thorough study of God's Word can be.

### Prestudy Prayer

As I study God's Word, approximately one third of the study time is spent in prayer. This prayertime is divided into four categories: before the study, while observing what the Scripture really says, while interpreting what it means, and when applying it to myself or those whom I'm teaching.

Just approaching my study time in prayer *changes me*. First, I pray about my personal preparation. Praying for *cleansing* before starting to study establishes a clear communication with God. Then expressing in prayer the hunger and thirst after righteousness that I feel in my heart assures me of "God's filling" (Matt. 5:6).

Next, it is important for me to pray, "*Lord, remove all preconceived ideas* about this portion of Scripture I am about to study." It is always possible that something I have heard or studied previously has not been correct. Praying for God to remove all preconceived ideas (for the study time) will enable Him to reveal fresh insights to me. I let my spirit soar as I thrill at new thoughts from His Word!

I also pray that God will *take control* of the study time so that all observations, interpretations, and applications will be *truth*. I must acknowledge my dependence upon Him if I want accurate, powerful, life-changing lessons for myself or those I will be teaching.

Then, *I ask God to be my Teacher*, inviting the Holy Spirit to be operative in me as I study. In John 14:26 Jesus said that the Holy Spirit would "teach you all things." Also, Paul prayed for the Christians at Ephesus that God would give them "the Spirit of wisdom and revelation in the knowledge of Him, the eyes of [their] understanding being enlightened" (Eph. 1:17-18). The Bible is more than a textbook of poetry, history, psychology, law, and letters; it is a living, personal message from God's heart to our hearts! And studying it thoroughly, deeply, and systematically produces *changed* people.

A good Bible study always includes three elements: *observation, interpretation*, and *application*. And as I diligently practice each part, God *changes me*.

### 1. Observation
*a. For teachers.* A great change comes over me as a teacher when I admit my fallibility. Having prayed for God to remove all my preconceived ideas, I am thereby made teachable. Then as I read the Scripture portion to be studied, I *observe* carefully what it really says, admitting the possibility of incorrect or incomplete preconceived ideas.

Since my experience in Hebrews 12 when Judy died, I am convinced that God not only allows suffering but that He sends chastenings our way. It is He who is doing the chastening. But because this is an unpopular truth with many Christians, I found myself at one time watering down this concept to "God allowing, not sending" in order to accommodate them. But while studying for my Bible class in 1 Peter, I was greatly relieved to observe the phrase: "Them that suffer according to the will of God" (4:19). This observation changed me into a much more confident teacher—having found confirmation of what God had taught me years before. So many of our ideas are built on what we think the Bible says, rather than on what it actually does say.

As I studied for that Bible class God gave me some additional help in 1 Peter 3:1 for my 14 months of living "without a word" before my daughter in 1968. For the first time I noticed how that verse started: "In the same way" (NASB) which referred me back to something that came before. (This is like "therefore," showing what a statement is "there for.") As I checked the preceding verses, I found that wives are to act in the same manner as Jesus did in His suffering. He, who did no sin and in whose mouth was found no guile, didn't retaliate when He was reviled or threaten when He suffered. No, Jesus just committed Himself to God who judges righteously (2:22-23). I had additional changing to do—to become more Christlike.

Then as I passed this observation on to my class members, two of them, whose husbands were being unfaithful, also saw God's answer for their own needs. When they reacted in a way that pleased God, they too could commit themselves and their problems to Him, the faithful and righteous Judge.

Pronouns are particularly tricky little words; they can tell us a whole story, for example: on Resurrection morning the angel, talking to the women at the tomb, said, "Remember how He [Jesus] spoke unto you when He was yet in Galilee, saying, 'The Son of man must be delivered into the hands of sinful men, and be crucified, and the third day rise again' " (Luke 24:6-7). That "you" tells us a whole story: (1) The women traveled with Jesus and ministered to Him in Galilee. (2) Jesus gave this teaching to the women (the angel doesn't mention the men to whom this most likely was given also). (3) Jesus taught the women directly while they traveled with Him to Jerusalem. (4) Jesus entrusted the women with some very important teaching. This little pronoun refuted several of my preconceived ideas about the place of women in the ministry of Jesus and changed my thinking considerably.

Plural pronouns can be enlightening. By observing the "us" in 2 Corinthians 2:11 I saw that Paul was talking about *himself* and the Christians at Corinth. "Lest Satan should get an advantage of us." I then realized that if Paul wasn't safe from the toehold of Satan in his relationship with the Corinthian Christians, I had better be a little more alert. Changed by a plural pronoun!

A teacher can get an accurate understanding of a situation by observing verbs. In Matthew 14:22 we read that "Jesus constrained His disciples to get into a ship and to go before Him unto the other side." Since Jesus deliberately sent His disciples into the storm, I reassessed my attitude toward the storms in my life. Does Jesus deliberately send me into storms so that I too can see the miracle of His walking on the water and the storm stilled?

Then again the little verb "drove" encompassed a whole theological truth. In Mark 1:12 we observe that "the Spirit immediately drove Him [Jesus] out into the wilderness" (RSV). And He was there 40 days, tested by Satan. Again my preconceived idea had to be changed by one little verb. The

Spirit didn't *hinder* Him from going, didn't *allow* Jesus to go; no, the Spirit *drove* Jesus to His temptation by Satan.

Another important rule for teachers to follow is: "Read the Scripture portion *before* reading any lesson helps. Carefully observing all God's Word has to say in the study enables teachers to evaluate lesson helps and commentaries in the light of the Scriptures."

Unless we actually observe first what the Scripture says, we are apt to accept gullibly all the teachings in other books—right or wrong, and be changed by them—right or wrong.

Accurately observing everything God says in an assigned portion of Scripture is the opposite of teaching by the piecemeal method, where a teacher skips through the Bible, taking a verse or part of a verse to prove a point. (This may be an acceptable method if each section has been carefully studied in context and if the premise to be proved is scripturally accurate.) Isolated phrases and sentences put together at a teacher's whim can be made to prove almost anything. Many false ideas, supposedly "Bible based," begin this way.

My neighbor was evaluating some Bible class study samples I had given her, and said to me, "We chose this one because it takes a portion of Scripture and teaches what it says. We don't like to jump around. If I took a bunch of letters from someone, cut out sentences here and there, and put them together the way I wanted, I could prove anything I cared to! "

While teaching this process to some senior highers, I evidently got a little carried away with my proving, for after Sunday School I received a phone call from an upset father. "What do you mean teaching our son that all the demons will be saved? " I hurried to explain that I was teaching the young people how *not* to prove something about demons. I had put three "pieces" of Scripture together—all true in their proper setting—and thereby "proved" that all demons will be saved.

1. "I know Thee who Thou art, the Holy One of God" (unclean spirit's words in Mark 1:24).

2. "The demons also believe, and tremble" (James 2:19).

3. "Believe on the Lord Jesus, and thou shalt be saved" (Acts 16:31).

Even the Scriptures themselves can be used to change us in a way that is contrary to God's truth and His will if we don't observe accurately what they say, all they say, and in context. We can be changed—incorrectly.

*b. For those I teach.* Lorna and Signe, my two prayer partners at that time, and I prayed for two years that I might teach a neighborhood Bible study class. But I had some changing to do before God would allow me to teach. I had to learn that the pupils too had the right to observe what God was saying to them and not to rely solely on what their teacher said. If I had used my lecture method, I would have given them what God had taught me through His Word instead of allowing them to discover for themselves what the Bible teaches. When I learned at last that the purpose of a Bible study is to let God be the Teacher, He gave me a wonderful class to teach every week.

When we came together in Ruth's living room, we first of all prayed that God would remove our preconceived ideas so that He could speak to our specific needs.

Then we read individually—silently—the Scripture we were to study that day, so that the teacher or whoever else might be reading aloud would not emphasize the words *they* wanted stressed. I offered no hints as to what God might say to them.

And this wasn't just a casual reading. It was the process described in James 1:25 of "looking into the perfect law of liberty" which meant seeking, desiring, longing for, as when Mary "looked" into the empty tomb that first Easter morning.

We had women from all denominations and walks of life in that Bible study, but none of them was a skilled Bible student. When they finished reading after our second lesson I asked, "Did God say anything to you that you didn't know before? " And 100 percent of them said Yes with gusto.

Later, after the reading, I introduced the teaching with, "What did God tell you?" They exploded with excitement. One lady tried to count on her fingers all the things God had said, but she didn't have enough fingers. I almost lost control of the group as they all talked at once. *They* had been taught by God!

Early in the study I learned how to make those who had never studied the Bible before feel that they were a part of the discussion. I would ask them the "observation" question and, just from reading carefully, they would be able to answer intelligently on what the Scripture had really said.

We had one very quiet member who sat through our first few lessons too shy to say a word. But all at once God spoke to her through the simple three-letter word *saw*. The fact that Jesus *saw* people burst upon her—how *He saw* Peter and Andrew and James and John. Then she commented that she was at the Bible study because so-and-so *saw* her and asked her to attend, but moved away before the study started. But another person *saw* her and picked her up and brought her here to study the Bible. After almost twenty minutes she stopped abruptly and apologized for monopolizing so much time. She had gained insight into Scripture—just by observing a little verb!

A teacher is humbled when God speaks dramatically to the class before she even gives her introductory remarks. That happened to me as I asked my usual, "Did God say anything to you?" question, and one member said, "Yes, He did."

"What did He say?"

"He said that I didn't know the Scriptures. Well, that's why I'm here—because my church doesn't teach the Bible and I want to learn the Scriptures. But God also said, 'You don't know the power of God either!' " (cf. Mark 12:24)

"Would you like to know the power of God?"

"Yes, I would."

"Right now?" (After all, we hadn't even *started* the lesson yet, and it certainly wasn't time for application.)

"Yes, right now." And before I even started to teach she bowed her head and accepted Jesus as her Saviour. *Changed*— just by observing the Word. Yes, God had some *changing* to do in me with this method of Bible study as well as in the pupils I was teaching.

Another important fact to *observe* while studying God's Word is "to whom a portion of Scripture is written." It makes a lot of difference who needs to be changed and also who is eligible to apply the Scripture to his life. At a Bible study in St. Paul, a woman observed "the eyes of your understanding being enlightened" from Ephesians 1:18.

"My family is not getting along well. How can the eyes of my understanding be enlightened so I will know how to run it better?"

"To whom did we learn this book was written?"

"To the faithful believers at Ephesus" (Eph. 1:1).

"Are you a saint—one who knows Jesus as personal Saviour? Are you *in* Christ Jesus?"

"No."

"Then you are not eligible for what Paul was praying for." And at that she decided to accept Christ—right there!

A well-known Christian author and speaker said to me, as we were discussing the way God speaks so specifically out of His Word, "Do you mean to tell me that somebody can find Christ just by reading the Bible?"

"Yes, sir, it really works."

## 2. Interpretation

If I'm going to understand and interpret the Bible accurately, I must spend time studying its meaning in addition to observing what the text says. I must rely on Bible scholars for word meanings from original manuscripts and for information on how the cultural setting influenced what was written.

Also, God has spoken to Christians down through the ages, and my failure to study what He has revealed to them makes me poor indeed. I am immeasurably richer when I learn from them, and am inspired by the insights they have gleaned. The early church learned these things immediately, for we find in Acts 2:42 that the new Christians "continued stedfastly in the *apostles' doctrine* and fellowship, and in breaking of bread, and in prayers."

And years later Paul admonished young Timothy to "give attendance to reading, to exhortation, to doctrine" (1 Tim. 4:13). In the interpretation we study in depth the meaning of a passage. Minimum study aids include a good commentary, a Bible dictionary, a Bible atlas, and a scholarly dictionary for word study.

God changes me into a *disciplined* person when I obey the command of 2 Timothy 2:15: "Study to show thyself approved unto God, a workman that needeth not to be ashamed, rightly dividing the Word of truth." To study takes discipline. Research is hard work, and time-consuming. It demands a reassessment of priorities—the giving up of some shopping trips, coffee parties, entertainment and recreation—some "good" but not "best" things.

Prayer at this point is essential. In order to be changed by my study the way God wants me to change, I pray, asking God to guard my mind as I read. Just because something is in print doesn't make it true. Then I pray for God to help me be selective. "Lord, lead me to just the books You want me to study." Indiscriminate reading of every book on a subject may not be good stewardship of my time, so I ask Him to show me what will be relevant to me and to those I will be teaching. Then I pray for His wisdom in interpreting and understanding the correct meaning. My greatest insight frequently comes not from reading but from praying.

But there must be a *proper balance* between inspiration and perspiration. I used to bring home all the reference books from my pastor husband's library for the study of next Sunday's lesson, stack them on the dining room table (the pile usually was at least two feet high), and systematically wade through them all that week. Then, after up to 25 hours of study, by Saturday I was ready to put the gleaned wisdom into outline form, dash it off to the church secretary to be mimeographed for the class members, and then go home to pray, "Dear God, please bless my notes."

I asked God to change that procedure, and He did. He taught me there was a proper balance between what other people had to say and what He had to say. A seminary senior, in tears, confided to me, "I've dissected the Scriptures so long that they don't say anything to me anymore." My college botany professor gave us some profound advice: "Remember, after you do enough dissecting, you no longer have a flower." This certainly can be applied to us sometimes.

But there is also the danger of all observation with little or no perspiration. By striking a happy medium and not neglecting either, God produced a good balance for me. To maintain this balance, I developed a *work sheet* on which I systematically recorded the various aspects of my lesson preparation. In three vertical columns I recorded: (1) my observations, (2) the meaning to those to whom the passage was written and the meaning to us, today, and (3) application for me and those I teach. This assured me of change through all aspects of study.

Interpretation of the Scripture portion is divided into two categories: What it meant to those it was written to, and What it means today.

*a. What it meant to those to whom it was written.* God changes my attitude toward Bible teachings when I understand their actual meanings. The meanings of words change through the years, and only by relying on scholars who have studied original meanings can I be assured of accurate understanding. Comparing several of the good translations is helpful also. To insure accurate instruction I must remember that paraphrases are good, understandable Bible helps, but not literal translations. I also keep in mind to whom the portion was written. Does 1 John 1:8 apply to non-Christians, or was it written only to Christians? And when the psalmist prayed, "Take not Thy Holy Spirit from me" (51:11), he was writing before Pentecost, so that it is not a way I ask God to change me today. Then, too, I must not assume that I can be changed by the study of only one portion of Scripture on a certain theme. I must study all His Word teaches on that subject, and not insist on being changed only by my "pet" Scripture.

*b. What it means to us today.* Only in the light of what the Scripture meant to those to whom it was written can I know accurately what it should mean to me today. We tend to interpret God's commands and instructions in the light of culture trends in the church and in our world. When I started teaching my first neighborhood Bible study I had to deal almost immediately with the cultures of different churches.

When someone asked the question, "What is sin? " the answers started flowing. "My church believes you can have one cocktail at a wedding reception." "My church allows alcoholic beverages for all adults." "My church only allows beer and wine." "We don't believe in any alcohol! " After agreeing to the rule that we would take as authoritative only what the Bible said and not what churches believed, the problem disappeared.

We are prone to put the emphasis on *today*, thinking that the moral climate of the age somehow influences what God demands of us. I remember hearing sermons condemning television sets when they first came out, and my husband recalls as a little child his grandfather storming into his home after his father had bought the first radio in the neighborhood, saying, "Well, I never thought I'd see my son on the way to hell." But attitudes change. Most of those who once violently condemned movies now sit glued to their TV sets as old reruns flash right into their living rooms.

God gave our Nancy a good answer to this problem when she was a teenager.

"Mother, is what was sin when you were a girl still sin? "

"Where are you reading in God's Word these days? " I asked.

"Ephesians."

"Let's take that Book and see what God says."

So, as we had done many times before, we both read silently until He stopped one of us. Suddenly Nancy said, "Stop. God gave me the answer in verse 4."

"What did He say?"

" 'That we should be holy and without blame before him.' It doesn't make any difference whether we lived at the time Christ was on earth or a 100 years ago, or whether we live today, we are to be blameless and acceptable in His sight."

God's standard does not change; His yardstick of perfection is not shortened by years or culture; His purpose to conform me to the image of Christ is the same yesterday, today and forever. When I know what God's instructions really meant to those to whom they were written, I can apply the same truths to my life today.

### 3. Application

The real change in me comes when I take the truths I have observed and studied and *apply* them to my life. Only when I apply the Scripture does God do the actual changing in my thinking and my actions.

There are reasons for reading the Bible historically, for an overview of a book or the whole Bible; but the real life-changing comes when we apply, one by one, the precepts that He tells us. "Precept upon precept; line upon line" (Isa. 28:10).

I had been teaching the same Sunday School class of sharp young adults for about 12 years when an unsettling thought started gnawing away at me: "Are those people any different because of all my hours of perspiring in lesson preparation? " Oh, they were a great group, and I would come away from the class with a heady sense of exhilaration from the lively give-and-take discussion on deep biblical subjects. In fact, that class was one of the joys of my life.

But the gnawing persisted—was actually growing—were they really different because of all my efforts?

Then the officers and I met to plan the year's program and curriculum. And I dropped the bomb. "I'm not going to teach this class anymore unless I see more evidence that the Scriptures are actually changing lives."

The only audible response was the swallowing of the others in the room. The stunned silence didn't deter me. I launched our paragraph study of the Book of Mark with a new determination. Either they would let God *change* them by what we were studying from His Word, or I was finished as their teacher!

After a couple of months, one Sunday morning I announced to the class that, instead of studying that day's lesson, I wanted them to share with all of us exactly how God had changed them by specific lessons we had studied. It didn't take long to see that God had been at work. One after another stood to share what God had changed in them because of specific Scriptures we had studied. My apprehension and fears were over. They *had* let God change them. Then Bill, our class president, looked at me and said rather meekly, "Did we tell you enough so you'll keep teaching, Ev? "

I remember the advice on counseling that Dr. Henry Brandt gave to the international leaders at Explo '72: "Only listen till the people coming for counseling mention a scriptural precept they're violating. Stop their conversation and give them the scriptural answer. Then send them off, telling them not to come back for more advice until they have *lived and applied* that answer."

During one of my neighborhood Bible studies, the women all were suffering some deep personal or family trial. But as we studied the Book of First Peter, we found an amazing thing happening. God gave answers *to live by* week after week to those who seemed to need help the most. I watched as they observed that those early Christians were suffering for a season but were to rejoice as the testing of their faith was preparing them for Jesus' return (1 Peter 1:6-7). Their attitudes changed. They actually learned to smile again.

Most of the women were enduring undeserved suffering (2:20), which was being caused by another family member. And I watched them change from being resentful, defensive, and wanting to retaliate to TAKING IT PATIENTLY because it was acceptable to God, and because Christ was their Example of suffering although innocent of wrongdoing. They applied what they studied.

But they were also watching for changes in me, their teacher, for I too was going through a deep family trial. One day while studying the lesson, 1 Peter 4:19, "Wherefore let them that suffer according to the will of God *commit* the keeping of their souls to Him," I discovered that the word translated "commit" was the same word as was translated "commend" in Luke 23:46. Jesus, agonizing as He gave up His spirit on the cross, cried with a loud voice and said, "Father, into Thy hands I commend My spirit." How God lifted my burden as I applied that truth to my own life! Although my suffering was so small compared to that of my Christ on the cross, I, with Him, committed the keeping of my soul to God. And He changed me.

I cannot expect those I teach to be changed by applying God's Word if I have not been changed by it first. But that is exactly what happens when I study His Word. The observations are thrilling, the studying is exhilarating, but the *change* comes when I personally apply what the Scripture means to my everyday life. The "Lord, Change Me" comes when I let His Words abide, take up their residence, in me (John 15:7). The change comes when I am a doer of the Word and not a hearer only (James 1:22-25). For when I look into the Bible and do not apply it, I am like a person beholding my face in a mirror and immediately forgetting the mess I see. But when I look into God's Word and do what it says, then I am changed into a blessed person. Changed—when I study His Word.

# 5

# Changed—When the Holy Spirit Reminds

Many times God wants to change me now when I'm reading or studying His Word, or when I'm with a group "reading until He speaks." But when I find myself in a situation where I need help immediately, then the Holy Spirit brings to my mind the Scripture that meets my need at that moment. One of the primary reasons for reading and studying the Bible is to provide Him with the Word to bring to our remembrance—*when we need it.*

Jesus said: "These things have I spoken unto you, being yet present with you. But the Comforter, who is the Holy Spirit, whom the Father will send in My name, He shall teach you all things, and bring all things to your remembrance, whatsoever I have said unto you" (John 14:25-26).

Now, some of the disciples would be recording the words of Jesus in some of the books of the New Testament. What a word of assurance this must have been for them. But was this promise of the Spirit's prompting given only to Peter, John, Matthew, and the other disciples who were with Jesus at that time? I think not. Prisoners of war and others who have had Bibles taken from them tell fantastic stories of the Holy Spirit recalling for them the Scriptures they had learned previously. This is one of the most powerful ways God has used the Scriptures down through the ages.

One of the surprises that came out of my analysis and the underlined and dated verses in my three Bibles was that

193

frequently the verse didn't have any immediate specific meaning to me. But when there was a need sometime in the future, the Holy Spirit pulled from my memory exactly the portion of Scripture that fitted the need.

We stay in the Bible, studying and reading devotionally, being taught by God so that the Holy Spirit can bring to our remembrance what He has told us. We tell our children that they can't expect God to help them recall answers on a test if they have never studied the material in the first place. Neither can we expect God to bring to our remembrance answers to our needs if we have not stored His truth in our hearts.

A couple of years ago I was fretting because I was remembering less and less as I grew older. But in a moment the Holy Spirit kindly reminded me of this verse on His bringing all things to our remembrance—His way of dealing with old age! Then I thought back on the chat I had with 82-year-old Corrie ten Boom the month before. "Evelyn," she said, "I never forget spiritual things."

### That I Might Not Sin

I view with awe my neighbor across our cul-de-sac who is working on the world's largest computer. My mind is boggled as he tells of the one million words it can work on at a time and the billions of facts its memory banks can store. But we as human beings possess the world's most sophisticated and complex memory banks—our minds—and they store up all the information acquired by us from infancy.

The psalmist says: "Thy Word have I hid in mine heart, that I might not sin against Thee" (Ps. 119:11). This is the process of tucking the Word of God deep down in our hearts by study and memorization. As we read the Bible, study it, and listen to sermons from it, we are not to dismiss what God says to us, but are to *hide* those spiritual truths in the deepest recesses of our hearts.

But those of us who know the pain of trying to recall some of the information we stored there as children, the college material that produced an "A" grade, or even a recipe that seemed so simple 20 years ago, realize the inadequacy of our human memory systems. As human operators we are frequently unable to bring forth even a tiny bit of stored information.

But when we need to recall a particular spiritual truth, we have a supernatural computer operator—the Holy Spirit!

When I recognize there is something wrong in my life and I know God wants to change me, I feed the problem into the computer of my mind. Then, when I ask God to give me a solution, the Holy Spirit often *reminds* me of a portion of Scripture—a verse or a single word—that shows me the specific sin that is causing my problem. Many times He flashes back: "pride" (Rom. 12:3) or "worry" (Phil. 4:6).

Occasionally, before I'm even aware that something is wrong, or before I know there is a problem to feed into my computer, my Supernatural Operator is already spelling out an answer to me. He knows the need or the problem before I ask, before I consciously formulate it into words. Jesus said in Matthew 6:8 that our heavenly Father knows what things we have need of *before* we ask Him, and the solution is recalled from my memory bank before I spell out my need. That's even less time than the 1.2 microseconds this largest computer in the world takes to summon answers! Yes, before I even realize my sin, the Holy Spirit is reminding, prodding, reproving with His gentle nudge or stating in no uncertain voice, "That's SIN!"

Our Supernatural Operator, the Holy Spirit, never makes a mistake. In one of our Kurt's junior high classes where the computer forms had the classifications "male," "female," and "other," some shocked students were classified as "other" by the not-too-friendly computer. And how I recall the agony of all the "Christensons" getting mixed up on the computer of our city's largest department store, just before our Jan's wedding. With all the shopping we had to do, we were suddenly lost from the face of the earth. And how embarrassed our senior high daughter felt when her school's computer assigned her to a boys' gym class! But the Holy Spirit never makes an error. Even when we feed in the wrong problem, He comes up with exactly the right answer for our specific need.

Reminding me of a scriptural answer when I ask for it, or even before I ask, is one of the methods the Holy Spirit uses to "reprove of sin," as Jesus mentioned in John 16:8. The psalmist in Psalm 119:11 gives the "why" for hiding God's Word in our hearts: "Thy Word have I hid in mine heart, *that I might not sin against Thee*." How else could God's Word, hidden, unseen, perhaps even forgotten, keep me from sin except that the Holy Spirit *recalls* it? This is the supernatural process of the Holy Spirit, more accurate than any computer that will ever be invented by man, reaching down and *recalling* for me exactly the answer I need from God's Word at the very time I need it.

My Spiritual Operator, the Holy Spirit, has a favorite one He spells out for me: "B-E Y-E H-O-L-Y; F-O-R I A-M H-O-L-Y" (1 Peter 1:16).

I hid this verse in my heart many years ago, and I'm surprised it isn't worn out from God's flashing it at me so often. But it gets to me every time. I immediately see my God high and lifted up, *holy*—perfect attitudes, actions, and reactions. And what I've stored in my memory bank from His Word comes clicking back to me. And I know how holy God is—and how holy I'm expected to be! Recalled—to keep me from sinning.

I remember one day while on vacation at our cottage I had a sudden eye-contact with a man. I flushed slightly, enjoying his obvious approval of me. The next morning I asked God to enlighten my understanding of the sin of this type of encounter. Slowly, as if on a screen in my mind, the words "Be ye holy; for I am holy" came forward until they were in focus. I asked God for complete cleansing, and immediately I was *changed*. Communing with God as He gave me several pieces of wisdom for my next book, I was suddenly engulfed with adoration of Him. Welling up from the depths of my being, flowing into every inch of my body was the prayer, "Oh, God, how good is vacation! Time to drink deeply of Your Word, to read good Christian books. Time to adore You rather than working under the tyranny of the urgent." Changed when the Holy Spirit recalled His "old faithful" verse.

### To Comfort Me

The Holy Spirit causes me to remember not only to keep me from sinning but also to supply needs in my life. When I find myself in adverse situations, He provides the Scripture I need to comfort me.

The night before I was to speak four times at a retreat high up in the Rocky Mountains, I was reading my Bible and these words spoke to me, "For He shall give His angels charge over thee, to keep thee in all thy ways" (Ps. 91:11). Angels? Why did I need angels when I was securely tucked into a warm bed in a nice private trailer?

But the next morning I woke cold and miserable. The electricity, and thus my electric heater, had gone off in the night; and, although it was only September, the first snow of the season had just fallen. Adding to my misery was a hard case of intestinal flu with its accompanying chills. Shivering violently, I piled all the blankets and coats in sight on me, trying to get warm. Then the Holy Spirit suddenly recalled for me the verse I had read the night before. "Angels? Wow, do I ever need them right now!" And just the thought of God sending His angels to hover and watch over me in that room changed me—warmed my spirit and made those difficult circumstances easier to take. His miracle of making me well enough to speak all that day was to come later, but right then I needed the assurance and comfort of the Scripture the Holy Spirit recalled.

While we were traveling overseas a few years ago, I came down with a severe infection in Jerusalem. As I was lying all alone in my hotel bed, looking out on the Mount of Olives, the Holy Spirit reminded me of Romans 8:28, and I knew that even missing the tour that day was being worked out by God for my good. Then He brought to my remembrance some of the lessons from God's Word that I had tucked down in my heart years before. Again, Romans 8:28—He brought good from the loss of those three pregnancies right after we were married. Then from Hebrews 12—the chapter that was so real to me at the time of Judy's death—He had taught me that even her death was for *my profit*. Lying there, I let God speak afresh about those lessons from His Word of yesteryears.

Surprisingly, instead of lying there rebelling at missing the tour to Bethlehem that day, I found my spirit soaring to the heavenlies with God—*changed*! He enveloped me with a tremendous sense of His presence—caring for, and speaking to me, personally. I spent hours listening to "Jerusalem sounds"—a cock crowing in the morning, a donkey braying in the distance—and had the unspeakable thrill of seeing the rising sun burst over the Mount of Olives, just as it must have done that first Easter morning! And God proved that the

Scriptures He was recalling would work again. Later in the week I was given a tour of Bethlehem by private car, and when I returned to Jerusalem I had the wonderful privilege of spending an hour alone in the Garden of Gethsemane, communing with my Lord.

### For Teaching Others
The Holy Spirit frequently brings to my remembrance Scripture I have hidden in my heart so that I can teach others the truths God has taught me.

Back in 1957 I was scheduled to speak at a women's meeting but could not get a message I felt God wanted me to bring them; every idea I had seemed inadequate. In desperation I arose early on the morning of the day I was to bring the message and sought out my old green prayer chair. Prayer and searching of God's Word produced nothing. Finally, in exasperation, I laid aside my Bible and picked up the newspaper. The headlines stunned me. Russia had sent Sputnik I into outer space! The frenzied race to *conquer* outer space was on. (How foolish that word "conquer" sounds now.) President Eisenhower, astonished that the Russians had projectors and propellants which could cast that 184-pound object into outer space, gave a message of comfort and encouragement to the American people on the front page.

But almost immediately the Holy Spirit recalled a portion of Scripture that I had hidden deep in my heart when I had taught Colossians to my Sunday School class: "For by Him [Jesus] were all things created, that are in heaven, and that are in earth, visible and invisible, whether they be thrones, or dominions, or principalities, or powers; all things were created by Him, and for Him; and He is before all things, and by Him all things consist" (Col. 1:16-17).

I had my message! Jesus *made* outer space! He put the stars and planets, the sun and the moon in place! Jesus *holds* them all together! He makes them run on course according to His will! We are not to fear some nation that can make a little piece of hardware circling our planet. But we are to put our trust in the One who created all that outer space, the One by whom it all consists—Jesus!

Just by recalling a portion of Scripture, that whole shocking news item came into focus. It lost its horror. I could go to that meeting and tell those frightened women that our enemy had invaded outer space before us, but Jesus had been out there creating it and controlling it from eternity past! *Changed*—when the Holy Spirit brought just two verses to my remembrance.

The Holy Spirit recalled a precious portion when I was asked to speak to a women's Sunday School class in Ambo, Ethiopia. None of them understood English, and I wondered what we had in common that I could talk about. As I looked out the window of their church, I saw a mountain in the distance. And immediately the Holy Spirit brought to mind *my* mountain verses from Psalm 121. They understood mountains!

Slowly, with the help of an interpreter, I related the story of how God spoke to me on my mountain. I told them that after having a slight heart problem I had gone to a doctor to find out whether it was advisable for me to travel through the Rocky Mountains in Canada on my way to Vancouver, British Columbia. A group of us were traveling in a caravan of cars, and everything went fine until we reached our first mountain. Suddenly I had trouble breathing and my heart started to beat wildly. We stopped at a motel and, while the others went to a restaurant, I spent the time in bed, gazing out at huge Cascade Mountain, which seemed to go straight up from my bedroom window. "Oh, God," I prayed, "please give me just the Scripture You want me to read. I don't want to be sick and unable to go on to Vancouver. I don't want to break up this caravan. Please give me something from Your Word." Then God flashed Psalm 121:1-2 in my mind. I reached for my Bible and read: "I will lift up mine eyes unto the hills. From whence cometh my help? My help cometh from the Lord, who made heaven and earth" (SCO).

Then I told those Ethiopian ladies, "I was looking up to the hills, but they hadn't helped me. In fact, they had caused my heart to act strangely. But there's a question mark after verse 1; my answer was in the next verse. My help comes from the Lord who *made* those high mountains. Then I decided to trust God for all the strength I would need to get across those mountains, and right away my heart was OK." Changed!

I told those Ethiopian women that when it was time for devotions the next morning I had the caravan stop on another one of those big mountains, and we all sat down while I read my "mountain verses" to them, telling them of my trust in the God who made all the mountains and who made—and keeps—me. Yes, the Holy Spirit had recalled just the Scripture I needed to teach that Sunday School in Africa that morning.

I was happy that I had tucked some verse down in my heart when I was doing follow-up counseling after a citywide youth evangelism week. On the last night the leader announced, "Mrs. Christenson will take all those who have finished their written follow-up books and teach them." My mind raced. How could I fill up a whole evening with teaching when all the subjects had been completed by these high schoolers? When a newspaper editor asked to interview a few of my young people, I silently thanked God for the few minutes I had to ask Him what I should tell them. Prayerfully, I waited for God to show me specifically what I should do.

Then the Holy Spirit recalled several scriptural truths I could share. Changed, I confidently told them that their completed follow-up program didn't mean that the battle was over for them as new Christians (Eph. 6). I reminded them that although temptation would come their way, there is always victory in Jesus (Phil. 4:13), and from 1 John I showed them that when we *do* sin God will forgive us if we confess it to Him (1 John 1:8-9). Then I shared how God would take all of these things, both good and bad, and work them all out for our good (Rom. 8:28).

When the evening was over, one of the other counselors came to me and said, "Whew! I'm glad he didn't give *me* that job. I don't even *know* those verses!"

How important it is to hide God's Word in our hearts so the Holy Spirit can recall it when we need to teach others. It is so great to keep sensitive to the Holy Spirit while teaching and speaking so that He can recall just the Scripture somebody in the audience needs.

### Just for Me
Sometimes the Holy Spirit recalls Scripture that is just for me. I'm not going to teach or share it with anyone—it's just for me.

As we drove down to Bethlehem that day I was given a private tour, I prayed, "Lord, bring to my mind just the

Scripture You want me to hear as I view the birthplace of my Saviour."

Looking at the shepherds' fields I expected to hear, "And suddenly there was with the angel a multitude of the heavenly host praising God" (Luke 2:13). But no Scripture came to my mind. And as we approached the town of Bethlehem, I waited for Him to recall Micah 5:2, "But thou, Bethlehem Ephratah." But there was nothing. I strained to hear God say something as we approached the Church of the Nativity—nothing. Then on the marble steps descending to the actual stable level— nothing. Breathlessly expectant, I stepped into the room where tradition states Jesus was born. Even as I pulled back the velvet wall hangings and touched the wall—there was still nothing. Regretfully, I walked up the stairs. Not one portion of Scripture recalled especially for me, from God in that precious spot. But as I stepped out into the sunlight of the courtyard once more—it hit! God recalled a total surprise: "And the Word was made flesh, and dwelt among *us*, (and we beheld His glory, the glory as of the only begotten of the Father,) full of grace and truth" (John 1:14).

The emphasis the Holy Spirit conveyed was on the word "us." I recoiled as my mind went to "me" with my filled teeth, eyeglasses, infection, and recent surgery. Then I looked around at the hunger and pain so prevalent in the Holy Land. Among us? As I almost felt the dirt around me, I wondered at that "Holy Thing" announced by the angel to Mary, being born into this. Yes, a part of it through the birth process. He *dwelt* among *us*?

Then God took my mind back to the preceding verses in that first chapter of John. Jesus Christ, who was God, and who had been with God from the beginning—in heaven's perfect environment where there was no pain, sickness, or death—had come down to earth right at that spot and dwelt *among us*. What a new picture God had given me of my Jesus—not the traditional Babe in the manger—but the holy Son of God who loved me enough to come down here and dwell among us. I was completely *changed*—with a new and deep appreciation of my Saviour's sacrifice—for me!

I've heard of some awful things that are supposed to happen to parents when the last child leaves the nest. The divorce rate for parents in this category goes up, and many mothers fall into an "I'm not needed anymore" depression. Just before leaving for college, our Kurt said to me, "I think this is harder on you than it is on me, Mother."

Two days after he left, Chris and I were driving along holding hands as we returned from a shopping trip that had carried us through what had been our family dinner hour with our children for 26 years. I squeezed his hand and smiled as I said, "Ye have not, because ye ask not" (James 4:2). The Holy Spirit had given us that verse for that weekend. And there had been some desperate "asking" as we saw Kurt's empty bed, the vacant spaces where his clock radio, stereo tuner, and desk lamp had stood, and as we "listened" to the silent bathroom that had resounded so vigorously every morning with splashing shower and buzzing electric comb.

On the last night of prayer together with Kurt, as we thanked God for the almost 18 years of joy, and then gave our son to God in a new and special way to make his own life outside our nest, I turned to a new kind of "asking": "Dear God, fill the void with Yourself," I prayed over and over. Then my prayer progressed, adding another dimension: "Dear Father, fill the void with *You and Chris*."

The results were incredible. God filled my life to overflowing with Himself and His love through other people. And after reading about Joseph taking such good care of the infant Jesus and His mother Mary, I prayed, "Thank You, Lord, for the way Chris protects me and the security I have in him."

Later that week Chris and I traveled together as far as Denver where I was to speak. Before he took off for the rest of his journey to California, he sat on the edge of the bed and said to me, "I don't know or understand all that is happening to us, but I sure like it."

"Ye have not because ye ask not," said the Holy Spirit. And how right He was! I was a completely changed mother and wife—just because I obeyed the Scripture the Holy Spirit recalled.

### Number One
But Romans 8:28 is by far the number one verse the Holy Spirit recalls for me. In fact, He has reminded me of it so often

that I have finally adopted it as my philosophy of life: "And we know that all things work together for good to them that love God, to them who are the called according to His purpose." God gave that verse to me at the time I lost my third pregnancy during our college days. He must have known then how my whole life would revolve around that verse—though I certainly didn't know it at the time.

I used to have to struggle to find the *good* in the seeming calamities of my life, but sooner or later I was able to see what God was doing and why He was doing it. And more and more through the years I am able to see the *why* of circumstances as soon as the Holy Spirit says, "Romans 8:28." What used to take time to figure out, now seems to come almost immediately and automatically.

And it works 100 percent of the time. When something especially bad happens, when the roof caves in or the floor falls out from under me, the Holy Spirit still persists, "*All* things." I cannot accept it just 90 percent of the time or even 98 percent of the time. I must accept it *all* of the time. It was hard at first, but as the years have come and gone, it has become easier. I guess it's a matter of faith. As faith is exercised, it grows stronger and stronger. And the faith, of course, isn't in a verse or even a verse turned into a philosophy of life. The faith is in the God of that verse—the One who is working out all things for my good. And the Holy Spirit is really recalling not a verse, but all that God has worked out for me for 30 years.

One of the greatest ways God changes me is by bringing to mind Scripture I have hidden deep in my heart. And He always picks the right Scripture at the right time. What a reason for staying in His Word daily—reading, studying, devouring it. And then what a challenge to stay so sensitive to the Holy Spirit's speaking that He can reach down and recall just exactly what I need at the very minute I need it!

# 6

# *Exchange— When I Ask God*

One of the most direct ways God changes me is by answering my prayers for myself. When I ask Him to change some specific trait in me, He frequently lifts that thing out and replaces it with a quality that He desires me to have. As God removes an attitude, a personality trait, or some characteristic of my old nature, and puts in its place His own attribute, the process is a dramatic one. He does not add a little of His strength to my weakness, or a little of His forgiveness to cover my sin. No, there is an actual *exchange* that takes place within me.

And this exchange takes place when I ask Him in prayer. Of course, the key to this process is my *wanting* Him to change me. Now, God's methods aren't always painless, but the end result is an exchange within me, which leaves me with an unexplainable sense of well-being. It is a life-changing process that fills me with His peace, joy, and power—when I ask.

### Strength for Weakness
Often we ask God to change us, but then don't *wait* for Him to answer our prayer. A secret I learned many years ago is that God gives me some things only *when I wait*.

Recently in a series of hectic days I had an unusually strenuous one. I drove to Wisconsin for an all-day prayer seminar, lectured for six hours, and then drove back home to Minnesota. I had just one-half hour to cook my dinner, eat, and get back on the road for another two-and-a-half hour lecture.

At bedtime, Chris, knowing my rigorous schedule, called me from his travels in Florida. "Just wanted to know how you made it through the day, Honey. How was it?"

"Oh, Chris, all I can say is that it was another miracle. By the time I had driven home from Wisconsin I was so exhausted that I could hardly raise my arms, my stomach was hurting, and it was hard to think straight. But—when I started to speak at Bethel College tonight, I suddenly felt as fresh as if I had had eight hours of sound sleep!"

What had happened? Before the evening seminar I took a few minutes to lie down and pray these words: "O God, *exchange* my exhaustion for Your strength." And it worked. God miraculously reached down, lifted my exhaustion, and then replaced it with His strength.

The same thing happened to me a few months ago at the Greater Los Angeles Sunday School Convention. The night before I left I had taught all evening, driven 50 miles, arrived home at midnight, and then had packed for the trip to Los Angeles. Early the next morning I flew out to California and dashed into the convention center just minutes before I was to speak. That evening I was scheduled to give my final lecture of that day at 8:30 P.M. California time. But that was 10:30 P.M. according to the time on which I was operating! Start again at 10:30? And continue lecturing until *my* 11:45?

During a short break between sessions, I dashed to my motel room, and suddenly realized that my staggering schedule had caught up with my body—my head felt fuzzy, and I was shaking all over. So I went to prayer—not just asking but desperately hanging on to God for help. Here again I practiced that threefold formula which never fails: 1. *Stop.* 2. *Ask.* 3. *Wait.* The results were fantastic. I bounced over to that final meeting and never felt a speck of fatigue all through the session!

Dr. Stephen Olford in his booklet, *The Secret of Strength*, explains that the word "renew" in Isaiah 40:31 ("They that wait upon the Lord shall *renew* their strength") actually means "the process by which the molting eagle *exchanges* its old feathers for new ones." We think of the renewing process as an addition of a little strength, but to God it is an actual replacement.

When we are fatigued, our tendency is to keep pushing and pushing, slower and slower, until we get the job done. But

God's formula is so simple. And it takes such a short time to *stop, ask,* and *wait.* However, there is a key to this formula: Ask, and then wait expectantly. This requires *faith*—not in the few minutes I might have in which to rest, but in the *One* who is to provide the strength. Hebrews 11:6 explains it so clearly: "But without faith it is impossible to please Him; for he that cometh to God must believe that He is, and that He is a Rewarder of them that diligently seek Him." It is God who *exchanges* my fatigue for His strength. And He does it when I stop, ask in faith, and wait expectantly.

### The Mind of Christ for My Fallibility
Another exchange takes place in me when I acknowledge my inadequate ideas, my shortcomings or sinful attitudes, and ask God for the *mind of Christ.*

The first step in this process is to recognize that there is something more or something better than I am now experiencing. My needs can be difficult to detect, for my inadequate thoughts frequently disguise a deeper problem, my shortcomings often excuse inactivity, and sometimes my sins actually feel good. When I finally acknowledge that something is wrong, then I can *ask* for the mind of Christ.

The day before I started a prayer seminar in the largest Lutheran church in the world, my son-in-law phoned and said, "Do you want to hear a funny story?"

"Sure," I replied.

"Well, Jan and I were being entertained in a couple's home, and our hostess mentioned Pastor Lindon Karo. 'How do you know him?' Jan asked in surprise. 'Oh I read about him in a book on prayer.' 'My mother wrote that book,' said Jan. 'Oh,' said our hostess as she glanced nervously around her house, 'if I had known, I would have cleaned my house better.' "

After Skip and I stopped laughing, he continued. "Then our hostess became quiet and preoccupied with her own thoughts. She blurted out, *'I feel as if I'm entertaining God.'* " And at that Skip and I roared with laughter. That surely was a funny story.

But when I hung up the phone, God said to Evelyn—pride! I dropped to my knees and pled with God to *give me the mind of Christ.* "O God, please forgive me for that terrible attitude. I'm sorry. Please give me the mind of Christ." Immediately God brought Philippians 2 to my mind. I knew what that portion said, but scurried for my Bible so I wouldn't miss a single word: "Let this mind be in you, which was also in Christ Jesus; who, being in the form of God, thought it not robbery to be equal with God; but made Himself of no reputation, and took upon Him the form of a servant" (vv. 5-7).

I was overwhelmed. Jesus *was* God (John 1:1). Jan wasn't God. I wasn't God—but Jesus, who actually was God, came to earth *as a servant*. My mind flashed to Mark 10:45 where Christ said of Himself that He "came not to be ministered unto, but to minister." This was the "mind of Christ" I was admonished to have in me—the mind Jesus had when He came to earth from heaven.

"O Lord," I cried, "change me. Make me *only a servant*. Please give me the mind of Christ." Immediately God answered. It seemed that He reached down and scooped out of me the attitude that must have been a stench in His nostrils. And flooding over me was an overwhelming sense of only being a servant. The next morning when I started my seminar in that large church and looked out over all those people, I had the most beautiful sense of being completely *their servant*— nothing more.

Pride over a funny story could have ruined the whole seminar, but God took that story and gave me what He really wanted me (and every Christian) to have—the mind of Christ. The mind of a Servant!

There are also other references in Scripture relating to the mind of Christ and the Christian. While I was teaching my neighborhood Bible study on 1 Peter, we as a class discovered much about suffering. In chapter 4, verse 19, we found that there are those who suffer according to the will of God. And in 3:17 we discovered that "it is better, if the will of God be so, that ye suffer for well-doing, than for evil-doing." And we were told in 1 Peter 2:20-21 that when we suffer for doing well and "take it patiently, this is acceptable with God." We are called to this because "Christ also suffered for us, leaving us an example, that ye should follow His steps." And I wrote in the margin of my Bible next to 1 Peter 4:1, "Lord, change *me*": "Forasmuch then as Christ hath suffered for us in the flesh, arm yourselves likewise with the same mind." As the teacher of the class, I also wrote by that verse, "key verse?" Is this the key to understanding the whole Book of 1 Peter? Yes, we are to arm ourselves with the mind of Christ so that we can see our suffering *as* He saw His.

Also, I found it interesting, and often disconcerting, to discover the mind of Christ in the four Gospels. Most of the time His reactions were so different from what mine would have been, His attitudes so much more lofty than mine, His thoughts so far above my thoughts. But what a privilege actually to be *admonished* in Philippians 2 to have His mind *in* us.

Whenever I'm in doubt as to how God wants me to change, I am always safe in praying for the mind of Christ. So often I'm aware that my attitude, reaction, or thoughts are not Christlike, but am not sure exactly what God wants to substitute for them. But I never ask amiss, when I pray for *the mind of Christ*.

### Prepared for Meetings

When I'm preparing to speak at a seminar, retreat, or a single meeting, I sometimes have trouble feeling a burden for the people to whom I'm to minister. Struggling to put myself in the right frame of mind usually proves useless, but I have learned what does work: asking God to exchange my attitude for His.

When one meeting follows hard on the heels of another and another and another, I occasionally find a lethargy setting in. Then, as I drive my car, or sit in an airplane winging my way toward a meeting, I pray, "Lord, give me a burden for these people. Please, God, take away this lethargy. Help me to feel Your burden." And God always answers that prayer. He *exchanges* my lethargy for His burden. I can feel it descend on me, almost like a weight, surrounding me and pressing from all sides. And I arrive at my destination completely prepared spiritually for the task He has given me.

I pray that same kind of prayer when I'm consumed by "the tyranny of the urgent." I find myself having to leave for a meeting in the middle of an important priority in my life. But it is time to switch gears, to let another priority have all of me. This is often difficult, but again, I pray for God to *exchange* the urgency of one priority for what He wants me to feel for this new task. And it always works.

I could hardly face a new evening seminar series which was to start on January 3, 1977. In addition to being completely engrossed writing this book, I had spent the day in holiday cleanup and washing our son's clothes for his return to college. I finally took the hour before dinner to get alone with God in my bedroom, seeking a spiritual lift for the new series. Then as I left the house for the seminar a sense of my utter inadequacy swept over me, and I asked Chris to pray for me. Driving down the freeway just a few minutes later I prayed in desperation, "Lord, change me; take away this frustration. Give me joy. Make me what You want me to be at this seminar."

Almost immediately there flashed a tingle of excitement. It flooded into my whole body. I could feel it physically. Then a smile of joyous anticipation spread over my face. I pressed a little harder on the accelerator—all at once anxious to get there! God had lifted all those undesirable feelings from me and exchanged them for His attitude toward the meeting. And I faced that audience absolutely thrilled—and felt their excitement and anticipation in return.

Sometimes God answers a prayer for exchange in unexpected ways. I worked for a month preparing for a "God's Living Word" retreat (mentioned in chapter 2). Without any emotion I was typing into the message outlines the material I had culled from the three Bibles I had used devotionally since I was 18. Then I realized what I was doing—I was recording just dates and facts, not God's personal, dynamic speaking to me through the years. I dropped my head onto the kitchen table and fervently prayed, "Oh, Lord, give me the emotion I need so that this message won't be just statistics and facts. Give me the feelings You want me to have."

Before I finished praying, the phone rang. It was my former prayer partner. "My daughter's baby died last night. She has just awakened, and a flood of grief and an overwhelming sense of being unable to face life has swept over her. She wants me to talk to you. Could you say something to her?"

I wept as I recalled our Judy. And I wept as I cared about her little baby. Then I told her about one of those underlined verses I had just listed for the retreat—from Hebrews 12. I told her that God never makes a mistake, and that He must have something great in store for her and her husband to allow them such suffering. I told that grieving young mother that God was doing this "for their profit," even though they could not understand it now.

And God had *exchanged* my humdrum listing of verses and routine typing with a deep, Christlike caring. I went to that retreat burning with the desire to impart to those women that God's Word is alive; it does have answers for right now.

God changed me in an almost violent way one night as I prepared for a retreat the next day. I had everything all in order on the pages of notes, but somehow I lacked a sense of urgency. It seemed to be just a run-of-the-mill preparation for an ordinary retreat. I realized that my heart wasn't as well prepared as my notes. So I prayed the simple but earnest prayer, "Lord, prepare *me* for tomorrow's retreat. Teach me what You want me to know and feel. Take away this feeling of nothingness."

Just then a deafening crackle resounded through our house, accompanied by a brilliant orange flash. As I sat stunned, the phone rang. My husband, calling long distance, said, "Just thought I'd let you know the tornado that was predicted for our area has moved past. You're safe now."

"Thanks a lot," I said weakly, "but our house has just been hit by lightning." I slowly hung up the phone, and sat in the total darkness. Then I bowed my head and thanked God for protecting me. After the firemen had examined the house and told us to keep alert for possible outbreak of fire, the children and I knelt by Nancy's bed. Eleven-year-old Kurt was the first to pray, telling God we were just going to trust Him that night and go to sleep.

As I awakened the next morning safe and sound, I had a new sense of God's protection. Driving to the retreat, I found myself following a car with a bumper sticker that read "Protected by Batman." I smiled as I thought, "*I'm* protected by God!" I arrived at that retreat changed. God, through a bolt of lightning, had *exchanged* my run-of-the-mill attitude for a vital, living sense of His protection and leading in my life.

Whenever I'm feeling inadequate for a job to be done and overwhelmed by an "I-can't-do-it" feeling, I quietly commune with God. I ask Him to give me His power, His enabling in place of my inadequacy. I ask this specifically for the task that I am facing, then claim Philippians 2:13, "For it is *God who worketh in you* both to will and to do of His good pleasure." And my attitude changes. I rise to do the task, completely able to do it. God lifts my inadequacy and fills me with *Himself!*

## Exchange: God for Money

Twenty-five years ago, in the apron-hankie-corsage era of payment for women speakers, Chris and I made a promise to God that we would never ask a fee for my speaking. We told Him we would pay for baby-sitters, hairdos, and transportation out of his pastor's salary—a promise we have never withdrawn, although he is no longer a pastor. Even in the early days of my prayer seminars when love offerings rarely covered expenses and prayer-letter mailings, we simply trusted God. Somehow I had always felt He would withdraw His blessings if I started serving Him for the money I might receive.

After my first book came out and my cassette tape sales increased, I was still completely detached from the income. Then people started ordering the tapes by mail. And gradually I became more and more eager to see how many orders the mailman brought. When Chris would ask what was in the mail, I would reply by telling him the number of orders I received.

Then one day as I was returning from a seminar, pushing harder and harder on the gas pedal to get home as fast as possible to see how many orders had come, God said clearly to me, "Evelyn, that attitude toward money is sin!" I was horrified. I slowed the car down and cried, "Please remove all of these thoughts and this attitude right now, Lord. O God, forgive me. O Lord, change me! Please, please, You remove this from me." And it was gone—not little by little as it had so subtly crept in; but in one sweep of His mighty cleansing hand—it was gone!

That night God had something to say to me out of His Word. As I was reading my Bible, tucking a thought in my mind to go to sleep on, a phrase in Matthew 6:24 almost jumped off the page at me: "You cannot serve both God and money" (NIV). For three nights I found myself peculiarly drawn to that same verse, from one translation to another. It was as if I wanted God to press it deeper and deeper into my very being. "I cannot serve both God and money!" Why not? God gave me that answer in the same chapter when Jesus was warning us against laying up for ourselves treasures upon earth and telling us to lay them up in heaven. Then Jesus gave the *why*: "For where your treasure is, there will your heart be also" (Matt. 6:21).

God didn't say that I never could be paid for my ministry. In fact, He has some explicit instructions about the workman being worthy of his hire; but the problem lay in *where my heart was*. And He *exchanged* my wrong attitude about money for His perfect one.

### Meekness for Self-Assertion

Sometimes it's a little risky to ask God to change me. I remember a pastor at a World Day of Prayer speaking on the topic, "Be careful what you pray for—God may answer your prayer." And I learned the truth of this back in 1967 when I asked God to give me a meek and quiet spirit.

While preparing a banquet message on Godlike characteristics in women, I was pricked by 1 Peter 3:4, where it says that we should be adorned, not with outward hairdos, ornaments and clothes, but with "a meek and quiet spirit." Recognizing something to be desired in my steamroller personality, I prayed for five consecutive days, "Dear God, please give me a meek and quiet spirit." This was the prayer on my lips and in my heart.

I must have thought God was going to "sugarcoat" me by some supernatural process, for I was completely unprepared for the method He used. Our sixth-grade daughter had a divorced male teacher who liked to take his female pupils to a wooded retreat for outdoor education. When I refused to let our daughter go to the woods with him alone, he was furious, and came to tell me so. When I answered my doorbell, I saw him standing there with his face ashen in anger. And for the next half hour he raved and ranted at me for ruining his reputation in the community by not allowing my daughter to be alone with him in the woods, etc., etc., etc.! When he finally walked out the door, I had what I had prayed for—a meek and quiet spirit!

Yes, God had *exchanged* my personality trait for the one of His choice when I had asked Him to. But, oh, the process!

## Forgiveness for Guilt

The most important *exchange* of all takes place when God takes our guilt and replaces it with His forgiveness, His cleansing.

While visiting in California in 1969, I heard a Sunday School teacher talk excitedly about an interesting concept in Psalm 103:12. Those were the days when we all were standing in awe of our space achievements, and she had found the concept of the Hebrew word *nasa* in that psalm. "As far as the east is from the west, so far hath He removed our transgressions from us." The word "removed" conveyed the Old Testament idea of sin being separated from the sinner. And the Hebrew word *nasa* translated "forgive" meant literally to "lift away." What a picture of the dramatic blast-offs of Houston's NASA space ships. The psalmist used the largest measurement which the earth can measure—"as far as the east is from the west," but NASA is now in the business of lifting off from Planet Earth completely!

But the comparison ends there. NASA tracks our satellites with unbelievably precise instruments and brings them back to earth again. But not God. Once He lifts them off, our sins are gone—forever. He doesn't even remember them anymore! God is in the business of replacing our sins with His forgiveness.

Of course, the ultimate of this exchange of guilt for forgiveness comes when we ask God to forgive all our sins and invite Jesus to become our Lord and Saviour. The greatest transformation of my life took place when I was just nine years old. At that time 2 Corinthians 5:17 became true in me: "Therefore if any man be in Christ, he is a new creation; old things are passed away; behold, all things are become new." Why is this transformation necessary? Jesus tells us clearly in John 3:18: "He that believeth on Him [God's Son] is not condemned; but he that believeth not is condemned already, because he hath not believed in the name of the only begotten Son of God."

As recorded in the Book of Mark, Jesus began His ministry in Galilee preaching *repent* and *believe*. Somehow today the emphasis is only on believing, and we tend to omit the first half of what Jesus preached (Mark 1:14-15). Then the night before He was crucified, Jesus told His disciples that He would send the Comforter who would "reprove the world of sin . . . because they believe not on Me" (John 16:8-9). Paul puts it so clearly in Romans 3:23: "For all have sinned, and come short of the glory of God."

But when God exchanges His forgiveness for this condemnation, the contrast is fantastic. Paul tells us that "there is therefore now no condemnation to them who are in Christ" (Rom. 8:1). Then in Colossians 1:13-14 he tells us that God has "delivered us from the power of darkness, and hath translated us into the kingdom of His dear Son; in whom we have redemption through His blood, even the forgiveness of sins." We exchange citizenship. And in Ephesians 2:1 we have the greatest exchange of all—life for death: "And you hath He [made alive], who were dead in trespasses and sins."

This exchange transforms our lifestyle according to the preceding verses. Theories and theologies are of little value if they do not produce *evidence* of their being true, if lives aren't changed.

Several years ago the churches of our city cooperated in a Teen Evangelism Crusade with Dave Wilkerson. About a thousand young people found Christ as their Saviour, and the local newspaper headlines said: "Teens Say Wilkerson Visit Resulted in Changed Lives." Then they quoted some of these young people.

"It has made me a completely new person," said a 16-year-old boy. "It has changed my life. I used to be a Latin Count. I used to feel like I wanted to beat up somebody all the time. I wanted to smash things."

A 15-year-old high school sophomore said, "I don't hate anybody anymore. I feel clean inside. I get along with my mom now."

"I am no longer self-centered. Christ is the center of my life," reported a sophomore girl. "Man! If I feel low, I pray to Him—and just like that! My emptiness is gone. I love everybody."

While we were chatting with Eldridge Cleaver the other night, he looked at me and said the same thing, "There isn't anybody I don't love now." What had so dramatically changed the lifestyle of this former Black Panther fugitive? We had just come from a meeting where he told of his years of running from U.S. justice, and then of the change—beginning with his dramatic experience on the shores of the Mediterranean in southern France to the time when he asked God to forgive all his sins and Christ to be his Saviour. Changed! Yes, he had *exchanged* a life of violent revolt for one of loving everybody— because God had *exchanged* in him his old nature for God's new one. It's almost as if God were in the heart transplant business. He lifts out the old heart and implants a new one.

But even after becoming a Christian there is the necessity for this exchange. John, who lived closer to Jesus on earth than any other person, included himself when he wrote in 1 John 1:8, "If we say that we have no sin, we deceive ourselves, and the truth is not in us."

Someone once said to me that we didn't have any record of the Apostle John ever sinning. "No," I replied, "except that he admitted it himself." His book of 1 John was written only to Christians, with clear directions on how "we" (John and other believers) can confess our sins so that God can forgive them (v. 9).

We spend so much time rationalizing and counseling in relation to what we did wrong, why we did it, what in our childhood made us do it, and on and on, that we lose sight of the fact that God says—confess it *as* sin, and I will remove your guilt. So many of our problems have an ultrasimple solution— confess what we have done or are doing as sin so that God can lift the load of guilt. Dr. Karl Menninger, well-known psychiatrist of the Menninger Clinic in Topeka, Kansas, treats this subject of guilt powerfully in his book *Whatever Became of Sin?* (New York: Hawthorn, 1973)

An interesting thing happens in my prayer seminars and retreats when I read a list of verses about sin from the Bible in preparation for confessing our sins to God in prayer. I watch faces change from a haughty "I don't have any sins to confess" expression, to a blinking in surprise, to horror, which says, "Stop, don't read any more. I can't take it."

I find it is good for me to pray through the lists of sins in God's Word. One of my favorite passages is the first eight verses of 2 Timothy 3. I stop to pray over each specific sin mentioned, asking God to reveal to me where and if that sin is in my life. I'm frequently surprised at what He tells me. But the process always works. I confess it as sin and God lifts the guilt from me. Exchanged!

This is a constant process in my life. God exchanging His presence for my loneliness—His power for my weakness—His healing for my illness—His hope for my despair—His peace for my anxiety—His love for my resentment—His grace for my suffering—His comfort for my sorrow. *Exchanged*—when I ask God.

# 7

# When I Ask Others to Pray for Me—I Change

When others pray for me, I change. So when I sense a need in my life I ask other people to pray. They in turn ask God to take over and do the changing, with amazing results. For the past nine years we have kept a record of all the requests that have gone through my prayer chains and groups for me, personally. Nothing has so overwhelmed me as the reviewing of these thousands of requests and answers. Whenever I read through them, I'm reminded anew that God really does change me when people pray!

### Bear Ye One Another's Burdens
"Bear ye one another's burdens, and so fulfill the law of Christ" (Gal. 6:2).

Does this law of Christ concerning our responsibility to one another include *only* physical needs—food, clothing, shelter? I think not. Many of *my* needs, yes, most of my needs are not temporal. Could Christ have had in mind spiritual, emotional, and mental as well as physical needs and burdens? How I used to appreciate the casseroles that were brought in for my family when I had had surgery, or a new baby, or when I was ill! But was that the *only* kind of support I needed? Was there more?

In 1968 while experimenting in prayer on the theme "What Happens When Women Pray," we felt it was an indication of spiritual maturity when the women started to pray for things that could not be seen with their eyes or felt with their hands.

217

God gave us a new dimension in our praying when we learned that there are other needs and burdens that don't have a fever, stitches, or a cast.

There are burdens that can be borne *only* in prayer.

The deepest need I ever had while in our pastorate was not physical. Nothing temporal was lacking, but there was a desperate need in my life. At the time, the grief was so deep that I did not think I could stand before the audience to speak at an annual Christmas luncheon in one of our churches. I had shared this burden with the women of my neighborhood Bible study, and they, sensing how difficult it was going to be for me, bought tickets for the luncheon. Then they came early enough to take a place closest to the speaker's table, and sat there upholding me in prayer every minute I was speaking.

The results were dramatic. I no longer felt alone and unable to cope, because I was completely undergirded and surrounded by their love and concern. I changed because the God to whom they were praying reached down and gave me the strength, courage, and even the joy and enthusiasm I needed to share with that luncheon audience. Yes, I *changed* when they prayed for me.

At a Sunday School convention luncheon last fall I had the same experience. Three of my advisory board members, sensing my special personal need that day, bought tickets and came to the luncheon. As I passed by them walking up to the speaker's table, I recognized immediately their "we're here praying for you" smiles. What a difference it made to be able to look down into their beaming faces—knowing they cared enough to spend money and time to come and help bear my burden. But the greatest part was what God did for me when they prayed. He came to that room and *changed* me with His power and strength.

Just sensing that other people are caring and praying for me is great. But God does what they never could do for me. He only has the power to meet my spiritual, emotional, and mental needs. He really *changes* me when others pray.

### Admitting Our Burdens
Some of our needs are obvious, especially physical ones; but many of our heaviest burdens are completely hidden to those

who would pray for us—unless we share them. How can we fulfill the law of Christ in all its potential if we refuse to admit our burdens to one another?

In order to benefit to the fullest from the prayers of others, we must *admit* our needs to them. In our prayer closets it is often difficult to confess our needs to God, but we find it almost impossible to admit a weakness or need to fellow Christians. However, this is a must if we expect to experience all the prayer support they are willing to give us.

When we first started our experimental praying in 1968, we all had a lesson to learn about praying for one another. One of our committee members had been taught to keep to herself her own needs and the needs or problems in her family, an attitude she found almost impossible to change. She was a terrific pray-er, but it stopped there. She could not admit that *she* had a need.

One day she had to leave our national committee meeting early because of a severe migraine headache. She knew that medication and rest would take several days to alleviate the problem. And she was having a baby shower at her house that night! As the time for the shower drew near, she found herself completely incapacitated. In desperation she finally decided to do what she never had done in her life: "Oh, God," she prayed, "if You want somebody to pray for me, just have them call on the phone. I won't call anyone, but if this is what You want, tell them to call me."

Almost immediately three women called her, one after another. "Hi. Just wondering if there is anything I could do for you tonight," each one said. Stunned, she broke the inhibitions that had been binding her and not once but three times said: "Please pray for me. I don't feel well. I need you to pray for me."

Admitting she had a need was hard, but God honored her honesty and humility. By the time the guests arrived, there wasn't a sign of her migraine headache or nausea. Changed!

Leaders sometimes find it especially hard to admit a need or a burden to other people. Often presidents, pastors (even pastors' wives), chairmen, and teachers feel they are to bear the burdens of other people they lead, but they find it difficult to ask those people to pray for them. Are they afraid of admitting weakness to those they lead? Are they fearful the people will think less of them as their leaders if they admit a need? I think just the opposite is true. The greatest leaders surround themselves with the strongest staffs, admitting their need to be supported by them. No man is an island unto himself. Some leaders bear so many burdens unnecessarily—just because they can't admit they have a need.

Yesterday morning my phone rang as I was getting ready to speak to 1,300 people at an all-day prayer seminar. It was the president of the national organization which had invited me. She was responsible for the day's activities and was to lead all the sessions. "Evelyn, I didn't sleep well all night. And this morning I have a terrible migraine headache. I can't even eat breakfast. Would you pray for me?"

As I went to prayer I wondered what would happen to all those people and all those hours of teaching without her leadership. I prayed fervently that God would undertake and have His perfect will in her body.

When I arrived in the convention room, I inquired, "How are you feeling? How's the headache?"

"Oh," she answered a little wide-eyed, "it lifted. It's all gone!" Changed! It was because she admitted she had a need that I knew I should pray for her. And it was because she admitted her need that God was able to answer my prayer.

Just last week it was only because I let a few tears fall and admitted I had a need that my secretary put her arms around me and prayed for me. And then I had the privilege of feeling God lift the burden that seemed so heavy—because she prayed. "O what needless pain we bear!" No human being can carry the burdens of others without having someone else bear his.

As president of our United Prayer Ministries, it is important that I admit my needs to my advisory board so that they can pray for me. Our prayer chairman calls every day for requests for my personal needs, problems, and burdens, then passes them through our prayer chains. In 1975 and 1976 the women on those prayer chains prayed for 1,119 requests—over half of them for me. I could never carry on the heavy schedule I have without all that prayer. When they pray for me I *change*—change into their guided, encouraged, empowered, healed leader—because they pray! I know—because we have all the answers to their prayers dated and recorded.

One of the thrilling things about our over 1,000-member Metro Prayer Chain in the Twin Cities area is that many Christian leaders request prayer. Admitting that they or their organization has a need activates over a thousand pray-ers—and activates God!

Even Paul, most likely the greatest Christian who ever lived, asked for prayer. In Ephesians 6:18-19 Paul asks the Christians to pray for him that utterance might be given to him, that he would be able to open his mouth boldly "to make known the mystery of the Gospel." And again in Colossians 4:3 he writes, "Praying also for us, that God would open unto us a door of utterance, to speak the mystery of Christ." In the conclusion to his first letter to the Thessalonians, his abrupt request is, "Brethren, pray for us" (5:25). And he begs the Christians in Rome to strive together with him in prayer for his deliverance from the unbelievers in Judea, that his service might be accepted by the saints in Jerusalem, that he might come to them with joy by the will of God and might with them be refreshed (Rom. 15:31-32). Paul was not ashamed to *admit* his numerous needs or to ask the Christians to pray *for* him.

Did Paul really expect to find himself and circumstances around him *changed* because people prayed for him? Why else would he have asked them to pray?

### Dependence

Perhaps one of the reasons we find admitting our needs to other people so difficult is that by doing so we are admitting we are dependent—dependent upon God and upon other people. We are a generation of "I can do it myself, God" Christians.

Whether we want to admit it or not, we are dependent on other pray-ers. In Matthew 9:38 Jesus said, "Pray ye, therefore, the Lord of the harvest, that He will send forth laborers into His harvest." Am I a laborer because someone, some time, some place, obeyed Jesus' command and prayed that God would send forth a laborer to the field in which I'm working? This is a humbling thought, and removes all the ego and pride about *my* ministry, *my* calling. Because somebody prayed, did I CHANGE into God's laborer?

If Paul was dependent on his friends to pray for utterance to be given to him, how much of *my* having utterance in my ministry is because somebody, or many people prayed for me? How dependent am I on other people's prayers for enabling me to teach my prayer seminars? In Ephesians 6:18-19 Paul asked prayer for utterance for himself and all saints—me! How much did I CHANGE because of them?

Frequently we don't know we have been depending on the prayers of others until we see the results. When Peter was in prison (Acts 12:5-19), he may not have been aware that "prayer was made without ceasing of the church unto God for him" (v. 5). Perhaps not until the chains fell off his hands, and he walked out of prison as the iron gate opened did he realize that God must be answering prayer. Or was it when the believers finally opened the door of the house and he saw them "praying without ceasing," that he realized why he was freed?

Scripture tells us in 1 Timothy 2:2 that we are to pray "for kings and for all that are in authority." So, whether or not they know it, leaders are dependent upon the prayers of those who obey this command. When God reaches down and *changes* kings and those in authority and the circumstances surrounding them even without their knowledge, they are dependent upon the pray-ers.

Or when we experience relief from some physical problem before it runs its natural course, it may well be that our fellow Christians are obeying the admonition in James to "pray one for another that ye may be healed" (5:16). When we are miraculously *changed* physically, how dependent were we on God's faithful pray-ers?

How much do I change because other people pray for me? Only eternity will tell. Only God knows who activates the process of change that takes place in me.

### Spiritual Warfare

Since the Father and the Son are one, I'm constantly amazed that God had need of Jesus' prayers on behalf of others. Jesus must have known that this is the process God uses, yes, expects, when others have needs, for in His high-priestly prayer He prayed for His followers and for us.

And in that prayer Jesus prayed that the Father would keep

them and us "from the evil one" (John 17:15). He didn't pray that God would remove us from the evil one's domain, Planet Earth; just that God would deliver us from him. Because Christ is our Example in all things, we too should pray this prayer for other believers.

Jesus also practiced this kind of prayer specifically when Satan wanted to sift Peter. He said, "But I have prayed for thee, that thy faith fail not" (Luke 22:32). But in spite of Jesus' prayer for him, cocky Peter—cocksure he wouldn't fall into the enemy's trap before the cock would crow—denied his Lord. Jesus knew the importance of praying for those who are tempted by Satan.

When Dr. Kurt Koch was in our Twin Cities a while ago to lead seminars in opposition to the occult explosion in America, he begged us to pray for him. He had just cancelled a series of seminars in New York and had to be flown back to Germany because of a severe physical problem that he attributed to the lack of prayer on the part of Christians in America as he spoke on this perilous subject. "Americans don't know how to pray in this battle," he told us. He pled with us to follow faithfully, fervently, Christ's example in His high-priestly prayer. Dr. Koch had changed—for the worse—because of lack of prayer.

In Ephesians 6:18-19 Paul's exhortation to pray always for all saints and for himself is part of the armor that Christians are to use in the battle against spiritual wickedness—the realm of Satan. In 1972 I bravely tackled a Bible study subject of "Ephesians in the Light of the Spirit World" (fools rush in where angels fear to tread), and experienced unusual resistance from the enemy. But in the margin of my Bible next to Ephesians 6:18 I wrote: "2/29/72. Great power first Bible study. Host of people praying. I could *feel* power. Never felt more when speaking." I had *changed* from an intimidated and harassed woman trying to prepare a Bible study that was a threat to Satan—*changed* into an empowered teacher. Because they prayed!

### Tell Me Your Secret

Many times after teaching my whole seminar on prayer in one day (five and one-half to six hours of lecturing), a pastor or priest will come to me and say, "Tell me your secret. How can you 'speak to convince' so many hours in a row? When I finish speaking for one or two hours on a Sunday morning, I'm exhausted. I'm completely overcome with fatigue. What's your secret?"

"I do have a secret," I tell them honestly. "It's my prayer support. It is all the women who so faithfully pray for me."

Yes, I do have a secret. On January 4 of this year after writing every spare minute during the holidays and then teaching a large first-of-the-year prayer seminar the night before, I awoke too exhausted to get out of bed. This was a rare occurrence in my life for I'm an early riser; but, as Chris put a towel over my eyes, I thanked God silently that he was going to a breakfast meeting that morning. Then, suddenly, surging through my body was strength, eagerness to get going on the day the Lord had given me. I was *changed*—there was a complete transformation. What had happened? The prayer chain members one by one were arising and having their quiet times with the Lord—and praying for me!

Not long ago I became aware that at exactly 6 o'clock every morning I felt a surge of God's power. Questioning the recurrence at the same time every morning, I casually mentioned it to one of the women who had been sending through the prayer requests for one of my prayer chains. I could almost see her blushing in modest humility over the phone as she stammered, "That's the time I pray for you every morning." I could feel the change come over me—as she prayed!

One day last fall this prayer request went through the chain for me: "Evelyn in desperate need of strength." Then the record of the answer made a couple of days later read, "Over 3,000 people attended her workshops. Ev stood and talked 14 hours one evening and next day. Experienced Isaiah 40:31. 'Those who wait upon the Lord shall renew their strength.' "

Last November 23 I asked the prayer chains to pray because I was already tired and facing an all-day seminar. I just reread the astounding answer recorded in our files, "Ev gained momentum as the day progressed." *Changed*? Yes!

When others pray for me, God, the omnipotent God of heaven and earth, reaches down and changes me—because they pray. Because they are willing to fulfill the law of Christ by bearing my burdens.

## For One Another

But the greatest joy in prayer is not just being prayed for, but bearing *one another's* burdens. Sprinkled all through our advisory board and other prayer chains are the personal and family needs of our members. What a privilege to pray for one daughter in distress, and then a year later to be praying for her as she leads a Bible study at Urbana—changed! And after praying for a member's arthritis surgery, to be told of the dramatic, almost painless success of the operation, or to pray for a Christian college professor's son from another state who was on alcohol and marijuana, and then to receive a thrilling letter that there is victory—changed! There was the mother with a stroke, the woman with the migraine headaches, the opening of a new Christian bookstore, and the responsibilities of the "Here's Life" city-wide prayer chairman—circumstances and people—all changed according to God's will for them because we prayed!

Yes, it's hard to admit we need to be changed and it's very hard to admit to other Christians that we need them to pray so that God will change us. Yes, it is a humbling process, but it's so rewarding. When others pray for me—I change!

# 8

# *When I Pray for Others—I Change*

The 14 months of silence from June 1968, didn't mean I gave up my intercessory prayer life learned so diligently during the previous six months. In fact, the paradox of this period was that it was at the peak of our telephone prayer chain ministry. But when I started praying, "Lord, change me," an unexpected change took place in my intercessory prayer life. As I prayed for Jan, I was praying for God's will, not mine, for her. Instead of superimposing my will upon her, I found myself praying for God to change her the way *He* wanted her to be changed. In the struggle of that long quiet period I learned a profound secret: *release*.

### Released
Releasing, I was to discover, was giving back to God something He had given me. Yes, Jan was a gift from Him. "Lo, children are an heritage of the Lord," we are told in Psalm 127:3. Though Chris and I had given her to the Lord before she was born (as we have all our children), this situation was different. It meant literal releasing—Jan was of legal age. I almost felt like Hannah as she gave her weaned child, Samuel, to the Lord. It was similar to what I experienced when the doctors told us that our Judy could not live. As I prayed for her that night, it wasn't until I *released* her to God for *His* will to be done that the battle was over. Not the grief—but the battle was over. I changed that night. I had released her to God!

226

Even the releasing of our children to God's care every day as they left for kindergarten and continued on through high school taught me so much about this process. Releasing them to God's protection and guidance when I couldn't accompany them to school, when my empty hand ached to hold theirs in this big, frightening world, was preparing me for the actual releasing that would take place in the future.

Releasing Jan to God intensified my prayers for her. So often what I do for a child is too little, too late. But God always does everything in the right way, at the right time. What I want for a child may be dictated by selfish motives—the best-paying job, the place of greatest honor, the highest grade, the biggest house—things the world equates with success. But not God. He always wants for them what will teach them the most, and that which will make them the finest gold.

I'll never forget what a mother of several teenagers once said to me. "I'm not sending my kids to a Christian college only to have them go to a foreign mission field, as my brother did, and leave *me* all alone in my old age."

I see this process of releasing take place in our prayer seminars so frequently. The most life-changing session we have is the one where we learn to pray in God's will. At the close we think of the most important thing in the whole world to us, and then give it to God in prayer. This is the point at which we release to God our right to that person or thing which is more important than anything else to us at the time.

While conducting a prayer seminar in a friend's church in California, I watched an astounding change take place in her pastor. His wife is a beautiful, talented, and charming hostess—but she is gravely ill with cancer. Throughout their pastorate, she has been his supportive co-worker. When I arrived for that seminar, I was introduced to the most heartbroken pastor I ever have seen. But a miracle happened while we were praying in our small groups after studying how to pray in God's will. That pastor released his wife to God for *His* will for her—not his own. As he came to the pulpit to close the session in prayer, I couldn't believe my eyes. "Is that man radiating?" I whispered to my friend. His face seemed literally to glow as he smiled at his congregation and told them what had happened. "He's radiating!" she whispered back. The wife hadn't changed—but the one who released her had!

Talking with a woman at a seminar yesterday, I listened as she told me that her husband who had had surgery several times had been told by his doctors that he could not get well. It was only a matter of time. She told me of her days and weeks of struggle and rebellion against God and of her refusal to give him up. "But," she said, "the miracle came when I released him to God. *I* was the one who changed. The battle was over." Then she added, "Oh, by the way, he's the gentleman you were just talking to over there. He's completely cured." But his recovery wasn't the only miracle. The miracle that happened when she released him to God was just as life-changing.

Perhaps the most difficult time to release our "human possessions" to God is when He is disciplining them. How we love to protect our children, our spouses, and our loved ones from God's discipline. At a recent retreat I was counseling a woman whose pastor husband had been having an affair with another woman. Having been discovered, he was in deep depression. She told me that she was asking God not to deal with him any more because she was afraid he wouldn't be able to take it. She was trying to protect him from God! I told her that the only hope for her husband was for her to *release* him to God, the only One who could convict him of the *sin* of his actions. Then her husband could assume his responsibility before God and confess his sin. But she should not have tried to control her husband's life—anymore than *we* can control other people. "Stop trying to play God," I told her.

The first time Jan faced final exams at college after I released her to God in 1968, I remember how different were my prayers for her: "God, don't necessarily give her all A's, but teach her everything she needs to know this first year of college." I remember Jan jokingly (but deep down inside, seriously) telling her friend not to have her mother pray for her. "She'll pray you right out of all A's." Well, I really wasn't the one who caused the one "B" that first semester, but in a way I felt responsible, for I *had* prayed that God would teach her *everything* He knew she needed to know. And He obviously knew (as I was to learn later) that there are more important things than all A's earned immediately upon entering college. Of course, all A's were as exciting to us as to her, but I had submitted to His will. I had released her for Him—not me—to teach her.

A missionary used half a box of Kleenex as she tearfully told me her story at a retreat. God had called her and her husband back to the United States and had given them a pastorate. She told me between her sobs that both she and her husband were absolutely positive that it was God's will that they were here. "But," she sobbed, "people won't release us. 'Once a missionary, always a missionary,' they say. It's the people *who pray for us* who won't give us to God for *His* will in our lives. They want to tell God where we should be serving Him."

How we love to play God in other people's lives—especially in those for whom we are diligently praying. But God wants *us* to change—to release them to Him for His will. Jesus taught us to pray for them that way in the Lord's Prayer in Matthew 6:9-10 when He said, "After this manner . . . pray ye . . . *Thy* will be done in earth, as it is in heaven."

When I was president of our faculty wives' association, we planned a "Lord, Change Me" retreat. While announcing it, I explained to the college and seminary faculty and staff husbands that we were going to draw apart at a retreat center and let God tell us from His Word what He wanted changed in us. "I don't want my wife changed. I like her the way she is," quipped one professor.

I held my silence, but how I wanted to say to him, "But does *God* like her the way she is?" There's a difference!

I praise and thank God for a husband who has released me to God for *His* will in my life. How beautiful our marriage relationship is, since Chris is interested not in what *he* wants for me, selfishly and personally, but in what *God* wants for me. Yes, it involves tremendous personal sacrifice to release a loved one to God, but the beauty of that submissive, changed life is great to behold.

### Releasing Our Spiritual Children

We often have a tendency too to be over possessive of our "spiritual children." I had been telling my telephone prayer chain chairman about talking long distance to a woman who had led many people to the Lord and was now physically and emotionally exhausted from trying to keep them all afloat. As she was discipling, mothering, and coaching, she found herself collapsing under the strain.

"Release them to God," I had advised her, "and let Him give them back to you one at a time for only those things He wants you to do for them."

The next day my prayer chairman called and said, "I took personally the advice you gave the other person over the phone. I suddenly realized that I was spoon-feeding my neighbors, feeling totally responsible for all of them all of the time. And I too am under a doctor's care, not able to take the strain any longer, so I just *released* these neighbors to God. I won't stop being concerned. I won't stop discipling and nurturing them; I'll only stop playing God."

Babies never learn to walk if adults refuse to let go of their hands. New Christians never learn to walk if we insist on carrying them. Although discipling is a necessary part of helping those whom we have introduced to Christ, there comes a time when we must *release* them to fly by themselves with God.

When we release our right to our own will for our "human possessions," we change—becoming submissive to God's will rather than demanding our will for them. But there is an added bonus in this process I had not counted on, and certainly had not sought. While God was changing me, He was also teaching me the effectiveness of *His* changing others for whom I was only praying, not "preaching at."

I saw myself in a new role—changed! On intercessor's knees, I found it much more effective to talk to God about things in their lives of which I didn't approve and letting *Him* handle them. Gradually I learned that there is more power in praying for people than in preaching at people, especially when I have released them for God to answer my prayers in any way He desires.

### Changed—While I Prayed

One of the greatest privileges for mortals on this planet is to be able to come boldly to the throne of grace (Heb. 4:16). When I exercise this privilege, I change. I see the worth God has placed upon me when He allows, yes, invites me to come into His presence in prayer. I, a mere mortal, have the overwhelming joy of bringing those for whom I'm concerned right to the throne of the God of the universe. I have the attention of the omniscient, omnipotent, omnipresent God—and this changes me!

The reason we are continuing our 24-hour "Here's Life" prayer chains in our churches now that our "I Found It" saturation is over is that many pray-ers have told us they don't want to give up the privilege of intercession. The joy they experienced on their 24-hour prayer chains, even when their hour to pray was scheduled in the middle of the night, was tremendous, they told us. The privilege of having access to God in that very special way is something many are not willing to give up.

Also, while I am praying for others, I am fulfilling the admonition of Colossians 3:1-2, "If ye, then, be risen with Christ, seek those things which are above, where Christ sitteth on the right hand of God. Set your affection on things above, not on things on the earth." Keeping my mind in the heavenlies, being transported mentally into the presence of God the Father and Christ His Son, changes me. When Jesus took Peter, James, and John up into a mountain to pray, we read that "as He [Jesus] prayed, the appearance of His countenance was altered" (Luke 9:29, RSV). It was *while He prayed* that Jesus' appearance changed. Matthew tells us that His face "did shine as the sun" (Matt. 17:2). And as I pray, God changes me. While I am directly associating with my holy God, high and lifted up, I become more Christlike, more conformed to His image.

We read in the Book of Acts that two of these same men were brought prisoners before the rulers, elders, scribes, and all the kindred of the high priest. And when they saw Peter and John, "they took note of them that these men had been with Jesus" (Acts 4:13, NIV). We teach our children they will be like the people with whom they associate. Is there really something different about us when we have been with Jesus? Yes, we are changed—even *our enemies* can tell the difference.

### Somebody Needs Me

Inherent in each human being is the need to be needed. It gives us a sense of self-worth, a zest for life, and a reason for living.

In our prayer seminars we discover the worth of ourselves as we practice intercessory prayer. As the urgent and often heartbreaking prayer requests are handed in, pray-ers find— many for the first time—that *someone* really does need them, and their prayers.

Corrie ten Boom told me that when she was five years old and had just received Christ as her Saviour, her mother said to her, "Corrie, now you are an intercessor." And she found that the people living around her home needed her prayers. What a great way for a little child to find her self-worth.

Trying to motivate and instill a sense of self-worth in teenagers at a prayer seminar proved to be a difficult experience. These were 200 members of a confirmation class who, along with a church full of adults, were learning to pray. But their presence was not voluntary, and the paper wads, bubble gum, and paper airplanes displayed on the first night showed me what they thought of themselves as pray-ers.

At the second session one of them came to me and said she had a prayer request. "My ten-year-old sister cannot hear," she said. Fearing I'd never be able to motivate them if God chose to answer some way other than healing her sister, I decided on a plan. I challenged those 200 teenagers by giving *them* the request. I told them it was *their* responsibility, *theirs* to do whatever they chose with it. I held my breath all that next week waiting for the outcome. At the next session my fears proved to be in vain. I found myself surrounded by a whole gang of the girl's teenage friends as she excitedly announced, "Guess what happened to my sister?" I waited with bated breath. "She can now hear without her hearing aid!" Those 200 teenagers had found the worth of themselves to someone in need.

After the last session of that prayer seminar, the pastor's wife came to me with tears in her eyes. "Do you remember the boy who was shooting paper airplanes and paper wads that first night? (How could I forget him?) Do you know what he just prayed in our little group? He prayed, 'Dear God, please teach my dad what You've just taught me!' "

## God Wants Me

Some of the greatest untapped potentials in our churches are our infirm members. Many of them were great spiritual giants while their bodies were still strong, but now that disease or old age has forced them to become inactive for God as they are confined to their rocking chairs, wheelchairs, or beds, their spirits often become as shriveled as their bodies. But I've discovered something exciting in our prayer seminars. Relatives and friends frequently bring these people to a seminar, and occasionally they even come by bus from nursing homes. I challenge these infirm Christians that God *still* wants them, and I tell them that they can once again exercise as much and perhaps more spiritual power than they did before. I love to watch these bypassed citizens of God's kingdom unfold like a rose as they rediscover that God wants them.

While experimenting in prayer back in 1968-1969, we assigned these people as prayer support for our neighborhood Bible studies. What a release of God's power and what changed results we saw in the Bible studies as the teachers and hostesses kept their "pray-er" up to date on all the needs and problems of the class!

One of our outstanding Primary Department teachers became physically unable to teach her class. Home-baked cookies and deep personal concern for every pupil had made her a teacher who was deeply loved. But after having to relinquish her class, she launched a new project from her hospital bed and home confinement—she spent the Sunday School hour praying by name for each pupil in her department and for the teachers and the superintendent. Almost immediately the other teachers began to report that amazing changes were taking place in that department. Discipline problems went almost to zero. Did God *want* her more in that capacity than teaching her class of primary boys and girls? Evidently. Yes, God had allowed her to be changed from an active to an inactive person, but instead of folding up in her confinement, she was changed into a powerful intercessor.

While I was conducting a prayer seminar in a large southern city, a psychiatrist told me, "You know, my profession isn't known for its cures, but I am discovering something interesting. I've been a Christian for only two years, but I've started to pray for my patients—deep, fervent prayer. And," she continued excitedly, "I'm finding that those for whom I pray," she took a deep breath before finishing, "actually get well." And *she* was a changed psychiatrist, overawed that God was actually doing something for her patients when she prayed for them.

When we first started experimenting in prayer in January 1968, the thing that changed the original "eight gripers" into motivated and faithful pray-ers was the discovery that God actually wanted them. And I have found this to be true through the years as I have taught thousands to pray. Watching people change from skeptical doubters to exuberant pray-ers, when they discover God is using *them*, is a constant thrill to me. A pastor's wife told me this morning that sometimes she prays for a need that only she knows about and for which no one else is praying, then *knows* it is *her* prayer that God is answering. The startling discovery that God is using *us* does change our sense of self-worth. We are changed—needed—people. And that makes us joyful people!

### Sweet and Bitter Water

When I become an intercessor, praying *for* other people, I find the truth of James 3:11-12 becoming evident in my life. I find it is impossible for two attitudes to be in me at the same time. "Doth a fountain send forth at the same place sweet water and bitter? Can the fig tree, my brethren, bear olive berries? either a vine, figs? So can no fountain yield both salt water and fresh."

When I pray for others, it takes my mind off my trivial or perhaps very real complaints. There is always someone worse off than I, and when I go into deep intercessory prayer for that person I change from a self-centered complainer into a person with genuine concern and love for that one for whom I pray. Somehow I can't concentrate on myself and pray out of love for others at the same time.

I find too that it is impossible to pray for and gossip about a person at the same time. One of the great results of a telephone prayer chain is that the pray-ers stop gossiping about other people's troubles when they start praying about them. Also, "roast pastor" is no longer a Sunday dinner main dish when we really start praying for him.

And I can't thank God for all the good things about a person and be filled with accusations at the same time. Somehow those two diametrically opposed attitudes can't be expressed simultaneously. This is one of the subtle results of thanking God for all our acquaintances—especially our enemies. During the process, *we* change.

I also find it impossible to pray for and be angry with a person at the same time. Could Christ have had something more in mind than the persons for whom He commanded us to pray, when He said in Matthew 5:44, "Pray for them which despitefully use you"? Could one of the results of praying for those who despitefully use us be that we, the pray-ers, are changed *as* we pray for them? But in order to effect this change, our prayers must be genuine. We cannot utter a few sweet words in prayer while the bitterness remains deep down inside. No, real prayer is the overflow of the heart.

The first step to take to insure the sweetness within is to forgive the person who has despitefully used us. It is at this point that we change on the inside. We are changed *when* we forgive others.

A retired missionary came to me yesterday and told me that the women in her church were studying *What Happens When Women Pray*. Tears came into her eyes as she said, "The crisis chapter of that book is the one about forgiving others. One thing after another is cleared up between people when they forgive each other. It is making such a difference in our church."

A woman attending a seminar in a Minneapolis suburb wanted me to play "Ann Landers" and advise her on how to tell her mother-in-law off. I asked her to wait until the next week when we would study how to handle such situations. The following session included the formula for forgiving others—and she prayed through! The next week she came bouncing into the seminar a completely changed person. A sweet spirit had replaced her acute agitation; a smile had replaced her troubled countenance. I never met the mother-in-law. Whether she continued to be her evidently rather miserable self or was changed as her daughter-in-law's attitude toward her changed, I will most likely never know. But this I do know—a radical change took place in the one who forgave her.

Two college girls burst into the dean of women's office after I finished teaching their prayer-week session on forgiving others. "I'm free. I'm free!" cried one. "I forgave her, and now I feel free!" Although I didn't have the foggiest idea who had been involved or what the problem was, the dean of women nodded and smiled an understanding smile. Something had been solved on that Christian campus. And the one doing the forgiving had the privilege of being changed. Free!

A very agitated woman from Germany came to Hansi ("the girl who loved the swastika"), telling her she could not stand her mother. They got along all right as long as the Atlantic Ocean was between them, but she had just received word that her mother was coming to America!

"Why don't you come to the prayer seminar at my church tomorrow night?" Hansi suggested. She came—and we just happened to be having the lesson on forgiving others. As the rows of people turned to pray together, Hansi found herself facing this angry woman. After having chosen her mother as the one person to forgive during prayertime, she looked up at Hansi and said, "Oh, now my mother can come from Germany!" Who changed? The mother? No, *when* she forgave her mother, *she* changed!

God wisely gave that little formula in 2 Corinthians 2:5-11 to those who have been grieved. We somehow feel that the person who grieved us is the one who needs to change, but God wisely places the responsibility on us when we have been despitefully used. There isn't anything in that formula that tells the person who has caused the grief what to do, but only what we, the grieved ones, must do. God knew all along that when we forgive someone and pray for him out of real love, we change.

Yes, when I pray for others, I change! *My* priorities, *my* rights, *my* attitudes, all change *as* I pray for other people.

# SECTION III—MAKE SURE IT IS GOD DOING THE CHANGING

# 9

# Source No. 1,
# Sensual

Now that we've looked into the methods God uses to change us, the haunting question arises: How can I be absolutely sure it is God who is changing me? How can I know that my lifestyle, the sum total of all my wisdom put into action, is really from Him?

God showed me the fact that the Book of James mentions four sources of wisdom from which I can obtain knowledge that will change me. And these four are constantly vying for my lifestyle; and I discovered that only one of them is God. Only one of the four is a trustworthy source of direction for the changes in my life. The other three are mentioned in James 3:15: "This wisdom descendeth not from above, but is *earthly* [from other people], *sensual* [from within our sensual selves], *demoniacal* [from demons]" (SCO).

Is there any way, then, that I can test the source of wisdom that is producing my lifestyle? James says the proof is in *what it produces*: "The wisdom that is from above [from the Lord] is first pure, then peaceable, gentle and easy to be entreated, full of mercy and good fruits, without partiality, and without hypocrisy" (3:17). This is in contrast to what the other three sources produce: "But if ye have bitter envying and strife in your hearts, glory not, and lie not against the truth. This wisdom descendeth not from above, but is earthly, sensual, demoniacal. For where envying and strife are, there is confusion and every evil work" (3:14-16, SCO).

Sometimes it is difficult to discern which source of wisdom has produced a change in me, because it is possible for the sources other than God to produce temporary satisfaction with the good life, but the end result in me will always be the opposite of what God wants to produce in me. Superficial happiness may be produced from one of the other sources of wisdom, but there will be an absence of real joy and peace down deep within me.

I discovered this frightening fact while reading devotionally in James 3 one Sunday morning several years ago. Anger over something a relative had said nine years before suddenly welled up within me. I had forgiven and been forgiven at that time, so why this recurrence of these feelings? As I read this portion of Scripture I knew God's answer: that attitude was not from Him! Horrified, I noted the other three sources of wisdom, and then realized that wisdom from God would not produce the anger I was experiencing. It had to be from one of the other sources.

In these final chapters I will discuss these four possible sources of wisdom which can produce changes that collectively result in my lifestyle.

One of the sources from which I can receive wisdom is my own sensual self—the part of me that is controlled by my senses. It is the natural man that Paul struggled with in his letter to the Romans, chapter 7. "For I know that in me (that is, in my flesh) dwelleth no good thing" (v. 18). "So then with the mind I myself serve the law of God; but with the flesh the law of sin" (v. 25b).

Christ, on one occasion when "He had called all the people to Him," painted a word picture of the human heart that was far from complimentary: "For from within, out of the heart of men, proceed evil thoughts, adulteries, fornications, murders, thefts, covetousness, wickedness, deceit, lasciviousness, an evil eye, blasphemy, pride, foolishness: All these evil things come from within, and defile the man" (Mark 7:21-23). James wrote about a source of sin that was within us: "But every man is tempted, when he is drawn away of his own lust, and enticed" (1:14). And Jeremiah lamented, "The heart is deceitful above all things, and desperately wicked: who can know it?" (17:9)

## Deceiving Myself

After reading what the Bible says about my sensual self, I'm appalled that I can deceive myself into thinking I know what direction my changing should take. A profound proverb says, "The way of a fool is right in his own eyes" (Prov. 12:15). And in Romans, Paul describes those who "when they knew God . . . became vain in their imaginations, and their foolish heart was darkened. Professing themselves to be wise, they became fools" (1:21-22). Then, because "they did not like to retain God in their knowledge, God gave them over to a reprobate mind, to do those things which are not convenient; Being filled with all unrighteousness, fornication, wickedness, covetousness, maliciousness; full of envy, murder, debate, deceit, malignity; whisperers, backbiters, haters of God, despiteful, proud, boasters, inventors of evil things, disobedient to parents, without understanding, covenant-breakers, without natural affection, implacable, unmerciful" (1:28-31). Are all these things really the end results of rationalizing and following my own feelings and senses? The possibility of any of these consequences being a part of my life sends me scurrying to God's Word for His direction on how to change.

What can I do about this sensuous self? God has some good advice for me. In Ephesians I read that henceforth (from now on, since I am in Christ Jesus), I am not to walk as other Gentiles walk, *in the vanity of their mind.* . . . But I am to "put off concerning the former [manner of life] the old man, which is corrupt according to the deceitful lusts; and be *renewed in the spirit of* [my] *mind*" (4:17ff). God wants to change me, wants to give me wisdom from Him that will produce the opposite of these sins of the flesh.

So in prayer I cry to God with the psalmist, "Search me, O God, and know my heart; try me, and know my thoughts; and see if there be any wicked way in me, and lead me in the way everlasting" (Ps. 139:23-24). "Don't let me be changed by what *I* think or feel. Give me the wisdom for changing that is from You."

## I Think

What I think really isn't very impressive according to God's Word. There is only one Truth, and that is God Himself. And the only absolute truth on which we can depend for the right kind of changes in our lives is found only in God's Word (John 17:17).

We have a rule about this at our house. Last summer I overheard two of our children discussing it: "Mother always said truth is truth. It doesn't matter if you believe it or not. And not believing it has nothing to do with the fact that it is truth, and it will not change from being truth just because we choose not to believe it."

Yes, whether or not I agree with something has nothing to do with whether or not it is true. My "I think" about a subject neither negates it nor insures its being true.

But we are so prone to believe our "I thinks" are very important. Many times what is billed as a Bible study turns out to be an exchange of our "I thinks." We read the Scripture portion and, using it as a springboard, dive immediately into the inner pool of our "I thinks" and begin a discussion of whatever comes to our minds. When we are finished telling what we think about the subject, other class members usually retain what they think, and I keep what I think. It may have been a great discussion, but no one acquired any new truth.

A rule for Bible study that assures us of getting wisdom from the only worthy Source, God Himself, is that we don't discuss anything that is not answered in the portion of Scripture being studied on a given day. The teacher, and hopefully the pupils, will have studied the actual meaning of the text, and the answers no longer will be the participants' "I think" but God's Word. Then we know that the changes we make in our lives based on that lesson are not from the "I thinks" of people but from God Himself.

I was conducting a retreat in an eastern state, and on Saturday morning we were to practice reading God's Word individually until He pointed out something in our lives that needed changing. The hearts of those women had really been prepared during their cabin devotions the night before. Someone had listed some excellent questions on "How do you react when . . . ?" The object was to discover if one's reactions were Christlike or not. But something went wrong. I sat in the corner quietly listening to their discussions. They became more and more heated as the women exchanged their

"I thinks"—disagreeing, ignoring, and vying for the floor. The next morning I asked how many could honestly say they learned something during the devotions the night before, and not one single hand was raised. But in another way they had learned a tremendous lesson, and were eager to listen to God that morning.

A professor at one of our large seminaries told me that the school was changing its teaching policy because the students had requested less group-interaction sessions and more teaching sessions. These students felt that there was far too much to learn to warrant so much time being spent in sharing their "I thinks."

However, this does not mean that we cannot learn from each other. Sharing can be a profitable source of wisdom—if the wisdom shared is from a worthy source. If the source has been what God taught that person, then the sharing will be profitable indeed. If the teacher says, "I think," the pupil well may respond, "So what?" And the same holds true when the teacher verbalizes his or her own feelings. They are not grounds for expecting or demanding change in the pupil. But when the teacher's source of wisdom has come from God or those who also learned from God, then the "I think" becomes positive wisdom.

This too is why we do not approach Bible reading or study with our minds full of our own preconceived ideas.  .

Asking God to remove preconceived ideas *before* writing would have helped the author of a widespread women's study to interpret and teach Genesis 1:26 and 28 correctly. Approaching the Scriptures with the preconceived idea that God gave the male the roles of dominion and procreation had blinded the author's eyes to the pronouns being plural, not singular ("them," and not "him"). The accurate reading gives male and female equal dominion and procreation roles and thus negates the basis of the thesis of the study. And looking up the meaning of the words *Adam* and *man* in this portion in a good Bible word study would have revealed that both words are plural—also disproving the preconceived thesis.

Sometimes our "I thinks" are produced by inadequate Bible study. A young male student assailed me after I had led a prayer seminar in his college prayer week. After teaching them, I had asked the student body to stand and make small groups for prayer. "You know very well," he exploded at me, "that nowhere in the Bible does it tell women to tell men to do anything."

"Oh," I said in surprise, "except Jesus and the angels on Resurrection morning both told the women to go and tell the men—not only that Jesus was not dead—but to go to Galilee where He said they would see Him too."

His preconceived "I think" had robbed him of seeing the truth about how the most important fact in the history of mankind—He is risen!—was revealed and then relayed to Christ's male followers.

\* \* \*

A lawyer in a class I was teaching on the Book of Mark came to me after class and objected, "Why are you teaching all this about Satan and demons? You know very well there's no such thing."

In our verse-by-verse study, I was not choosing topics but simply teaching whatever subject was covered in the text, and the first few lessons had all included some encounter with these beings.

I replied, "You are a very intelligent man. I want you to do something for me. Take at least the Book of Mark, and all four Gospels if you have time, and write down as if you were preparing a legal case every time Satan or demons are mentioned, who said what, how each reacted, who was victorious, etc. When you have finished, tell me your decision about the reality of these things and I promise to abide by your decision as to whether or not I will teach about them."

By the next Friday a note had arrived in my mail box: "Dear Mrs. Chris: Please forgive me. I only thought I knew what the Bible said about that subject. I hadn't really read it."

\* \* \*

Sometimes we take a perfectly good word from the Bible (such as *chastisement, suffering, submission, healing, God's justice*), dive immediately into our pool of "I thinks" and weave them subtly and securely around that word, leaving the impression that all of our "I thinks" about the word actually were included in the scriptural meaning of the word.

Also it is important to base a theological premise on *all* the Scriptures dealing with the subject and not from our ideas from just one Scripture portion. It is easy to believe that prayer should be made only in a closet, only holding up holy hands, only kneeling down or only lying in bed when we take what that particular Scripture has to say about prayer. But, in order to get a true, complete picture of scriptural prayer, all Scripture on that subject must be viewed collectively.

So also it is easy to get a lopsided view of women staying home and being keepers at home, whereas many of Paul's co-workers were women. Priscilla traveled with Paul (Acts 18:18), taught Apollos, and the four Gospels abound with women traveling with Jesus. And these same women made up a large part of the 120 waiting and praying together with the men after the ascension of Christ back to heaven (Acts 1:14). Then we next see them still with the apostles and other men at Pentecost with the Holy Spirit falling on *all* who were in that prayer group, and *all* of them speaking to the visitors in Jerusalem from many different countries—in their native tongues. Peter explained this phenomenon not as *being* drunkenness, as was supposed, but as the fulfilling of Joel's prophecy: "But this is that which was spoken by the prophet Joel; 'And it shall come to pass in the last days,' saith God, 'I will pour out of My Spirit upon all flesh: and your sons and your *daughters* shall prophesy, and your young men shall see visions, and your old men shall dream dreams: And on My servants and on My *handmaidens* I will pour out in those days of My Spirit; and they shall prophesy'" (Acts 2:16-18).

Many of these verses, you may have noticed, have to do with the role of women within the church. Lest someone suspect that I as a woman am anxious to advance my own "I think," I will assure you that the issues growing out of these passages are the ones that have been coming up week after week in the prayer seminars around the country.

Many women have shared with me how they have allowed someone's "I think" to thwart their usefulness and to render them almost subhuman. Bookstores are filled with women's books, some advocating total submission to men, others suggesting ways a wife may manipulate her husband to "keep him happy and save the marriage"; still others suggest that Christians abandon male-female roles altogether.

Few topics of late have been so popular—or so polarizing. Because so many men and women are being hurt because of a misunderstanding of male-female roles in the home and church, it is especially important for all of us to put aside our "I thinks" and allow God's Word to speak.

Ideas are only as good as their sources. It is possible that the interpretation we are familiar with has been only some speaker's or teacher's "I think." But when we let God speak, having had our minds cleared of our own preconceived ideas, we receive from Him exactly what He wants to teach us—the method He wants to use to change us.

Sometimes we even back up our "I thinks" with Scripture that we feel supports our own ideas. "The heaven, even the heavens, are the Lord's; but the earth hath He given to the children of men" (Ps. 115:16), was used by many to prove that man was confined to this planet in the solar system and that he would never be able to land on the moon or any other planet. But this "I think" idea was shattered on July 20, 1969, at 10:56 P.M. Eastern Daylight Time, when Neil Armstrong uttered the now almost immortal words, "That's one small step for a man; one giant leap for mankind" as he put the first, but not the last, human foot down on the moon. This process of disproving one's "I thinks" and proving the Bible has been going on for centuries.

Galileo, the 17th-century scientist, believed the now-accepted fact that the earth is not the center of the universe. But in 1633 the Church forced him to kneel down and, with his hand upon the Gospel, renounce his belief because of what "they thought."

Sometimes we superimpose a change on others because of what we think the Scripture means. I remember being told of a minister, who ran a home for displaced children and young people, having sexual relations with the teenage girls in his care. He firmly believed he was doing the right thing because he thought they needed to experience love (a good scriptural concept). These girls were changed because of his "I think," but certainly not according to the kind of love God would have used to change them. This type of "I think" is spelled S-I-N.

*How Smart Are You?*

While I was being entertained as the guest of honor at a dinner party in a large southern city, a young man trained in handwriting analysis suddenly asked me, "What's your I.Q.?"

All conversation ceased as those around me listened for my answer. "Sorry, no way am I going to talk about that," I replied, embarrassed at the silence.

"Oh, come on, I've already analyzed your handwriting, and I know how smart you are."

I suddenly realized he meant business and was ready to tell me all he knew. "OK. I'll tell you how smart I am." He smiled a little "I won" grin as all eyes focused on me. Slowly and very deliberately I said, "I'm smart enough to know that I don't know" (I could almost feel the shocked silence). "But," pointing upward, toward God in heaven, I added, "I'm also smart enough to know who does know." Proverbs 3:5-6 says: "Trust in the Lord with all thine heart; and lean not unto thine own understanding. In all thy ways acknowledge Him, and He shall direct thy paths." Yes, I know I don't know how to direct my own life. When I lean on my own understanding, I become more and more stubbornly entrenched in my own ambitions, rights, and ideas.

How, then, can I avoid getting my lifestyle from wisdom that is within myself—a source that produces bitter envyings, strife, confusion, and every evil work? (James 3:16) God has promised if I *don't* lean on my own understanding, He will take over and direct my paths. Then He will teach me through Bible study, guide me through devotional reading, and recall Scripture when I need it. And He will give me wisdom when I admit I need it and ask Him for it—wisdom that changes me according to His perfect will.

# 10

# *Source No. 2, Earthly*

Another source of wisdom by which I am changed that James mentions is *earthly*. This is not that which attacks me with fiery darts from Satan's emissaries, nor my own "I thinks" welling up from deep within my sensual self, but it is the wisdom that bombards from the world around me. This is the constant barrage of communicated suggestions which pellet me from every angle: people, books, newspapers, radio, and television. The parade is endless and unrelenting. Bit by bit they push, press, chisel, and invade until I am changed—unsuspectingly—into a composite of their messages.

The advertising media have learned the power contained in suggestions that flash so rapidly on my TV screen. I am not even aware of them, but I am motivated to get up out of my chair and go to the kitchen for something to eat or to go out and buy their product. These hidden persuaders are not only on TV; they are subtly at work on me all day long from a myriad of sources.

In Romans 12:2 Paul refers to the results of this process as *conforming* to the world. He writes, "And be not conformed to this world." To conform is to become similar to, to bring into harmony or agreement with, to act in accordance with. CHANGED! Changed to conform to what? The *world*. The age in which we live. The principles and practices of this present order of things. The world becomes our source of wisdom which in turn changes us into conformity to it. Paul warns us against this. James says that this wisdom "descendeth not from above [from God], but is earthly" (3:15).

Peter puts it this way: "Wherefore gird up the loins of your mind . . . as obedient children, not fashioning yourselves according to the former lusts in your ignorance" (1 Peter 1:13-14). What are these former lusts? Paul defines them in Ephesians 2:1-3: "And you [Christians] hath He quickened, who were dead in trespasses and sins; Wherein in time past ye walked according to the course of this world, according to the prince of the power of the air, the spirit that now worketh in the children of disobedience. Among whom also we all had our conversation [way of life] in times past in the lusts of our flesh, fulfilling the desires of the flesh and of the mind; and were by nature the children of wrath, even as others."

## Bombarded by a Relentless Parade

What becomes commonplace changes me. I can remember the times when I hurt inside if anyone took God's name in vain, when I winced at some of the four-letter words so commonly used on TV today—words I never allowed to enter my home by any other way. I never tolerated a child's playmate or a crude adult friend using those words, but now I am frequently unaware of the vile language so casually used on our TV.

And God's standard for marriage is steadily eroding as the ever-present marriage triangle on TV now involves not just the bad guy but our heroes, the "nice guys." Sleeping overnight with someone else's wife or husband doesn't carry a hint that it might be wrong. Soap operas constantly feature the third person in the marriage relationship, and on one of the current top ten programs a divorced mother and her two daughters talked freely about not "doing it" until "Mr. Right" comes along. And little by little we are a bit less shocked as we grow accustomed to that kind of lifestyle.

In today's popular music there has crept in a gradual changing of moral values. We find ourselves actually sympathizing with the lovers who have to keep their "beautiful" love a secret till they both are free from the selfish culprits to whom they are married. And the young woman alone in her room at night convincingly laments that there is some man out there missing what she has to give.

I recall the startled expression on the face of a member of my Sunday School class when we read Jesus' words in Matthew 5:28 that "whosoever looketh on a woman to lust after her hath committed adultery with her already in his heart." Horrified, he exploded, "Does it really say that?" Yes, God's "flee fornication" still stands, no matter how much the world tries to change our thinking.

I wonder how many Christian young people are getting their moral standards from this relentless parade, and how many adults unwittingly lower their ideals because of this invasion by the world. And when does turning our heads and ignoring it change into condoning? *Changed*—first in our thinking and then in our actions.

### Gullible—If It's in Print

A returned missionary shared with me that he felt God was calling him to translate good literature to send to the nationals he had just left. "They believe anything that is in print," he lamented. But it happens here in America too. A national denominational women's executive said to me one day, "What can we do about the gullibility of our women? Now that women are 'thinking for themselves' they are reading and studying everything they can get their hands on. And they are believing anything, as long as it's in print, swallowing everything printed under the name of 'Christian.' " What a sad commentary on our discernment abilities.

We should test every book we read by the Bible's standards, but the tendency today is to make the Bible's teachings fit into those of a book—secular or religious. In a Sunday School class a teacher was using a popular secular book, attempting to conform biblical concepts to the ideas expressed in the book. After a few sessions of this study, a doctor's wife became extremely agitated and said, "I personally studied this material in a seminar conducted by the author, and by 9:00 A.M. he was 'bombed.' And we Christians are evaluating the Bible by what this alcoholic's book says!" Many of us act as if the Bible is on trial, whereas we should judge every book by what the Bible says. And this includes Christian books. An internationally known Christian psychologist startled me one day when he said that he didn't know a single Christian book that did not have in it something he considered to be contrary to the Scripture.

And we must evaluate *all* the teachings in a book. A national Christian radio personality told me last week that she had been reprimanded for reviewing a certain book on the air. In her hurried perusal of that book, she had missed the one antiscriptural teaching in it. But she learned that it was necessary to check out all the teachings of any book before she reviewed it. I've heard people say in defense of an author, "But that book has so much good in it." Great. Take what is good and true, and accept it. But we must reject anything, even from our favorite author, that is not consistent with biblical truth. A lot of truth in a book doesn't automatically make everything in the book true.

### Source of Wisdom When We Teach

Discerning an author's source of wisdom is also wise. When an author has been taught by God, what he has written can be a valuable source of wisdom for my changing. But I must be alert to things in print which are a result of the author's having received wisdom from Satan's realm or from his own "I thinks." If the teachings in a book are contrary to the Scriptures, the source of the author's wisdom could not have been God, but from one of the other three sources—sensual self, demonic, or earthly.

Many times our preconceived ideas, our "I thinks" about what we want the Scriptures to say, color our interpretation. I was appalled as I read a Christian couple's paraphrase of Proverbs 31 in a Christian magazine. It obviously was their idea of the perfect wife, but it had little to do with the actual description of the virtuous woman recorded in the Bible portion. They wrote, "Your own clothing will be modest, but chosen in colors to please your husband," while the Bible actually said she made herself coverings of tapestry and her clothing was silk and purple (v. 22). And they said, "There may be many beautiful and intelligent women in the world, but I wouldn't trade you for any of them," whereas the Bible says the virtuous woman opens her mouth with wisdom (v. 26). Again they wrote of her buying fresh fruits and vegetables and, in consultation with her family, organizing the day's responsibilities. But the Bible said she considers a field and buys it—an independent businesswoman (v. 16). And the purpose of her making fine linen and girdles was to sell them to the merchants—not only for her family. This virtuous woman must have been an intelligent and clever businesswoman, for even the civic leaders in the gates praised her for her work.

A pastor's wife recently said to me, "I get that doctrine all straightened out until I go back and read so-and-so again." How easy it is to accept gullibly some author's "I think" about the Bible and be changed by it, not stopping to test it by what the Scripture actually says. But wisdom is only as good as the author's source, and is only worthy as a source of change for us if God has been his teacher.

Several years ago a teacher at a parent-teacher night said that our first-grade child had picked a book from the school library which she, a Christian teacher, questioned. Knowing we were a preacher's family, she said, "Oh, Honey, you don't want to read *that* book, do you?" "Well," was the reply, "we don't have to *believe* everything we read." Did that little first-grader know something many adults have not yet learned? Do we accept without question and are we changed by anybody's printed wisdom regardless of its source?

Those of us who write and teach have a grave responsibility to make sure of our source of wisdom. To admit we are wrong and change our teaching is admirable; but in doing so we must admit that our former source of wisdom could not have been from God for it expressed an opposing view.

This puts an awesome responsibility on my shoulders to make sure that *before* I teach others my source of wisdom has not been my "I thinks"—the results of being squeezed into the world's mold or the contemporary Christian culture, or by what is acceptable thinking and behavior in my specific Christian community. Or that my teaching has not been colored by the sensual welling up from within me. And, of course, the really frightening responsibility is to make sure my source is not from demons. Satan is an angel of light (2 Cor. 11:14), and some of his subtle persuaders look so right and feel so good that I sometimes have trouble catching those deceptions. But if I pass those on as I teach, they become heresy. I'm sure most antiscriptural teaching is done in complete innocence, the teacher having been convinced that his or her source of wisdom was God. But Paul warns us in 2 Corinthians 2:11 that we are not to be ignorant of Satan's scheming ways.

Then the question comes, *how can we retract and correct teaching that we have received from the three sources of wisdom other than God*? I may be able to reach a few, but the seeds I have sown multiply and in turn are scattered by those I have taught. How imperative it becomes for me to pray *before* I teach, asking God to remove all my preconceived ideas which may have been from the other three sources, and then to ask Him to guard and guide my mind as I study and teach.

There are some excellent books for husbands and wives these days that are God-inspired and tremendously beneficial. There are others that have not been inspired by Him. Here again, the author's source of wisdom makes the difference— God's holy Word or Hollywood. Is it advice that will change me into what God wants me to be? One husband complained to me, "My wife is acting like God is the Hugh Hefner of the sky." Also, where the author is in his or her personal life at a given point in time may not be the direction God wants us to take. We may be changed—but not according to God's will! Someone may be "teaching for doctrines the commandments of men" (Mark 7:7).

### Test by What It Produces

Inadequate Bible study and basing our teaching on an inaccurate premise of what we think the Bible says produces the wrong kind of changes in our lives. Many women have come to me angry, depressed, or in tears because they studied material that was not accurate according to the Scripture, and they had tried to change into the persons God did not intend them to be.

An extremely frustrated and guilt-ridden author and teacher came to me one day because what she taught a woman had produced a husband who, instead of becoming the head of the house, had taken a gun and blown his brains out. Silently, I questioned the source of wisdom resulting in such tragedy. Reading through just the first six pages of her study course, I found a long list of things that I did not believe were scriptural, including the basic premise of the whole study. I went to prayer asking God to reveal the mind of Christ to her—not what Evelyn thinks for I can be right *or wrong*, and what God is saying to me for my life might not be what He is saying to her.

If our new lifestyle produces rebellion in our mates, it is good to check the source of wisdom that is affecting our changing. One husband whose wife had been following step-by-step a course of study finally exploded, "Honey, I married you because you were a bubbly, outgoing, beautiful hostess. I loved you the way you were. Will you please stop this idiotic behavior? I can't stand you this way." The changes in her life had infuriated him. And many husbands have been insulted and embarrassed that men in their social circles or neighborhood have all been receiving the same planned treatment each week. Discovering that their friends' wives and their own were changing their behavior toward their husbands in exactly the same way has caused deep hurts.

If what we teach produces bitterness, confusion, guilt, embarrassment, rebellion, insult or even divisions among Christians, we need to check the source of wisdom from which we are deriving our teaching. James 3:17 and 18 tell us: "But the wisdom that is from above is first pure, then peaceable, gentle, and easy to be entreated, full of mercy and good fruits, without partiality, and without hypocrisy. And the fruit of righteousness is sown in peace of them that make peace."

### Not to Manipulate

My motive for changing is not to manipulate other people. When I pray, "Lord, change me" I am only concerned with my changing into what He wants me to be. Peter said my changed actions and attitudes will *affect* the people around me. Others will change as they see and observe my "chaste and reverent behavior" (1 Peter 3:1-2), but God takes care of changing them. I am responsible for me.

Some of the books and studies for women these days are designed to manipulate the husband into a certain response when the wife follows a certain pattern of behavior. One course of study teaches the wife how to manipulate her husband so that she with him will qualify for a higher place in heaven. And another study switches from God's plan to that of movie stars for manipulating men, husband or not.

One man said to me recently, "I am insulted that my wife is trying to manipulate my behavior in this way."

God's Word abounds with instructions for both husband and wife which are sufficient to produce all the joys, privileges and beauty of the marriage relationship. Letting God change us into warm, loving, responsive mates physically, emotionally, and spiritually is His will for us—not the manipulation of one another, but for each to be changed into what He wants us to be. Paul says in Colossians 2:8, "Beware lest any man spoil you through philosophy and vain deceit, after the tradition of men, after the rudiments of the world, and not after Christ."

### Squeezed into Their Mold

One of the ways we conform to this world is described in J. B. Phillips' version of Romans 12:2: "Don't let the world around you squeeze you into its own mold."

We are exposed these days to courses of study that would squeeze us into the mold of the world. Many of these courses, in the areas of mind expansion, philosophy, and social behavior, are strictly from a worldly perspective with no consideration as to God's teachings. In them a clever, persuasive teacher can present the material in such a way that it produces dramatic changes in thinking and actions—frequently opposite from God's way of changing.

We tend to believe a teacher if he or she draws a large crowd. And we instinctively feel all those people can't be wrong. But as I read through the text of Mr. Sun Myung Moon's speech given to the standing-room-only crowd at Madison Square Garden recently, I realized the error of this thinking. He cleverly twisted and misinterpreted Scripture to "prove" that Jesus did not come to earth to die, the cross was not God's will for Christ, the crucifixion was a mistake, and Jesus thus could not save us totally. Then he went on to "prove" that Jesus was not coming back in the clouds but would be born again as the third Adam in the flesh.

A distraught leader of a large denominational district rally told me her daughter had left home to live at Mr. Moon's headquarters in our city. After I spoke to the gathering on this subject, the denomination's leader stood up and said, "I hope you paid attention to Mrs. Christenson, for right now, this week these Moon representatives will most likely knock on your door. It is our community they are saturating this week with their philosophy." Moon's followers are missionaries to Christians—trying to squeeze us into their mold. Trying to change us—but not as God would have us change. God's Word says, "Let no man deceive you with vain words" (Eph. 5:6).

### Advice from Other People

As a young pastor's wife in our first city pastorate, I was eager to please everybody, and slacks were still questionable attire for women. But on our first Christmas in that pastorate my mother-in-law gave me a pair of lovely maroon wool slacks. I immediately put them on to go to the train station to meet an arriving relative. Just as I stepped out of our front door, an elderly member of our church passed by, stuck her nose in the air and said, "Harumph. Women in pants!" Then she strode defiantly on past our house in the howling wind. Should I rush back and change into a skirt and be late for the train—or chance it?

As I stood on the train platform with the winter storm raging about and the plaid of my new slacks getting louder by the minute, I suddenly shrank back into the shadows. Another female member of our church! But I was too late. She bounded over to me and sighed, "Well, at last we have a pastor's wife with enough sense to dress for the weather!" Which one was right? Which one's reaction should I heed? It couldn't be both. In my confused state I dug out my Bible and once again found the answer from God—Acts 5:29: "We ought to obey God rather than men [people]."

This past Christmas my husband and I sat looking at the family picture on the Christmas card from our former assistant pastor and commenting on what a lovely family they are. He is now the assistant to a successful national leader of thousands of people. "Oh to think I advised him not to go with that man," recalled Chris. (At the time Chris gave that advice that new boss was a relatively unheard-of youth leader.) "That's why we obey God rather than men," I commented.

I went home and cried after receiving advice from another person at a retreat. In an exercise of giving something to each other she said to me, "I give you a spirit of adventure."

I was crushed. "Lord," I prayed, "have I missed it that much that people think I need a spirit of adventure?" Reviewing that very month, I realized how wrong that advice had been. I had turned fifty—which in itself took a lot of courage. And I enrolled in my first seminary class, started speaking on a then very misunderstood subject in churches and schools—"The Dangers of the Occult," organized my first St. Paul telephone prayer chain, conceived and planned the first of the annual Founder's Week luncheons for women at our college and seminary—and on the list went.

I'm sure I needed advice, but a spirit of adventure was not it. I could have used "Learn to say no," "One thing at a time," or, "Try eight hours of sleep some night." But a spirit of adventure—hardly. I'm sure the advice was well-intended, but missed my real need completely. Psalm 118:8 says, "It is better to trust in the Lord than to put confidence in man." Advice from other people can chisel away at us until we are reduced to a fraction of all that God intended us to be. God's wisdom enlarges, matures, and fulfills us.

However, the worth of people's advice is determined by their source of wisdom. There is much Christian counsel that is worthwhile and beneficial. But all advice must be evaluated in the light of the advice God gives in His Word. If the counseling is contrary to the Bible's instructions or from the person's "I thinks" it can never change us into the persons God intends us to be. "And my speech and my preaching was not with enticing words of man's wisdom, but in demonstration of the Spirit and of power: that your faith should not stand in the wisdom of men, but in the power of God" (1 Cor. 2:4-5).

How precious is the counsel of the godly to us, and how good to be changed by it; but even Job (Job 13:1-2), Christ (Matt. 16:21-23), and Peter and John (Acts 4:18-20) had to firmly reject being changed by the advice from people so that they could follow God's instructions and leading in their lives.

Changed? Yes! But by the only infallible, consistently reliable Source—the Lord.

# 11

# Source No. 3,
# Demoniacal

As I discovered in James 3 the four sources of wisdom by which I could be changed, the most horrifying one to me was the wisdom from demons. Although I was well aware of this subject doctrinally, the sudden realization that it was possible for me to receive and be changed by wisdom from demons completely unnerved me.

Then I began to wonder. How much of the "confusion, strife, bitterness, and evil work" in my life have been caused by an input from Satan's kingdom? The possibility of demons literally shaping my lifestyle by the wisdom they were giving me suddenly loomed as a dark, threatening menace. I thought of the anger over a remark made years before that had seemed to come from nowhere as I read my Bible that morning. God had forgiven, and when He forgives, He forgets. So who dug up something settled nine years ago? Not God! I looked at the other three sources. Not the earthly source from other people—I was alone in my living room. My own "I think"? I couldn't make any sense out of that one since the incident hadn't been a part of my thinking, at least not that I was aware of, for nine years. I was left with just one source of wisdom that was producing that un-Christlike attitude in me—demons!

### Spirit of Discernment
One evening we had taken Corrie ten Boom to dinner at the top of our new IDS tower in Minneapolis. Ignoring the breathtak-

ing view across our city, she suddenly asked, "What is the gift of the Holy Spirit least sought after these days by Christians?" Several shook their heads, wondering what Corrie was going to say. "I think I may know, Corrie," I said. "Is it a spirit of discernment?" (1 Cor. 12:10) Her eyes lit up. "Yes!" And she was off on one of her wonderful little sermonettes on a subject about which she was feeling deeply.

God had shown me this three years before in 1 Corinthians 12:8 and 10, "For to one is given by the Spirit . . . discerning of spirits." At that time I had prayed that He would give me that gift, the ability to identify the source—which spirit it was that was producing my lifestyle and that of others.

Then Corrie said, "It's a poor soldier, indeed, who doesn't even recognize the enemy."

Peter recognized and discerned the source of wisdom which caused Ananias to lie: "Why hath Satan filled thine heart to lie to the Holy Spirit?" (Acts 5:3)

Perhaps Peter recognized this source so easily because Jesus had identified it in him when Peter in his rebellion declared that Jesus could not go to Jerusalem to die—doing His Father's will (Matt. 16:22-23). Just saying, "I don't believe that can happen to a Christian" doesn't change the truth of our enemy's tactics one bit. We do receive wisdom from demons.

### By What It Produces

I learned from the Book of James that I can identify and discern the source of wisdom by what it produces. Bitter envyings, strife, confusion, and every evil work are always the input of Satan's kingdom. How frequently I have to claim God's "sound mind" of 2 Timothy 1:7, when I find this state of confusion in me, and let God change me!

I also discovered that fear is another product of this demonic source of wisdom. Several years ago, while reading our Bibles until God spoke, another woman and I were puzzled as to why God stopped us both at 2 Timothy 1:7. I tucked this truth down in my heart, but didn't need it until the following September. While conducting a retreat near Banff in the foothills of the Canadian Rockies, I was to speak on a Sunday morning on the subject of victory over Satan. On the night before, our campfire sharing time near the horse corral was broken up by a pack of wolves. Around midnight when I returned to my bedroom in the far corner of the lodge a sense of uncanny fear came over me. I felt I was not alone, though a thorough search in closets and under the beds revealed no one. Turning out all the lights except the one over my bed, I took my Bible, zipped up my sleeping bag, and began quoting 2 Timothy 1:7: "For God hath not given us the spirit of fear, but of power, and of love, and of a sound mind." Then, telling Satan to get out of the room (James 4:7) and claiming 1 John 4:4, I went to sleep—a beautiful, restful sleep—and awoke the next morning changed, with actual tears of joy in my eyes. Completely changed by recognizing the source of that fear—and claiming the Scripture God had given to me six months earlier.

I saw this fear displayed in a college student from the University of Montana who was sitting next to me on a plane flying to California. He was telling me how deeply he was into meditation.

"Tell me, do you ever hear anything?" I asked.

With a fear in his eyes that I cannot describe, he said, "Lady, if I'd tell you everything I've heard, they'd come with a straitjacket and take me away. I hear bells, voices . . ." and with that his voice trailed off. It wasn't hard for me to discern the source of that fearful lifestyle, but he wasn't interested in changing it.

As I teach young people on this subject, I can usually tell which ones are getting their wisdom from some supernatural source other than God by the peculiar fear they exhibit. As many share their problem quite readily with me, I show them from the Bible that this way of life is not from God. What a joy to watch them change as they pray, asking God to forgive them. And I know the change is complete when the big smiles spread over their faces, demonstrating their happiness.

Yes, the gift of the Holy Spirit least sought but so needed these days is the gift of discerning the spirits—it enables us to discover the sources of wisdom that will change us, and to avoid those which will not change us for the better.

### Test the Spirits

Now for the question: "How can we tell which kind of spirit is changing us?"

The Apostle John gave us a good test of the spirits: "Dear friends, do not believe every spirit, but test the spirits to see whether they are from God, because many false prophets have gone out into the world. This is how you can recognize the Spirit of God: Every spirit that acknowledges that Jesus Christ has come in the flesh is from God, but every spirit that does not acknowledge Jesus is not from God" (1 John 4:1-3, NIV).

John warned us not to believe every spirit; not to accept wisdom from those that are not of God, not to be changed by what they teach, say, or suggest to us.

And we are to test them according to whether or not they confess that Jesus Christ came in the flesh, that is, He took on a body with flesh and blood for the purpose of shedding that blood on the cross to defeat Satan (1 John 3:8). Every spirit that does not confess that Jesus is come in the flesh is not of God.

God said in His Word that "without shedding of blood there is no forgiveness" (Heb. 9:22, NASB). But because Jesus did come in the flesh, He redeemed us from sin by shedding His blood on the cross. "Forasmuch as ye know that ye were not redeemed with corruptible things . . . but with the precious blood of Christ" (1 Peter 1:18-19). (See also Matt. 26:28; Col. 1:14; Eph. 1:7.)

Sometimes it's difficult to discern what people who receive wisdom from demons really think of Jesus. A woman in our area, a popular speaker at local occult conventions, supposedly receives messages from dead loved ones by automatic writing. Our local newspaper quoted her as saying that God was great, the great Creator, etc., but farther down in the long article she was quoted as saying, "But the confusion comes when we try to put a *body* on 'it.' God can be an 'it' force in the universe, but don't put a body on 'it.' " This reveals what she thinks of Jesus having come in the flesh!

I was hoping someone dressed in a colonial costume would approach me at the Philadelphia airport when I was there on July 6, just two days after our 1976 Bicentennial birthday, and I was not disappointed. A lovely young girl in a bonnet and a long dress started telling me about our country's spiritual heritage. I beamed back and said, "Yes, I love God, and love and serve His Son, Jesus." At that she gave me a long speech about how great a teacher Jesus was and how wonderful He was. As I nodded in agreement, she continued, "And He was one of the ways to God." I blinked and started to listen more closely. "Oh, yes, He was *one of the ways to God*. There are many ways to God. Let me tell you about mine. I'm a Hare Krishna girl. . . ."

"Hold it, honey," I interrupted. "I think you are doing a very diabolical thing here in Philadelphia at this, our nation's birthday celebration. Our country was founded on belief in God through Jesus, and you are saying how great He was and at the same time that He is just one of the ways to God. But Jesus said of Himself, 'I am the Way, the Truth, and the Life: no man cometh unto the Father, but by Me' (John 14:6). Now, He is either a barefaced liar, or He is who He said He is—the *only* way to God." What the Hare Krishna followers think of Jesus!

Krishna, whom she follows, says in chapter ten of the *Bhagavad Gita*, "I am the prince of demons." Test the source of that kind of wisdom before believing and being changed by it. Jesus said in John 8:44 that Satan was a liar and the father of lies.

Sometimes it is difficult to test the spirits. Three people supposedly dressed in costumes such as Abraham and Sarah might have worn came to one of my prayer seminars. They would not let me touch them as I tried to shake their hands in welcome because, they said, they were from Am.

"Where's Am?" I asked.

Surprised at my ignorance, they replied, "Oh, that's heaven. God sent us to earth, and He has been saying 'Evelyn' to us. When we saw the sign for your prayer seminar in front of this church, we knew you were the Evelyn."

I immediately started to pray for protection and discernment. (Several others in the audience sensed the need and prayed also.) After the seminar the female of the trio threw her arms around me to give me "a double portion of God's power." Perhaps I'll never know the source of those three, but I immediately knew and sensed the protection of Jesus Christ.

### Doctrine of Demons

False teaching seems to be taking on a new dimension these days. The investigation of inner space and outer space (not authentic exploration) is producing a new kind of wisdom. It's possible to listen to lectures by "beings" from outer space, browse through endless shelves of do-it-yourself inner exploration, attend teaching sessions on the power of the mantra, reincarnation, dreams and the inner world, and astrology as cosmic patterning. Or we can bask in the Caribbean sun on a yoga vacation with Swami Vishnude Vananda or retreat to a Buddhist monastery in the Catskills. The September 6, 1976 issue of *Newsweek* put it this way: "There are more than 8,000 ways to awaken North America."

A University of Chicago anthropologist claims 20 million Americans belong to "fringe religious cults" such as the Hare Krishna movement, spiritualism, and Scientology. The market is flooded these days with cheap or expensive ways of changing with "wisdom" from every source mentioned in James 3 except the true God in heaven.

Paul warns us against the *doctrine of demons*, in 1 Timothy 4:1: "the Spirit explicitly says that in later times some will fall away from the faith, paying attention to deceitful spirits and doctrines of demons" (NASB). This is not the doctrine *about* demons, but the doctrine *of* demons.

After a recent prayer seminar a woman in her 20s said to me, "I was deeply into TM, but recently while meditating I heard a voice say, 'That is of the devil.' Now, I'm from a church where we never talk about the devil, so that word could not have come from within me. It had to be God." God warning about being changed by the wrong source?

A faculty member of a southern Christian college asked for prayer at a prayer seminar. She had just returned from doing research for a postgraduate dissertation in Iowa near where the Maharishi Mahesh Yogi has established his university. Anxious for any mind-expanding help she could get, she took the TM course and practiced it, but God spoke to her, telling her that this was of Satan and was not for Christians. She immediately renounced the practice. But what she asked us to pray about was that her secret mantra (that Hindu-worship word) kept bonging and ringing in her head. No matter what she did or how hard she tried, she could not get rid of it. She had been changed in a way she didn't want to be changed.

According to *Time* magazine (March 1, 1976), students

enrolled in TM classes at their high school in Maplewood, New Jersey brought fruit and flowers to be placed on the altar before the picture of the late Guru Dev. Then, kneeling at this ceremony performed at the TM center in Union, New Jersey they were given a mantra, the secret word that must be repeated to aid meditation.

These students were being changed, not by their own "I think" but by other people whose source of wisdom was not the God above. They were being changed by worshiping a pagan god.

Jesus said this method of meditation is used by pagans when they pray. But He told His disciples, "But when ye pray, use not vain repetitions as the pagans do" (Matt. 6:7, sco). Repeating one word over and over is not a method Jesus would use to change us.

However, there are biblical methods of meditating on our God who is in heaven. The Scriptures abound with examples. Dr. Herbert Benson, cardiologist and assistant professor of medicine at the Harvard Medical School, discovered that, although meditating with a Hindu mantra did beneficially lower blood pressure, meditating in ordinary ways without a secret religious word also produced the same beneficial results. Christians call it prayer. The danger comes not from meditating, but from the spiritual powers to which we open our minds.

A professor in one of our large theological seminaries said, "If you want to find demons today, go to the pulpits of our churches on Sunday morning." I questioned the possibility of such a thing until I heard a sermon based on the best seller, *Jonathan Livingston Seagull*. Although the author himself speaks freely of occult healing power (having actually stopped the flow of blood with supernatural power when he cut himself) and of a "voice" telling him what to write in the book, his philosophy was used as a basis for many sermons. And one local pastor leads a group in "healing from the cosmos" every Tuesday evening. At 11 P.M. they meditate and get vibrations from their California headquarters, giving them power and the ability to see auras around people. Are preachers immune to this source of wisdom, or are they unusually vulnerable because they influence so many other people?

The book, *UFO Missionaries Extraordinary*, compiled by Hayden Hewes and Brad Steiger, could cause much deception about Jesus' second coming. In an interview with Bo and Peep in chapters 7 and 8, in which two "people" claim to have existed before and to have been sent to a woman's womb from the heavenly kingdom by a spacecraft that came close enough to earth to make contact, there are profuse references to Jesus and the Bible. They say they are part of a preparation for Christ's coming. Their teachings sound so plausible and are so near what Christ taught. When Jesus really comes back and Christians are taken up to be with Him, will people turn back to this book and believe those Christians went to the next level in a space ship?

A fine Christian woman with an important job for God in our area called me and said, "I've just read the *Reader's Digest* condensation of the book *Life After Life* by Dr. Raymond A. Moody, Jr. It's about people who died, left their bodies and then were brought back to life. They all (unless they committed suicide), whether Christian or non-Christian, had such a beautiful experience. There was nothing unpleasant, no judgment, and a warm being of light was seen by most of them. We Christians may have to reevaluate our position on what happens after death in the light of all that evidence!"

Taken aback, I recovered enough to say to her, "You are in a very important position for God in our city right now. You are especially vulnerable. Let me pray about this and I'll get back to you."

A few days before reading that book condensation, I had asked God to guard my mind and give me wisdom as to its truth. After the phone call, I prayed asking God to give me His answer to that book. Immediately it came to mind, "It is appointed unto men once to die, but after this the judgment" (Heb. 9:27). I suddenly realized what God was saying, "If those people are back here to tell the story, they did not really die." The death process was not complete. It is after we *really* die that there will be judgment—and eternal damnation for those who do not know Christ. The whole biblical teaching, of the wages of sin being death, must be discarded if there is only pleasantness, warmth, and light after death. Jesus said in John 3:16, 18: "For God so loved the world, that He gave His only begotten Son, that whosoever believeth in Him should not perish, but have everlasting life. . . . But he that believeth not is condemned already."

The "doctrine of demons" may not be popular with some Christians today, but in December 1971, a completely new thought illumined me as I was reading 1 Timothy 4:6: "If thou put the brethren in remembrance of these things, thou shalt be a good minister of Jesus Christ." Looking back to see what "these things" were, I realized Paul was talking about the *"doctrine of demons."* I don't like that subject either, but if I put other Christians "in remembrance of these things," I will change into a better minister of Jesus Christ.

### How We Open Ourselves to Wisdom from Demons

"Where did we go wrong?" lamented a mother of a college girl who had left her Christian college to enroll in and later become a teacher in a local school for witches. I'm sure this is the question being asked by many agonizing and anxious parents. There are many ways Christians can open themselves to wisdom from demons, sometimes without being aware of what is happening.

There is much actual teaching of occult practices in our public schools and universities these days. During a question-and-answer period at a workshop conducted by an HEW member in Washington, D.C. last spring, I heard a schoolteacher from a large Florida city ask what could be done about the occult practices that were being taught in public grade schools by immigrants who brought their voodoo and witchcraft practices with them to Florida.

And a public school administrator in another large city told me she was terrified that we would get prayer legalized again in the schools. She told me that she knows personally Satan worshipers and witches who are teaching in their schools and added that in a democracy if Christians get the right to lead their pupils in prayer, so will the Satan worshipers and witches. And, she said, if our children are exposed to that kind of praying year after year, I'm not sure we'd ever recover them.

A rather new source of wisdom coming to our area is called "The Way." A distraught mother told our prayer chain chairman that the people of this movement were teaching her daughter that she should follow them if she wanted to be like Jesus, because He disobeyed His parents when He was 12. That wisdom didn't come from God. They were seeking to change that little girl to be just the opposite of what the Bible says about obeying parents.

How many people discerned that the "I Got It" bumper-sticker was the slogan of Werner Erhard's "est" and not at all related to the Here's Life "I Found It" slogan? Instead of accepting the fact of new life in Jesus Christ as deliverance from past sin, Werner Erhard believes that there isn't anything but spirituality, which is just another name for God. He denies the past and thinks we should ignore the future consequences of our actions. Having removed moral and ethical considerations Erhard decided he was "God in my own universe."

"Why did God stop all 18 of us individually on the word 'sorcery' in our cabin as we were reading Galatians 5 until He spoke?" asked a retreat chairman. "You had better tell *me* why," I answered. Then came a startling discussion of how they were using occult practices, such as Ouija boards for advice, in their farming procedures. Wisdom from God? In prayer those women confessed this as sin. God changed them by stopping them all on the same, very frightening word—sorcery.

Sometimes we deliberately ask for wisdom from demonic sources. Perhaps the most common way these days is by reading horoscopes. Millions of Americans get their daily lifestyle from the newspaper columns. God forbade this ancient practice, along with many other occult practices which are prevalent today, in instructions to Moses as the Children of Israel were entering the Promised Land. God said that those who do such things are an abomination to Him (Deut. 18:9-12).

At a retreat we were attending, a pastor's wife became concerned because there weren't any newspapers available. "I won't know how to run my life today," she moaned. "I won't be able to read my horoscope." Being susceptible to the power of suggestion from a source God calls an abomination to Him is dangerous indeed. And it certainly can't lead us in the direction God would have us go.

Believing and following predictions of psychics is another way of getting wisdom from a source other than God. We are warned, in Deuteronomy 18:21-22, that unless everything which is prophesied comes to pass, that prophet is not of God. Check the percentage of accuracy! The *National Enquirer's* article of July 6, 1976, revealing the predictions of 10 leading psychics for the second half of 1976, included the information that Castro would be ousted; Frank Sinatra was to emerge as a national hero after foiling an assassination attempt; the Six Million Dollar Man, the Johnny Carson Show, and Kojak would no longer be on TV; Billy Graham would suffer a heart attack forcing him to end his career; a gigantic earthquake in California would tear apart entire mountain ranges revealing the biggest gold deposits ever discovered—all before the end of 1976! And we gullibly swallow and mold our life-patterns—are changed—by that source of wisdom!

A frightening number of our children and young people are opening themselves up to wisdom from demons through occult practices these days. Students in a Christian school were disrupting their school playing Mary Worth—calling forth this witch's image on mirrors in darkened restrooms. At their parents' request, I explained to them that the people who practice this (and get wisdom from Ouija boards, tarot cards, séances, and all the other methods they told me they were using) are an abomination to God. How they changed that day as they asked God, one by one in audible prayer, to forgive and deliver them from this.

A mother told me that her daughter had solved a slumber party occult practice. She discovered that the other girls had no power when she prayed. And when they found out that she was the cause of their "games" not working, then they wouldn't allow her in the room when they were practicing them.

Another mother told me her daughter worried for years over a palm reader's prediction that she would die by age 16.

Satan engineers our behavior without violating our free will. Weeping, an 18-year-old girl told me she had given her body for Satan worship with all its obscene acts because she was dating a boy who was involved in it. At the time, a pain had come in the pit of her stomach, and she had not been able to get through to God in prayer or understand anything in the Bible. After breaking up with the boy and renouncing Satan worship, she tried desperately to free herself from Satan's clutches and these symptoms, but could not. I prayed for her, using the same simple words Jesus prayed in His high-priestly prayer in John 17, "Dear Father, deliver this dear one from the evil one." Then, according to James 4:7, I just said, "Satan, in the name of Jesus of Nazareth, get out of this dear girl."

The change was instantaneous and dramatic. She grabbed her throat as if choking, became a little light-headed, and then jumped up and threw her arms around me. "It's gone. The pain's gone. I'm free! " Changed by Jesus Christ!

A graduate of a Christian college, someone I know, was watching a TV program on Satan worship from San Francisco. He foolishly said, "If you're real, Satan, prove it." And Satan did. For over a year, though he struggled against it, power and direction for his life came from voices speaking to him in the shower and through inner compulsions. It is possible to voluntarily open ourselves to direction from Satan's kingdom.

Books on occult practices abound even in our best bookstores. Anyone desiring to be changed in this way has only to buy a book describing in detail the method he has chosen. But this is not new. Acts 19:19 tells us, "Many of those also who used [magical] arts brought their books together, and burned them before all men; and they counted the price of them, and found it fifty thousand pieces of silver." A huge sum compared to the worth of our Christ to Judas—sold for *thirty* pieces of silver.

Yes, we do receive wisdom from demons in so many different ways, sometimes by deception, sometimes by unknowingly opening ourselves, and at other times, deliberately. But the results are the same—change into a lifestyle opposite of what God would choose for us.

## Keep Your Mind on Jesus

An unusual demonic influence was described to me by a distraught woman in a Western city who had 14 immediate ancestors who were witches. They had practiced voodoo and palm reading on her from the time she was two years old, and a pastor had recently cast out the demons, but she was left with what she described as a hole in the pit of her stomach. I had no idea what she was talking about, but promised to meet her the following Saturday. On Thursday morning I awoke early and begged God to give me an answer for her. And He started recalling Scripture—Colossians 3:1-3, "Seek those things which are above, where Christ sitteth on the right hand of God"; Philippians 2:9-11, "That at the name of Jesus every knee should bow"; Ephesians 1:3, "In heavenly places in Christ"; Ephesians 1:19-22, "When He raised Him [Christ] from the dead and set Him at His own right hand in the heavenly places." I jotted the references down in my notebook, and when I met her I said, "The Lord gave me some answers for you out of His Word."

"Great," she said. "He gave me some too."

"Mine are in my notebook. I'll turn it face down on the desk while you tell me what Scriptures He gave you."

"God told me I was to get my mind off those demons and get it on Christ. He gave me Colossians 3:1-3; Philippians 2:9-11; Ephesians 1:3, 19-22." Exactly the same verses God had given me!

"And the hole in my stomach disappeared too. All week long you have been teaching us how to pray and study the Bible. All you've talked about is Jesus. And the void in the pit of my stomach has been filled with Jesus."

What a change. She started that week confused, bitter, and frightened, but finished it radiating her newfound peace and excitement in Jesus.

In August of 1972 I prayed for the first time, "Lord, keep my mind from the evil one." Jesus prayed this prayer for us in His high priestly prayer, "Father, I pray . . . that Thou shouldest keep them from the evil [one]" (John 17:15).

God also provides us with the armor to withstand in our battle against these "principalities, powers, rulers of darkness of the world and spiritual wickedness in high places" in the battlefield of our minds (Eph. 6:12-18).

When I keep my mind in His Word, the sword of the Spirit, I have the weapon for the battle. One of my favorite verses is 1 John 4:4, "Greater is He that is in you [Christ], than he that is in the world [Satan]." When I am experiencing an onslaught of fiery darts, I quote it, and I immediately change into a victorious—not vanquished—soldier for Jesus. One day, just reading that "Jesus . . . went about . . . healing all that were oppressed of the devil" (Acts 10:38), lifted the oppression I had been experiencing.

Kathy Barrow, the beautiful singer sponsored by World Vision, said to me the other day as we were talking about this battle, "I know how it comes out." And pointing to her Bible said, "I have read the end of the Book! " (See Rev. 20:10.) Yes, even Satan knows Jesus came to earth to destroy his works (1 John 3:8), and that Jesus said, in Matthew 25:41, "Depart from me, ye cursed, into everlasting fire, prepared for the devil and his angels." And even the demons recognized Jesus as He started His public ministry, crying, "Art Thou come to destroy us? I know Thee, who Thou art, the Holy One of God" (Mark 1:24). Victory in Jesus!

Sometimes I feel my shield of faith needs to be as powerful as the heat shield of a space capsule to quench the fiery darts of Satan. But it never fails because my faith is in a Person, the risen, glorified, Lord Jesus Christ.

All this armor listed in Ephesians 6 is to protect my thought life—to withstand the wisdom of Satan and his emissaries, the demons. But there is no mention of falling, only standing and withstanding when I wear God's armor! James did show us that frightening source of wisdom—from demons. But he also gave us a promise: "Resist the devil, and he will flee from you" (James 4:7).

It is imperative to admit the reality of this source of wisdom and be alert to discern it, but it is equally important to keep it in its proper perspective. It's good to remember the advice the mama spook gave to the baby spook, "Don't spook unless spooken to." Even though "the whole world lies in the power of the evil one" (1 John 5:19, NASB), it is also true that the earth is only God's footstool. This little speck of dust in the universe we call Planet Earth is temporarily Satan's domain, but the heaven of the heavens cannot contain my God (1 Kings 8:27). And He lives in me!

Yes, it is possible for me to be changed when I receive and respond to wisdom from demons. But this is not a necessary process in my life. I have been given all the resources and power I will ever need to resist this source of wisdom and be changed only as God wants me changed—with wisdom from Him.

# 12

# *Source No. 4,*
# *the Lord*

"And be not conformed to this world; but be ye transformed by the renewing of your mind, that ye may prove what is that good, and acceptable, and perfect, will of God" (Rom. 12:2).

Transformed! The opposite of being conformed to this world!

"Lord, is this what You had in mind when You led me to pray, 'Lord, change me' so many years ago? God, do You mean I can actually be transfigured just as Christ was on the Mount of Transfiguration? (Matt. 17:2) It's the same Greek word, Lord. Really changed like that?

"I guess You meant it, Lord, because You said, '*Be ye* transformed.'

"You wouldn't have said that if You didn't mean it, Lord. Is this what You've been doing all these years? Transforming me?

"Lord, I know You are the only Source of wisdom worthy to be used to produce my lifestyle, and You've taught me all these ways to obtain Your wisdom; but *how* have You been accomplishing this transformation in me? It's been a huge task, Lord! How have You done it?"

### The Source Is Also the Means
We have an oil painting of my husband's favorite verse on one of our walls, and every time I walk by it I am reminded of how the Lord accomplishes this changing, this transforming in me: "For it is *God* who worketh in you both to will and to do of His good pleasure" (Phil. 2:13). The Source of wisdom to change

me is also the Means. It is God Himself who is working in me, producing the change. When I try to pick myself up by my own bootstraps I can fall so flat on my face. Even when I know how to change, doing it myself is practically impossible.

But there is a Person involved. A divine Means. Back in November 1971, I wrote "Lord, change me" in the margin of my Bible by Hebrews 11:6. Then I added, "I believe You will do it." "Without faith it is impossible to please [God]," but the faith is not in the seeking or the changing process; faith is in a Person. God will reward me and work in me when I diligently seek Him. God is the divine Means for my changing.

"How, then, Lord, do You bring about this changing?"

### By the Renewing of Your Mind
How does God accomplish this transformation in our lives? When we accept Christ we become a new creation (2 Cor. 5:17). The Book of Romans was written to those who had become new creations (1:7); and, according to Romans 12:2, there is a process that should be going on in the lives of these people, for the phrase "be ye transformed" is in the present continuous tense. And these new creations have within them the potential of this ongoing process of being transformed.

These new creations are to be transformed *by the renewing of their minds*—not "in the vanity of their own mind, but by a change in their pattern of thinking" (Eph. 4:17, 23). It is in the realm of our thinking that we are bombarded by the three wrong sources of wisdom listed in James 3:15, but it is also in this realm that God does His changing.

Proverbs 23:7 tells us, "For as he thinketh in his heart, so is he." To realize that I am actually the sum total of all that I think is frightening. But it is also exciting, for God is in the continuous process of changing what I think—and thus changing me. He is providing both the wisdom and the means to change my thinking. And the result is a transformed me!

### I'm Unique
How I thank God that He created me a unique individual. Nobody else is just like me. And God's finished product, "Me," is different from any other He has planned.

But I must realize that every other Christian is unique too

and God is changing them according to His divine blueprint. I have a tendency to feel that if some changing is right for me, then God must want everybody else to change in the same way. But that is not true. The way the Lord changes me does not automatically become a pattern for every other person. Only the omniscient God of heaven has clearly in mind the finished product for each of His children, and I must let Him, not Evelyn, be every individual's Source of wisdom. I must direct others to the Designer of their individual blueprint—the Lord of glory.

And having God's unique blueprint in my spiritual genes also makes me responsible; accountable for all the potential He put in me; answerable to God for how I let Him change me into what He ultimately wants me to be. "So then every one of us shall give account of himself to God" (Rom. 14:12).

This places the ultimate responsibility on each individual before God. In the final judgment each person will answer for himself. God has only children, no grandchildren. I will be accountable *only* for me—only for what I have allowed God to do in and through me. "Oh, Lord, change ME!"

## Changed—So That . . .

Change for the sake of change doesn't make much sense. In the natural realm, the new isn't always better than the old. Romans 12:2, however, gives us the reason for our being transformed. And this is not only better but best. "Be ye transformed by the renewing of your mind, *that ye may prove what is that good, and acceptable, and perfect, will of God*" (italics mine). This is that will of God which is in itself pleasing to Him and which results in actions on the part of His children that are pleasing and acceptable to Him. Changed so that all the words of my mouth and the meditations of my heart are *acceptable* in the sight of my Lord (Ps. 19:14). Changed, so that I will be and do what He wants.

Changed, also, that others may observe my behavior—which has been changed because my thinking is acceptable to God (1 Peter 3:1-2). So often our lives reflect "do as I say, not as I do," but the Book of 1 Peter says my husband (and other people) are changed and won when they see my changed life.

A psychiatrist who attended one of my prayer seminars

wouldn't accept anything I said until she saw me in action with other people. Not knowing she could read lips, I questioned her intense gaze from the other side of the room as I interacted with and counseled several different people at a dinner party following the seminar. My speech at the seminar was of little value to her until she saw me prove myself in action. James says a person who is really wise *shows* it out of a good life (3:13).

The first spring we lived in our house in St. Paul, I came down to the dining room one morning to see it alive with brilliant color. The whole room was aglow with little rainbows all over the walls, ceiling and furniture. The rising sun had come far enough north to be directly in line with my small kitchen window, the dining room door and then our crystal chandelier. And the piercing white light of that morning sun was producing hundreds of rainbows by diffusing through all the crystals every color of the spectrum. I swung the chandelier ever so slightly, and the colors danced and flashed around the room. I stood spellbound at the spectacular sight.

How similar that is to God's penetration of my life. Webster's *New World Dictionary* defines *white* as "the color of radiated, transmitted, or reflected light containing all of the visible rays of the spectrum." And God too is the sum total of all that exists. He is infinite. One of His attributes is infinity—that quality of being limitless, to which nothing can be added. And He enters me as pure white piercing light. God in me, my Source of change, wanting to *radiate* through me all the visible rays of the sum total of all that He is. God's acceptable will for me is that I will let Him change me until I sparkle and glow and radiate Him into my whole environment. But I must be yielded to Him.

### Thermometer or Thermostat?
Changed—so that we become a thermostat, not a thermometer.

So much of the time we are like thermometers, registering the temperature of the atmosphere around us. We respond to a cold shoulder, a chilly remark, a cool reception with a plunge of our own thermometers. Or a hot accusation influences us to flash back with a hotter retaliation. We find it difficult to keep cool heads with heated arguments going on around us, and a warm, suggestive look frequently fans into a burning temptation. But when we let God change us into what He wants us to be, we become thermostats—changing the climate around us, not just registering it.

And when it is God who sets the dial, our environment always changes for the better. When the suggested change comes from our sensuous self, Satan's kingdom, or from other people, the temperature extreme may get worse instead of better. But when God changes us, a cold piercing glance turns into a tender look, a sharp tongue utters a soft answer, an aloof stance melts into a loving caress, a clenched fist into a squeezing hand.

But we must have complete confidence in the divine Changer. He always knows when the temperature needs changing to better the environment, and He always knows just how many degrees to turn the dial.

### My Spiritual Barometer

For over 20 years my spiritual barometer has been 1 John 1:4, "These things write we unto you, that your *joy* may be full." The amount of time I spend in God's Word, letting Him change me, seems to register on my spiritual personality indicator. The more time I spend seeking after God's wisdom, the more joy He produces in me.

As I grow older I find that fewer things cause a "tingle" in the pit of my stomach. The first snow of winter, bare feet on the first spring grass, the first squeeze of my teenage boyfriend's hand all produced an exhilarating sensation. But these impressions seem to diminish with age. However, there is one thrilling sensation that becomes stronger every year and seems to come more frequently with passing years—the thrill of having God speak to me out of His Word!

God changes me as I turn to Him for advice on how to change. Proverbs 2:10-11 is underlined in my Bible: "When wisdom entereth into thine heart, and knowledge is pleasant unto thy soul; discretion shall preserve thee, understanding shall keep thee." In the margin I wrote, "*Pleasant*—not rebelling against or negative to but my spirit soaring in JOY." Yes, God's wisdom is written down for me so that I might be changed—that my joy might be full.

## The Next Plateau

God always changes me to lift me to a higher level. Sometimes God's changing takes me through hot fires, deep valleys, grief or suffering; but after a while the "God of all grace" makes me perfect, established, strengthened and settled (1 Peter 5:10). These unpleasant experiences have prepared me for the next and higher plateaus of my life.

After an extremely deep valley in our family, I recorded in my Bible my cry to God, "O Lord, when is after a while?" But it was exactly a year later that I added the note, "*Now* is God's after a while! Great joy again!" It had taken a year for God to do His changing in me and turn that difficult circumstance back to normalcy.

When the violent learning season is over, God settles me down—but not where I was before. As I'm changed, according to His will, He places me on the next plateau that He has prepared. There's always an open door and always power to go through it when I am changed into what He wants me to be.

In June 1968, when I prayed, "Lord, make me the kind of wife *You* want me to be," instead of removing my speaking engagements, God did just the opposite. He opened a whole new life of ministry. He had an exciting succession of open doors ready for me (and many since then). And through those 14 months of searching, letting Him *change me*, God was preparing me for those doors He was waiting to swing wide open for me.

But even going through His open doors sometimes requires sacrifice. A woman in my group on a World Day of Prayer, commenting on "If any of you lack wisdom, let him ask of God" (James 1:5), said, "Sometimes I don't want wisdom. It's easier to sit in a corner and do nothing than to know what to do and then have to do it."

As my advisory board and I pray through each new door God seems to be swinging open for us, I realize more and more that obedience requires sacrifice. And it involves sacrifice on my husband's part, also. But God always gives more than I give Him. He has rewarded my obedience with more joy, acceptance, and respect for each other than Chris and I have ever known before. And God is changing me bit by bit into becoming more like that virtuous woman in Proverbs 31 of whom it says, "The heart of her husband doth safely trust in her" (v. 11).

### For My Good

When God gave me my life verse, Romans 8:28, in 1946, I had no idea how good the things He was working out for me would be. As I look back, I can see so clearly the way He has picked up the shattered glass of my life and carefully fashioned the stained glass window He is now making of me. Lost babies, surgery, heartaches, grief—all have been used by God to change me. And always for the better.

How I thank Him for the privilege of growing older so I can reflect on what He was really doing. And I'm sure I won't begin to understand all of this until it is explained to me in heaven. God, the Source and the Means of my changing, working out all these things that change me—all for my good.

### Therefore

This morning I was very tired and felt I could not get out of bed to start the day. As I lay there communing with my God, He brought Isaiah 40 to my mind. Reaching for my Bible I was sure it was verses 28 to 31 about our strength being renewed that He wanted me to read. But I started reading at the beginning of that chapter and found something completely different.

My heart soared as I read about my God—*who He is*! Nobody taught Him. "All nations before Him are as nothing. . . . [He] sitteth upon the circle of the earth, and the inhabitants thereof are as grasshoppers . . . [He] stretcheth out the heavens as a curtain. . . . Lift up your eyes on high, and behold who hath created these things . . . the everlasting God, the Lord, the Creator of the ends of the earth, fainteth not, neither is weary. There is no searching of His understanding" (Isa. 40:17-28). I clutched my Bible to my heart as tears came to my eyes. Who He is!

Then I noticed I had written in the margin of my Bible by Isaiah 40, "12/23/71, see Romans 11:36 to 12:2" with the "2" underlined several times. Turning to Romans, I discovered that I had written on that same day "12:1, therefore." God had connected these two passages for me in 1971.

Now whenever we see the word "therefore" we look back to

see what it is "there for." In Romans 12:1-2 Paul is "therefore" beseeching us to give God our bodies, not to be conformed to this world, but to be transformed by the renewing of our minds. So what is this transforming process "there for"?

Looking back to the four preceding verses I found what it is "there for"—because of *who God is*. And the words are quoted from Isaiah 40! I am to be transformed by the renewing of my mind because of *who* God is.

"O the depth of the riches both of the wisdom and knowledge of God! How unsearchable are His judgments, and His ways past finding out! For who hath known the mind of the Lord? Or who hath been His counselor? Or who hath first given to Him, and it shall be recompensed unto him again? For of Him, and through Him, and to Him, are all things: to whom be glory forever. Amen" (Rom. 11:33-36).

## A Process

I wish I could say that I have arrived, but I can't since this word "transformed" in Romans 12:2 isn't a once-for-all happening. It is a *process*. And whenever I feel that I have arrived, or that I am just about what God had in mind for me to be, He starts changing me again. And this process has been going on all my life.

When I was a little girl I longed for God to change me—into an angel. My sister, brother, and I each had a special Christmas tree ornament that was our very own. We could hang it any place we wanted on the tree. Mine was a beautiful pink angel. And I would hang it on a low branch, way inside, near the tree trunk where it could not be seen except from my favorite, private spot—under the tree. Lying on my back, I spent hours gazing at that lovely, fragile, glass angel and dreaming my favorite dream: "If only I could be an angel!" How I wished I had been made an angel instead of a little girl.

But the words in a song, "Holy, holy, is what the angels sing," that became popular when I was a young teenager, brought it all into focus for me:

> "But when I sing redemption's story,
> They will fold their wings;
> For angels never knew the joys
> That our salvation brings."

Although created in beauty, power and intelligence, no angels will ever have the privilege I have of being changed by God, step by step, into conformity to the image of His dear Son, Jesus (Rom. 8:29). The angels probably aren't going through the often hard, deep and fiery changing process, but neither are they *becoming conformed to Jesus' image!* Nor have they been promised some day *to be like Him.* Yes, they see Him now and have seen Him for eternal ages past, but they are still not like Him. But I, a mere mortal, *when I see Him will be like Him.* "When He shall appear, we shall be like Him" (1 John 3:2). Whether I leave this world through death or am changed "in the twinkling of an eye" when my Jesus returns, the process will be complete.

"Behold, I show you a mystery; we shall not all sleep, but *we shall all be changed.* In a moment, in the twinkling of an eye, at the last trump; for the trumpet shall sound and the dead shall be raised incorruptible, and *we shall be changed*" (1 Cor. 15:51-52).

I shall be perfect as He is perfect! My long "Lord, change me" struggle will be over. I will be like Jesus!

"Dear Father, I have so far to go. I fall so short of what You want me to be. Please keep changing me on this earth until there won't be so much left to change when I see my Jesus. LORD, CHANGE ME!"